# BETTER LATE THAN NEVER

BETTER LATE THAN NEVER

# BETTER LATE THAN NEVER
## The Reparative Therapeutic Relationship in Regression to Dependence

*Lorraine Price*

**KARNAC**

First published in 2016 by
Karnac Books Ltd
118 Finchley Road
London NW3 5HT

British Library Cataloguing in Publication Data

A C.I.P. for this book is available from the British Library

ISBN-13: 978-1-78220-319-3

Typeset by V Publishing Solutions Pvt Ltd., Chennai, India

Printed in Great Britain by TJ International Ltd, Padstow, Cornwall

www.karnacbooks.com

*Dedicated to my children, my grandchildren, my clients, and my therapist who have taught me more experientially than is possible for any book.*

# CONTENTS

# ACKNOWLEDGEMENTS

The writing of this book has been a continuation of my research work. I want to thank those who have supported me through all of this, particularly my husband, Ian, for his continued and tireless support. My friends Julie and Doug, who have kept me going when things were difficult, and Denis, Lorna, Jo, Lionel, Rosemary, and my other friends and colleagues at SPTI. Thanks to Collette, who has supported me in the final stages of this book and made its completion much easier for me. My thanks also go to my friend Sue who has patiently shared her wisdom with me. Finally, my appreciation and thanks to two people without whom my work would not have happened, Dorothy and Richard. Dorothy has tirelessly and generously supported me both practically and emotionally throughout the whole process of this work. She has kept me going and has sat at my computer for many long hours. She deserves an award. Richard has loved me through it and taught me many things. He has understood who I am even when I have lost sight of me.

Thank you to you all.

# ABOUT THE AUTHOR

**Lorraine Price** worked in the civil service and local government before training as an Integrative Psychotherapist and supervisor. She is currently Programme Leader of the MSc in Integrative Psychotherapy programme at the Sherwood Psychotherapy Training Institute, Nottingham. Lorraine has a private practice near her home town of Lichfield, Staffordshire and a supervision practice in Ireland. She is accredited both with the British Association for Counselling and Psychotherapy (BACP), the United Kingdom Council for Psychotherapy (UKCP), and the Irish Association of Humanistic and Integrative Psychotherapy (IAHIP), and is also an EMDR practitioner. Lorraine also successfully completed her Research Doctorate in Psychology with De Montfort University in 2014 where she pursued her ongoing interest in the effects and treatment of early infantile trauma upon clients in psychotherapy, therapeutic regression, and the reparative capacity of the therapeutic relationship.

# INTRODUCTION

*My story as the beginning*

"The teller of chaos stories is, pre-eminently, the wounded storyteller, but those who are truly living the chaos cannot tell in words" (Frank, 1995, p. 98). I first came across the above quotation in Etherington (2003). It caught my attention because I see myself now, in my role as a psychotherapist, as a fellow wounded storyteller, helping others to heal and to find words for their chaos, which can then be shared with another. My interest in psychotherapy began with the need to understand myself and my personal story. It feels important then, at the beginning of this work, to identify some of my own story and its impact upon me and my work. Prior to entering therapy I had some behavioural and psychological "symptoms", my anxiety was severe and manifested in panic attacks and at times I feared madness, believing that only madness could account for such loss of the ability to control my behaviour, thoughts or emotions. I was unable to tell a cohesive and comprehensible story of my life, which accounted for my feelings of fear, shame, pain, and distress. In my early adulthood I recognised that my family was dysfunctional, critical, and shaming. I was a late and unexpected arrival and my mother was depressed; this depression was intensified by grief when my older sister died in a car accident. My father suffered from unresolved post-traumatic stress disorder as a result of his experiences in the Second World War, compounded later by the loss of my sister who was the apple of his eye. My mother was passive in the face of his domineering behaviour and experienced chronic anxiety and depression. She was unable to meet me emotionally as an infant, and unable to protect me from my father. As an adult, I now recognise that I sought a relationship that would complete me, that is, one which would fill the "hole in my soul" (Tomkins, 1963), which I now understand resulted from an absence of a cohesive self. I sought completion in friendships, in romantic relationships, in marriage, in becoming a parent, and in God, all failed to give me any sense of security at my core. Without a narrative for my experience, unconscious, buried memories, and emotions emerged in panic and anxiety, as I had no words to express or explain what I was experiencing. The process of therapy for me involved reconnecting with elements of my pre-verbal self in the presence of a loving "other" who could respond to and repair the cumulative traumas of my infancy. My story has similarities to those of many of the clients I have worked with. My interest in researching was to understand my own process and also to be more able to effectively help my clients to repair the wounding that they had experienced. As a child, my natural and age-appropriate dependency needs were not met by a holding and containing other, my mother could not contain her own anxiety let alone that of a dependent child. Instead I grew up in fear, and felt shame for my vulnerability and dependence. I learned how to close down to my emotions and developed a "false self" and a degree of self-reliance and this helped me to survive and develop, but left emptiness and fear shut off inside me. Over time, my personal therapy became a place of safety for me and the process of my repair began. For the first time I was able to have needs, express them and be responded to. I was able to enter a relationship with my therapist where I could learn to appropriately depend upon a trustworthy other and the previously shut off aspects of myself could begin again to grow and develop.

## Types of clients

The types of clients I am concerned with here are those whom Winnicott (1958a/1984, pp. 279–280) describes as those who must address "the early stages of emotional development before and up to the establishment of the personality as an entity" and that therapeutic work must account for "a very early development of a false self". Therefore, with such a presentation, regression to a therapeutic dependent relationship is necessary to allow development of the previously undeveloped "true self". Van Sweden (1995, p. 208) recognises the difficulty of determining if a client requires such a process, because "the false self presentation disguises the severity of the patient's trauma". He describes potential presentations as follows: "A sense of futility about life, feelings of hopelessness, a belief about no one ever being there, and inability to form meaningful personal relationships, the manifestation of ego deficits, and a variety of other personality disturbances, including depression and/or eating disorders."

## What is the nature of this therapy?

The therapeutic process I have described can be seen as a regression to a relationship where dependence on the other, the therapist, is needed and appropriate. When the client experiences regression to a needed relationship it allows a reprise of the dependent phase of their developmental history. This offers an opportunity for containment and holding by the therapeutic other. In this regressed experiencing, the therapist is emotionally available and alongside the client in the experience in a way that did not occur in their infancy. Because the client needed to be appropriately dependent in infancy, and this was not allowed or possible, it remains searched for in adulthood, leading to relationships characterised by excessive need, control, and fear of abandonment, or conversely, an extreme independence. The therapist's presence and availability allows this re-experiencing, permits the repair of damaged aspects of self and can allow progression towards integration and psychological health.

## The significance of story

Importantly, this therapeutic process helped me to conceptualise my psychological damage through the emergence of my story. An understanding of the interpersonal nature of the development of the mind and how it responds to trauma can help here. Trauma leads to dissociation affecting aspects of the brain, which in good health communicate with each other, but in trauma become split off and fixed (Siegel, 2015). Having such understanding and a narrative gave me a framework upon which to hang my experiences, helping me to apply theory, and to understand some of my behaviours and psychological processes. Having a story gave me a map with which to find my way in the world, and a template to build on in future work, and also made it possible to have a shared understanding with others. Winterson (1985, p. xv) expresses it thus: "Once you can talk about what troubles you, you are some way towards handling it. I know from my postbag that *Oranges* (Winterson's novel) has given a voice to many people's unspoken burdens. And when you have found your voice you can be heard."

From 1990 onwards, therapists, social researchers, and others became interested in narratives, narrative therapies, and narrative studies of lives. They were interested in how people constructed their lives through social contexts. From a non-medical perspective narrative ideas aim to understand a client/participant/social group in the context of their environment. Zilber et al. (2008) explore embedded narrative and acknowledge that narrative psychology recognises the importance of context in understanding and interpreting identity stories. They highlight that narrative theoreticians emphasise that identity stories are constructed intersubjectively (Gergen, & Gergen, 1987). Object relations theories construct the self as occurring in the intersubjective field, and human development theories place the development of self in early infancy. These theories and narrative theories can be seen as fitting together in combining the client's history, the here-and-now and the therapeutic response to their story.

Etherington (2000) highlights the importance of narrative in helping clients to understand their development and history. In constructing the client's narrative, therapist and client can develop a shared language which enables the client to feel understood and to make sense of their early life and current relationships.

Erskine (2007, p. 5) sees the necessity within the therapeutic relationship for the recreation of narrative in both verbal and non-verbal ways. Through empathic attunement, validation of the client's experience together with an understanding of their developmental state "is essential in forming an emotional connection that facilitates a communication of pre-verbal experience".

Understanding one another needs a shared language; in this case the language of both theory and experience, the difficulty for these clients is that they lack a conceptualisation and language for their experience because it falls before memory is established. Helping to develop a narrative, a story through which the experience can be understood, is one of the roles of the therapist in this work. Winterson (2011, p. 40) describes the use of story as a means of sharing a reality and an experience, and how she has used stories as a means of personal healing.

> I had no one to help me, but T. S. Eliot helped me. So when people say that poetry is a luxury, or an option, or for the educated middle classes, or that it shouldn't be read at school because it is irrelevant, or any of the strange, stupid things that are said about poetry and its place in our lives, I suspect that the people doing the saying have had things pretty easy. A tough life needs a tough language—and that is what poetry is. That is what literature offers—a language powerful enough to say how it is. It isn't a hiding place. It is a finding place.

Personally, I have found that the shared experiences and the words of others when I was unable to find my own words have helped me to feel connected to others who understood what I was experiencing.

As a practitioner of integrative psychotherapy, using a relational/developmental approach, the use of self is an important concept and the key factor in successful therapy and healing. I use myself to feel into the worlds of my clients, noticing my thoughts, feelings, and behaviours in relation to both myself and my client, and working with unconscious processes, as a means of understanding hidden aspects of their story. Reflexivity recognises the importance of personal influence, transparency, and openness to self-exploration. I have therefore continued with this use of self within my research and within my book and I have allowed myself and the process to be changed as a result. As Dale (2010, p. 17) comments: "I have tried therefore to be reflexive, that is transparent about my own processes, and how they have changed and developed as the process has moved on."

## The development of this book

My personal experience, my training as a psychotherapist and my work with regressed and distressed clients developed my passion to understand this process, and to determine the most effective ways of working therapeutically. This in turn led to PhD research. My research explored the experience of regression to dependence through interviews with research participants who were practicing psychotherapists. Using a heuristic approach and my personal reflexivity, I intended to use myself within the research process in the same way that I use my personal experiencing, my countertransference, in my clinical work. I gathered my data for my study from practicing psychotherapists who themselves had received psychotherapy, experienced this regressive process, and applied this knowledge and experience when working clinically with distressed and regressed clients. The data from this study, the arising theoretical concepts and the recommendations for professional practice form the basis of this book with a view to developing the therapeutic work with adult clients presenting with symptoms of cumulative infantile trauma, that is, those adults who in their infancy did not meet an optimal environment which would have allowed for a healthy development of self.

## The importance of the legacy of psychoanalysis

I consider that as the field of contemporary psychotherapy has developed, "the baby has been thrown out with the bath water", meaning that the importance of concepts from analytical exemplars, such as Winnicott, who recognised the significance of early infantile experience to adult clients in psychotherapy, have been largely overlooked in the move to embrace either humanistic relational concepts or cognitive interventions. I aim to re-establish the importance of these "archived" aspects of theory in order to illuminate the processes emerging from this study. Johnson (1985, p. 4) identified that many therapists of his generation prematurely gave up on psychoanalytic psychotherapy. He commented, "large portions of analytic writing are unnecessarily obscure, dominated by an imprecise and often archaic jargon". He also recognised that the newer therapies lacked in terms of theory, limiting the capacity of the work. My aim is to reintroduce these important theoretical concepts, but set them in the relational and developmental frame, which is integrative psychotherapy.

Modern integrative psychotherapy has an important relational tradition, but some of the significant concepts, which I consider necessary when working with clients with early relational trauma may have been insufficiently emphasised, lost or overlooked. This may be because training has focussed on appropriate developments in the understanding of intersubjectivity, relational depth, and therapeutic repair, but has resulted in the side-lining of this body of theory and research from the psychoanalytic tradition. This knowledge of human relationship, both intrapsychic and interpsychic, is essential for psychotherapists working with this client base to absorb.

Klein (1987, p. xv) identified that "our need for others has its roots in our earliest experiences, and is bound up with our deepest feelings". Object relations theories upon which this book is theoretically underpinned are concerned with the relationships that we develop as a result of our need, and about how these relationships affect our lives. Object relations theories consider that our earliest relational experiences guide and define our subsequent adult relationships. Therefore, understanding is the key to unlocking the relationship patterns that can be seen in later life. Winnicott (1896–1971), for example, as both paediatrician and psychotherapist, observed similar behaviours in both his infant patients and in his adult psychotherapy clients.

During my training and personal psychotherapy the work of Winnicott and others was significant in that I came to understand that my inner disturbance resulted from deficiencies in my early childhood. This aligned with my prior beliefs that my feelings and behaviour as an adult resulted from the family circumstances in which I was brought up. In my practice as a psychotherapist I was asking how best to address these troubling and hard-to-understand experiences which have been conceived of as representing a return to the difficulties first experienced in the mother/infant relationship (Winnicott, 1965b; Balint, 1968; Van Sweden, 1995; Erskine, 2011).

This book addresses the need for a theoretical base which integrates theories and identifies the processes occurring in this therapeutic work. This need was clearly identified by the findings from my research study. As a practitioner seeking to understand the regressive processes being experienced by my clients, my Integrative training was very helpful in enabling me to use and develop my relational/developmental framework to apply theory in practice. I now share my journey with the profession as a whole, bringing attention to this significant area of client work which seems to be disregarded or misunderstood.

## The evolving nature of knowledge

Professional therapists are trained and motivated to expand and develop their knowledge and experience. Van Sweden (1995) identified that this search may be motivated by complex patients, "[…] there will always be those patients for whom our current proficiency is not enough" (p. xvii). Since Van Sweden wrote this experience, knowledge and understanding have continued to evolve. Some of this evolution has been towards understanding the intersubjective nature of the relationship and its healing potential, and some has been towards treating the majority of patients minimally, where cost is the prime consideration, as in the upsurge in cognitive behavioural therapies. Whilst I have no doubt that for some people these minimal interventions are relevant and effective, for others the complexity of their presentation requires other, more significant forms of help.

I use here an excerpt from an unpublished poem by Jessica Charles, called "Heart sick". It describes the emotional pain and turmoil experienced as a result of infantile trauma.

> Emotions descending from deep within the body, residing in every cell, painful imprints, buried deep. Feelings erupt into insurmountable pain, anger, rage, a burning agonising anguish, anxiety, despair, overwhelming the psyche, provoking an inability to think, swamping the entire being. Then numbness, coping strategies surge into existence, alcohol, drugs, gas, smoking, diazepam. An inconsolable wave of desperation amalgamates into a frantic attempt to blunt out feelings, a longing for an unreserved numbness to mind and body. What other ways are there to deal with these debilitating feelings?
>
> Heart sick like thick black tar concreted in your chest, restricting the natural flow of energy. Guarded from allowing love in or love out, feelings buried so deeply from the vulnerability of being hurt.

The process of my research over the past eleven years has also evolved and will continue to do so. My hope is that increased understanding of these complex clients will result in more effective therapy.

## How to use this book

All therapeutic relationships are different and there is no map for relationship, in this book I do not aim to provide one. However, I do aim to provide a guide for the process of regression to dependence, using each chapter as a "close up" of a particular area. Mitchell (1988, p. 15) highlights this point: "Theories are not facts, observations or descriptions—they are organizational schemes, ways of arranging and shaping facts, observations, and descriptions."

This book is ordered in the way I think is most useful to the reader. I begin with an introduction to me and to my work. Subsequent chapters each address an area of interest in relation to regression to dependence. I begin by explaining what I mean by regression to dependence in Chapter Two, followed by chapters on shame, terror, relational repair, and boundaries. In my final chapter I summarise the work and present my findings from research into this area.

This book is useful for practicing psychotherapists and supervisors, trainee psychotherapists, psychotherapy training programmes, and those with no formal training, but having an interest in the subject. Researchers who are interested in the heuristic process and reflexivity may also benefit. My research has contributed to the theory and practice of psychotherapy and will be of interest to a range of audiences. Members of other disciplines may also have an interest in these findings, such as Social Scientists involved in understanding the development of personal identity, identity process and the development of self. Those who work with trauma survivors may wish to consider the impact of earlier developmental trauma upon recovery. Mental Health professionals may also consider these findings when service users do not respond to other treatments or protocols.

Each chapter of this work contain excerpts from interviews with my research participants and I explore relevant theory to allow the reader to develop a way to conceptualise the process I am describing. This is the same stance that I will advocate later for therapists to adopt, that is, to develop an understanding of theory relevant to this process in order to fully understand and effectively work with these clients. The references which are used within this book all appear at the end of the entire work.

## Terminology

Theorists and practitioners refer to their clients, and themselves, in different ways according to their theoretical orientation. In my practice I refer to "clients" and "therapist" or "psychotherapist", and I have used these terms throughout this book, except in quotes from theorists using different terms, such as, "patients", "analysand", or "analyst".

# CHAPTER ONE

# In search of understanding: theoretical explorations

## *Presenting issues*

My client presented with anxiety and panic attacks. She was otherwise high functioning, intelligent, and with a good immediate family support system. As her story unfolded, I understood that she was searching for change, for something transformative and had tried to find it in her relationships with men and her children. At the beginning of therapy, she wanted an end to her anxiety at any cost. She recognised feelings of inner emptiness, which were permanently with her. In the countertransference I felt a strong maternal pull to nurture her, which I have come to recognise as being frequently present when working with clients whom Winnicott (1958a/1984, pp. 279–280) described as needing to address "the early stages of emotional development before, and up to, the establishment of the personality as an entity". I saw the yearning in her eyes, a yearning for relationship that therapists often experience in clients with borderline process, and although some of her relational history and inner processing indicated such traits, there was no evidence of chaos in her current history, in fact she seemed overly controlled. She did not push boundaries or waiver in her committed relationships, it emerged that her "false self" and toxic shame kept her more borderline tendencies in check. She felt that there was something broken in her and she wanted help to repair this. As I got to know her I saw some of her attempts at intimacy fail and, as our relationship developed I saw her attempts at intimacy with me cause her great fear and difficulty. This client had difficulty in articulating her pain and trauma, and she was bound by shame processes. It seemed impossible for her to allow that she had needs or emotions. This client's history and her presentation for therapy indicates the presence of infantile neglect or trauma.

Over time, I have recognised that there is no one classic presentation of such clients. Some clients may have more borderline traits, seen in the great fear of abandonment and desire for and avoidance of closeness and intimacy, while some may seem more schizoid, holding no sense of the possibility of relationship. Johnson's (1994) description of the oral character seems to be most frequently be identified. These clients have not been allowed to fully inhabit the appropriate dependent position in their infancy because of abuse and neglect, more subtle failures of attunement, or the emotional unavailability of the caretaker and so continue to search for it into adulthood. In some clients their deep need of relationship is evident on first meeting, but for some high-functioning, adapted clients it is effectively defended against, and out of awareness, to emerge much later in the work.

## The concept of regression to dependence

My theoretical model is Integrative, which brings together theories that are compatible within a relational/developmental philosophical stance. My initial training directed my interest towards object relations theorists and it was the work of Balint (1968) and his understanding of the "Basic fault" which sparked my interest. Balint described the necessity of working with the client at a level of relationship which existed prior to the development of the fault that is at the level of primary anxiety, as Winnicott (1958a/1984) would view it, in order to repair infantile wounding, so allowing the client the possibility of a new beginning. This is the concept of regression to dependence; the return to a relationship having similar characteristics to the parental relationship in order to offer a repair and to enable progression of previously fixated and unresolved relational ways of being.

## Connecting theory to practice

My previous study (Price, 2014) has been concerned with finding understanding of this process and ways of applying it in my clinical work with clients, connecting relevant theory to practice and so finding ways of making meaning of the experience, such reflexive practice in psychotherapy is an act of research. This endeavour has a parallel process to the client's need to understand and to find narrative for their experiences. Shaw (2008, p. 10) recognises the research aspect of psychotherapists in their day-to-day work. He highlights the importance of the "therapist's body language, the counter-transference that is felt in the body, seeing it as a valuable tool which can be shared in the therapeutic encounter".

## Relevant theory

There is a lack of literature emerging from Integrative sources, yet I recognise that this is the nature of integration, that theorists and theories develop and change, and new theories emerge, becoming theorised as a new therapy rather than being integrated. I found what I was looking for within the object relations movement, offering me a base from which to begin to understand the clients' processes. Working relationally involves the therapist as an active participant in the relationship, and so the therapeutic stance of psychoanalysis, where the therapist is positioned as a mirror reflecting the client back to themselves, would not be appropriate. The application of theories from object relations within a relational therapy enables understanding of infant developmental processes and provides a template for the identification of infantile wounding and a plan for repair. There is an increased interest in the relational component of therapy, even within theoretical orientations that have previously eschewed the importance of the relationship to the therapy, such as cognitive behavioural therapy. Mitchell (1988) calls this the "relational turn", recognising the importance of the relationship as a healing factor. Integrative psychotherapists focus on the therapeutic relationship, but to work with regression to dependence requires a more in-depth knowledge of infant development, and of the connection of the original dyadic relationship between caretaker and infant and the therapeutic relationship between therapist and client.

Object relations theory identifies the self as developing in relation to its early environment, the caretaker, (Winnicott, 1965b/1984; Fairbairn, 1952; Mahler, 1968; Mahler et al., 1975) and others. Once the influence of this dyadic relationship is acknowledged, then theorists move towards the construction of the importance of such a relationship and the consequences when it is considered as insufficient for optimal development. It is the therapeutic relationship then which can offer a vehicle to repair those individuals whose early infantile environment has resulted in wounding to their very self.

Psychotherapists as far back as Ferenczi (1923) have understood that psychotherapy needed to be more than an intellectual reconstruction; it needed to be an emotional reliving. The problems presented by our more distressed clients occur as a result of deficiencies in early environmental provision. Love, acceptance, and nurture are essential for a child's healthy development and such a relational stance is also essential for clients. Ferenczi (1923) considered that where there is a trauma there is always a split in the personality, whereby part of the personality regresses to the pre-traumatic state. He believed that no analysis was complete unless it had penetrated to the level of the trauma, a position that Winnicott would later also hold.

Ferenczi's ideas were further developed by Klein, Balint, Winnicott, and others who started to construct theories about the mind, using information gathered from infant observation. Mitchell (1988) explains how theoretical traditions from object relations, self psychology, and other interpersonal theories complement each other and can be seen as being within a multi-faceted relational matrix. He makes an important point, that the basic features of an integrated relational approach were not constructed from previous theoretical traditions which were applied to clinical work; rather they were discovered within the practice of psychotherapy. It is the practice of psychotherapy, for myself and my participants, which has necessitated the search for theoretical understanding.

## The metaphor of the baby

Infantilism concerns the central role played by concepts of early infantile development to psychoanalytic theory. Freud assumed the successful negotiation of early infancy, seeing the source of psychological conflict occurring later at the oedipal level, but recognising that aspects of a person's life can be understood in the light of their infant experiences, and if they are, then puzzling and hard to understand experiences, feelings, and behaviours can be illuminated when viewing the client as having aspects of the child within. Van Sweden (1995, p. 33) considers that the primary mother/infant relationship should be dealt with in order for the adult client "to repair pathology stemming from difficulties in the early mother–infant relationship". Ferenczi (1931) recognised the unmet needs of childhood existing within his clients, and Bollas (1987) links the mother's provision for her infant with the therapist's stance within the relationship. Object relations theories are concerned with the relationship of people to other people and to things which are meaningful for them and how these relationships affect our later lives. Klein (1987, p. xvi) seeks to understand what life was like in early infancy, and "what implications does this have for our later years, when we can no longer call on others in quite the same way to take care of the baby which still survives in us?" and "what does this tell us about the help which psychotherapists and psycho-analysts can give if, in later years, we find we are compulsively recreating the relationships which were first developed between the baby-self and the parent adult". Winnicott (1958b/1984), as both paediatrician and psychotherapist, observed a correlation between his infant patients' way of being, and his experience of his adult psychotherapy clients. He considered that where there was infantile environmental failure it was defended against by a "freezing of the failure situation" (p. 281). This resulted in an experience of a failed dependency stage, which was then seen to re-emerge within the therapeutic setting as regression to dependence. This re-emergence and its re-enactment exhibited attributes similar to those of the infants he worked with. He theorised that "in the emotional development of every infant complicated processes are involved, and that lack of forward movement or completeness of these processes predisposes to mental disorder or breakdown; the completion of these processes form the basis of mental health" (p. 159), making a link between infant development and psychiatric states. This theory, translated into clinical work, results in the concept of regression to dependence, and the possibility of relational repair facilitated by the therapeutic relationship. Recognising the conceptual correlation between the caregiver/infant relationship, and the therapist/client relationship means that using the metaphor of the baby, that is working with the perceived infant ego of the client enables understanding and the development of a shared language for the therapeutic process between therapist and client, and begins to bridge the gap between conceptual knowing and application to practice.

Mitchell (1988, p. 127) identifies that "psychoanalytic experience has shown that the scattered and complex fragments of the analysand's background are often powerfully integrated and illuminated by viewing them in terms of infantile experiences". Mitchell recognises that viewing obscure and puzzling presentations in the client as if the client was a child can help to organise fragmentary experiences into "coherent, understandable patterns" identifying this as "using the metaphor of the baby". He highlights the difference between Freud's baby and the modern baby; Freud's baby being riddled with conflict, the modern baby being a relational baby, where conflict only arises when there is a lack of parental provision. This is important to theories of developmental-arrest, as in Winnicott's "deficiency disease". Mitchell (1988, p. 139) accounts for this shift in understanding of the baby by seeing it as a product of scientific advance coming from the field of infancy research. Object relations theory considers that the primary drive of human beings is for relationship, where relationship has been deficient then the relational needs of infancy, which are necessary for developmental provision, remain active within the adult client. Having reached the concept of these needs, the work of Winnicott, Balint, and other object relations theorists begins to offer insight and understanding into the application of these conceptualisations.

## The possibility of therapeutic repair

Balint (1968) and Winnicott (1958a/1984), in particular, recognised that some patients required assistance to deal with the early stages of emotional development before, and up to, the development of personality as an entity. These are the patients whose reparative need is in the dyadic relationship and who need "management" according to Balint (p. 87) and the "mother actually holding the infant" according to Winnicott (p. 279). These regressive experiences, where "talking therapy" (I believe they mean the interpretation aspect here) is neither useful nor therapeutic, offer an opportunity for reparative experiencing. The therapeutic task is simply to be in tune with the client and their developmental needs, to acknowledge and validate, to be fully present within the relationship, and to offer some appropriate gratification.

In the following chapters I will describe the process of regression to dependence in detail, addressing the possibility of repair within the therapeutic relationship.

# CHAPTER TWO

# Regression to relationship: a return to dependence

I just went into complete collapse, there was a whole lot of things happening in my life [...] that was like the crash point, but there was a whole lot of other stuff, that everything had just got too much, and I [...]suddenly just couldn't stop crying. I think I was anxious long before I got to therapy, I was very anxious [...] literally feeling that my body doesn't, isn't together, that my arms and my body don't function together, that my legs don't function together.

[...] an overwhelming [...] sense of a kind of lostness and disconnection [...] of regressing to a kind of wordless state [...].

[...] I couldn't find the language, though [...] and I know I knew, but I didn't have the language for it [...].

These excerpts from my research data describe a sense of disintegration and collapse that echoes theorists' descriptions of a return to an unintegrated state (Winnicott, 1958a/1984; Van Sweden, 1995). Such regressive experience is viewed by Winnicott (1958a/1984, p. 261) as a return to infantile experiencing, which, when processed within the therapeutic relationship, offers the potential

9

for repair, "The advantage of a regression is that it carries with it the opportunity of correction of inadequate adaptation-to–need in the past history of the patient, that is to say, in the patient's infancy management." A relational/developmental theoretical perspective seeks to repair early environmental failures, seeing some clients as having sustained psychological damage very early in their infant development resulting in a variety of relational difficulties throughout later life. The presentation of these clients may include:

- feelings of alienation,
- fear of emotional dependency,
- having difficult intimate relationships,
- fear of abandonment and of being alone,
- feeling that life has no meaning,
- feeling panicky and anxiety ridden,
- feeling that they are living behind an emotional façade,
- feelings of sadness and loneliness even though being a high achiever,
- omnipotent defences and avoidance of vulnerability.

It was with these clients, whose struggle I recognised both personally and as their therapist that I found myself challenged to find ways of working effectively.

As I have already mentioned in chapter one, clients who may benefit from allowing a therapeutic regression to a dependent relationship do vary in their presentation. The therapist may experience the client as having a deep yearning or hunger for relationship. Some clients fit the oral dependent picture, all are heavily defended, often with primitive defences, and are easily shamed. There may be difficulties in holding on to object constancy that is, being unable to conceive that people or objects are consistent, trustworthy and reliable especially when they are not present. This is a developmental skill, which is usually learned in infancy and results from having experiences which confirm the caretaker as reliable and trustworthy and the relationship as ongoing and sustainable.

In this chapter I will identify aspects of theory, moving through historical perspectives towards more contemporary theorists, which are relevant to working with these issues. I will explain the place of transference and unconscious process in integrative psychotherapy and describe theoretical understanding of ideal infant development, which supplies a good environment in which the innate potential of the infant can develop. I will also introduce theoretical understanding of the influence of early environmental failure upon infant development, and the potential for trauma as a result, such ideas that are now supported and informed by neuroscientific research. Having explored infant development I will then describe what I mean by "regression" itself, and "regression to dependence", and how this offers the prospect of psychological progression.

## Seeking answers in theory

My Integrative theoretical orientation owes much to object relations theory and it was into this field that I first looked for answers. How to more effectively help such clients is an important question for me, and a question that has occupied the thoughts of practitioners and theorists for many years. The original psychoanalytic position presented by Freud viewed the mind as monadic, that is, a unit operating and developing by and of itself. Later relational theorists viewed the development of the mind as occurring in the relational matrix. Mitchell (1988, pp. 17, 19–33) considered that the "mind has been redefined from a set of predetermined structures emerging from inside an individual organism to transactional patterns and internal structures derived from an interactive, interpersonal field". He writes that "the individual mind is a *product* of as well as an interactive participant in the cultural, linguistic matrix, within which it comes into being. Meaning is not provided a priori, but derives from the relational matrix. The relational field is constitutive of individual experience". He explains that "for Kohut, as for Winnicott, the establishment of reflexive stability is the central motivational thrust in human experience, and relations with others and the roles they play in this pursuit is the primary context for human experience".

As a paediatrician Winnicott (1958b/1984, pp. 170–171) observed similar processes occurring between mother and infant, and between himself and his psychotherapy patients. When studying human relationships he stated that the "paediatrician and the psychiatrist badly need each other's help", feeling that "those who care for infants [...] can teach something to those who manage the schizoid regressions and confusion states of people of any age". "I am saying that the proper place to study schizophrenia and manic depression and melancholia is the nursery."

Those practitioners using object relations theory to understand the experiences of their clients' view that the troubling symptoms experienced by some of their clients have their roots in their early infantile relational experiences and the experiences of trauma which resulted. Erskine and Trautmann (2002) describe the process of integrative psychotherapy referring to the integration of theory with a perspective of human developmental tasks and needs. The theoretical foundation focuses on child psychological development, the understanding of attachment patterns and the lifelong need for relationship. In this formulation of the therapeutic process it is considered appropriate for the therapist to use his or her self-experiencing to assist the integration of developmental process through the client's childhood needs, their experience process, and interventions, including touch and holding, as dictated by the perception of the client's developmental age regression. The rationale for this is further supported by reference to Fairbairn's (1952) argument that the need for relationship is a primary motivation in human behaviour and the disruption of contact results in needs being unmet. Developmental research shows that the sense of self and self-esteem emerge out of contact-in-relationship (Stern, 1985). Other theorists (Erikson, 1950; Mahler, 1968; Bowlby, 1969, 1973, 1980) wrote of the significance of the early infant relationships, through which experiences of self and other emerge.

Interest in the nature of human relatedness led Bowlby (1969, 1973, 1980) to understand that the nature of human beings is to be drawn together. He considered that for the infant to survive its need for its mother to supply the physical and emotional needs was primary. It is this intersubjective view of the mind that underpins relational/developmental psychotherapy and, therefore, this book, but I am mindful of Mitchell's (1988, p. 22) point that "current thinking about infants, like all psychoanalytic ideas, is a blend of facts and theories and is presented here as an example of a way of thinking, a conceptual strategy, not as incontrovertible truth". Mitchell (1988) recognises Bowlby's contribution, but highlights that "biological, physiological and psychological" primacy of the early relation of the child to its caretakers has emerged from another field entirely—infancy research, and it is from this field that Winnicott, a paediatrician and psychotherapist, finds his experience and understanding.

These, along with other object relations theories are used to underpin the theoretical stance within this work.

The group of patients which are the focus of this study was identified by Winnicott (1958a/1984, pp. 279–280), who emphasised that the therapist must specifically address "the early stages of emotional development before and up to the establishment of the personality as an entity". He considered that the treatment techniques developed by Freud and Klein were ineffective because of the level of maternal deprivation experienced by such patients. This resulted in an inability to benefit from traditional psychoanalytic technique because they would require the ability to identify thoughts and feelings and verbally communicate them to the analyst. These theoretical constructs seemed to describe the clients that I was seeking to help.

Theorists such as Ferenczi, Balint, and Winnicott had encountered such clients and concluded that treatment was possible for these patients, but would require different techniques to enable the patient to come to "a regression in search of the true self". It should be noted that at this time therapy was not relational in the way that it would be understood now, that is, where the self of the therapist and the relationship between therapist and client play an important part within the therapeutic relationship. The object relationists were advocating a move away from the traditional analytic techniques which were prevalent at the time, but even with these adjustments which were suggested for particular clients, the therapy would still have been much more formal than would be recognised by many therapists today.

In his seminal work on regression to dependence Van Sweden (1995) identifies the following four premises which lie behind his theoretical stance: a) that in working with clients with pre-oedipal disorders of maternal deprivation a change from aspects of the usual analytic stance of abstinence and interpretation is necessary; b) that the early months of life are the main focus of the therapy, and that the transference relationship is the vehicle through which these early experiences are replicated and worked through; c) that complex defences have developed resulting in a high functioning client which may mean that these deficits are missed in the therapy; d) that the therapist's response, survival and containment of the return of the client's primitive experiences within the therapy can result in progression, enabling a second opportunity to achieve ego integration. As an integrative psychotherapist I would agree with this stance, but my way of being with a client would be different from that described by Van Sweden, as I do not practice as an analyst, I do not hold an analytic stance with any of my clients. When working with regression to dependence, I may adjust the boundaries of my usual therapeutic stance, particularly those around contact outside sessions and touch. Stewart (2003) considers that work on this area of analysis has not received the recognition it deserves because of the adaptation of technique that it requires, and the necessity of the therapist living without knowing for long periods. Mitchell (1988) would recognise the importance of object relations theory in understanding human development and the connection between the client's infancy experience and their needs of their therapist, he would question the concept of seeing a client as having past omissions and developmental gaps repaired. He believes that this is a distortion which omits the adult relational needs of the client. He cautions against the highlighting of regressive needs above other aspects of the relationship. I think this is an important point, however in looking at the relationship overall and over time, the regression to dependence relationship has phases of intensity, but at any one time all relational facets may be present to some degree. It is essential to remember the importance of the person-to-person relationship (as opposed to the transferential one) and the normal relational needs which present in any relationship. In my experience, rather than seeing a regressive phase which is clear and distinct, which clients approach and then move away from, I have experienced an overarching movement to deeper levels of regression over the course of therapy and I have also noted that clients may move in and out of regressed states within any session. Bollas (2013, p. 1) describes working with patients in the process of breakdown and the difficulties for the analyst when patients tip into psychosis. He makes an interesting statement though, about regression to dependence, "if the analysand regresses to dependence in a rather ordinary way—lessening defences, opening up the self to interpretive transformation, abandoning disturbed character patterns—the self will usually break down in a slow and cumulative way".

Clarkson (2003) identifies five facets of the therapeutic relationship, these are: a) the working alliance; b) person to person; c) transference/countertransference; d) developmentally needed; and e) existential. She considers that all of these facets may be present at any time. The regression to dependence process has a focus in the transferential/countertransferential and developmentally needed facets, but will also involve the working alliance, the person to person, and possibly the existential.

Before exploring further the process of and rationale for regression to dependence it is necessary to look in detail at some history of the development of psychotherapy, and then at how psychotherapists understand and are informed by aspects of developmental psychology.

## Historical perspectives

Freud (1900a, 1905d, 1915c, 1933a, 1940a) formulated that psychopathology developed from conflicts as the individual moves from the dyadic relationship between mother and infant, to the triadic relationship of the mother, father and child, "three-person psychology". He considered that instinctual drives were the motivation for individuals, only co-incidentally moving them towards others. This concept meant that the therapist's role was to be non-judgemental and emotionally uninvolved, viewing themselves as mirrors on which the unconscious ideas and beliefs of clients would be revealed. Clients were helped with their psychological difficulties by bringing the drives that were in the unconscious into consciousness, therefore allowing the client to understand and work through their issues. The therapeutic task then was to help the client to become aware of these unconscious processes, making them conscious and under the command of the will, and therefore available for change. To achieve this the client must be able to recognise and verbally communicate thoughts and feelings to the therapist. Any emotional impulses would be spoken rather than acted out, with behavioural acting out being seen as resistance to the therapeutic process, this then requires a high degree of sophistication in the psychological processes of such clients. This meant that more disturbed and distressed clients who acted out and who were unable to verbalise their experiences were considered un-analysable. There were other theorists, however, who were willing to try to work with clients who did not fit these criteria.

Ferenczi, (1931, 1932/1988, 1933) a student of Freud, was known for working with such clients. He, and other object relations theorists, have sited the roots of psychological disturbance within the dyadic relationship, considering that clients who were not available for interpretive psychoanalysis could still be effectively worked with if there were changes to the way in which the therapy proceeded, and in this way started to move away from the analytic stance to what I consider to be a more client-led model. He believed that in order to heal, some clients needed to regress to a former developmental state, prior to the time when they were psychologically damaged, whereas Freud would have viewed these regressions initially as resistance to analysis.

The therapeutic dyad being used to reveal unconscious processes enables both client and therapist to identify deficits within early relationships, and through the therapeutic process have the potential to allow relational deficits to be responded to and repaired. Thompson (1943, p. 64) cites Ferenczi's understanding of this process "With patients in whom a severe depression dominates the clinical picture from the start the regression is likely to go further, and demands may be too primitive for the ego to mediate", considering that the inability to work with such clients was more to do with the lack of skill on behalf of the therapists rather than the patient's incurability. Thompson identifies Ferenczi's understanding of therapeutic repair "the patient is ill because he has not been loved, and that he needs from the analyst the positive experience of acceptance, i.e. love". Van Sweden (1995) also highlights Ferenczi's perception of the relationship in regression (1931, p. 137) as "like that of an affectionate mother" and thought that "adult patients, too, should be free to behave in analysis like naughty (i.e., uncontrolled) children" (p. 132). He considered it necessary to focus the analysis upon the child ego state within the adult, considering that the analyst's presence was important within the relationship and that the process between therapist and client would enable past traumas to be re-lived emotionally within the therapeutic relationship. The traditional unyielding stance of psychoanalysis was considered by Kohut (1971, 1977) and Gill (1982) to be experienced by the client as rejecting and could repeat the wounding received in infancy.

Klein, (1957, 1959) a contemporary of Freud, considered the relationship with the mother to be the formative one, and that the source of psychological disturbance was in the dyadic relationship. This stance was also held by other influential theorists such as Winnicott, Fairbairn, Guntrip, Balint, and Kohut. These theorists (known as The British Object Relations School) viewed the dyadic relationship as developmentally key and the therapeutic relationship as fundamental to the successful outcome of therapy. Balint (1959, 1968) placed high importance on the value of the regressive experience seeing that in the therapeutic setting it offered an opportunity for reparation. Both Klein and

Winnicott were in a position to observe the behaviour of infants, and drew conclusions about their internal experiencing as a result of these observations. Through his experiences as a paediatrician Winnicott highlighted similar behaviours in his adult patients who were in distress to those that he saw in distressed infants. This was a move away from Freud's understanding of the infant living in a completely narcissistic state and unable to distinguish the other as separate, towards a model of psychology which focuses on the dyadic, intersubjective relationship between mother and infant. This relationship, once formed, is considered to be carried with the individual into adulthood.

In his paper on the "true and false self" (1960, p. 141) Winnicott comments that:

> Experiences have led me to recognise that dependent or deeply regressed patients can teach the analyst more about early infancy than can be learned from direct observation of infants, and more than can be learned from contact with mothers who are involved with infants since what happens in the transference (in the regressed phases of some patients) is a form of infant–mother relationship.

He considered that "it is possible to establish a clinical link between infant development and the psychiatric states, and likewise between infant care and the proper care of the mentally sick" (Winnicott, 1958b/1984, p. 158). His observations of what he considered to be normal infant development led him to believe that "The mental health of the human being is laid down in infancy by the mother, who provides an environment in which complex, but essential processes in the infant's self become completed" (p. 160).

"Two-person psychology", the psychology of the in-between of relationship, the intersubjective, was the focus for Balint (1968) based on his analytical experiences with patients, putting the interaction between caregiver and infant at the centre of developmental theory, and identifying the possible source of some adult clients' difficulties as being the experiences of their early infancy (Van Sweden, 1995). When attempts to connect in infancy fail, Hedges (1994b, pp. 4–5) considers that they remain "imprinted on the psyche". He views these infant scenarios as reappearing "in the psychoanalytic relationship as replicated transference modes of interacting that pervade our character and body structures." It is these theorists, in making the link between infancy and clients in therapy that form the underpinning for this theoretical stance and so allow for the concept of therapeutic relational repair.

Participants in my research into this subject have described their regressive experiences:

> [...] well I wouldn't have known that it was going to be regression when I went into the therapy, I thought I was perfectly adult. I didn't know what therapy was anyway, but I realise looking back now and at the time I knew I was very anxious. It reached a point where I would just walk through the therapy room door, and I could just feel myself becoming two or younger [...] not a nice feeling, tremendous, I definitely needed to go there.
>
> Well, I recognise that if I was in situations where there was a lot of anger around me I completely dissociated [...] in terror, which was about my dad's rages [...] and I wouldn't be present, but I would look like I was, and that happened to me at work, and you know, all over the place really, and I think I spent a lot of time dissociated in a way that I don't any more [...] without [...] and it was around rage as if there was anger around, and I would sometimes dissociate in the train.

These experiences are viewed as a return to early infancy reprised within the therapeutic relationship. It is clear from these extracts that the participants understand their experiences through the construction of the infancy narrative. Their therapists are likely to have held this view of the phenomena, and their own training would have also supported this view. Clients who are not therapists may not hold this perspective until it is introduced to them through therapy (Stern, 1985). Other theoretical orientations may view these experiences differently and I will comment upon this further in the conclusion of this chapter.

## Transference

"Those who do not remember the past are condemned to repeat it" (Santayana, 1905).

If we accept the object relational stance in asserting that the way that infants develop and behave and the way that regressed patients behave have similarities, then knowledge and understanding of developmental theory can be seen to supply important information for the therapist. The early relationship with the mother, or primary caregiver, recognised as the key relationship for infant development, can be seen as a model for the sort of setting and the type of relationship required to address issues which stem from this period. It is this developmental theory, which is the basis for working with regression to dependency, and the concept of transference and countertransference which means that a new experience between therapist and client is possible.

Transference was initially seen as a defence against remembering when it was first described by Breuer and Freud (1895d). Later (1905d), it came to be seen as one of the main elements of psychoanalysis, where it was recognised that some patients' communications were in response to archaic relational conflict rather than as a response to some current environmental situation. Transference can be defined in this way: "The transference/countertransference relationship is the experience of 'distortion' (Freud's word) of the working alliance by wishes and fears and experiences from the past transferred (carried over) onto or into the therapeutic partnership" (Clarkson, 2003, p. 11). Jacoby (1984, p. 17) views transference thus: "In his relationship to the analyst the patient repeats and relives the love, hatred, aggression, and frustration he experienced as an infant in relation to his parents." In this formulation patterns of relating which originated in childhood are seen to be repeated by the client in their significant relationships, including the therapeutic relationship. Maroda (2004) defines transference as the conscious and unconscious responses, affective and cognitive, of both therapist and client. Levy and Scala (2012, p. 400) define transference as "a tendency in which representational aspects of important and formative relationships (such as with parents and siblings) can be both consciously experienced and/or unconsciously ascribed to other relationships" (Levy, 2009).

Further insight into the process of transference within the therapeutic relationship can be found in the work of: Heimann (1950); Langs (1976); Racker (1982); and Cashdan (1989).

Such transference can be seen in the following quotation from one of my research participants who is describing how important the therapist has become to her, and the significance of the relationship:

> [...] I also couldn't bear the idea of her having other clients [...] I
> just convinced myself I WAS the only one, and she only had the

others because she'd got to earn a living, and that way I could just tolerate it. […]

The understanding of early infancy narratives and infant psychological development enables us to recognise a parent/infant transference within the therapeutic relationship, rather than seeing it as something akin to romantic jealousy. Clarkson (2003) identified the transferential/countertransferential (the experience of the therapist) relationship to be the unconscious wishes and fears transferred onto or into the therapeutic partnership. Therefore, the client will eventually bring their wishes and fears for relationship into the therapeutic arena for re-enactment and resolution.

It is considered by therapeutic approaches which recognise and work with the transferential aspects of the relationship that the client may be able to tell the unconscious components of their story through the unfolding of the transference. The therapist's task then is to understand their part in the story. The emergence of transference within the therapeutic relationship and the potential re-enactment of the mother/infant relationship within the therapy then has the potential to be beneficial in the client's development. From this construction the client presents their story into the relationship in a "live" way and this allows the possibility for whatever failed in the early relationship to be seen and repaired in the current therapeutic relationship. Theoretically then an understanding of the processes involved in that early infant relationship is necessary. The therapist's response, their countertransference, will be explored later in this chapter after I have presented theories describing the type of infancy relationship which can be considered as enabling an infant to develop their full potential.

## Infant development

### The good enough mother

The theory of the ideal parent/infant relationship sees the infant, with its inherited potential, ready to meet a facilitating environment which is responsive to it, initially totally, then appropriately, given the rate of development of the infant. In this ideal setting the infant is not challenged with more than the level of its development can tolerate, allowing the infant to develop a "continuity of being" (Winnicott, 1960, p. 47).

The alternative to this is reacting, and reacting interrupts the "continuity of being" and annihilates. The mother, who is the facilitating environment, recognises the infant's needs and level of development through her attunement, and only allows such stimulation as is tolerable to the infant. In this setting the infant is able to process such experiences as occur, and to make meaning of them. Winnicott describes it as "the ego-support of the maternal care enables the infant to live and develop in spite of his being not yet able to control, or to feel responsible for, what is good and bad in the environment" (p. 37). He considers that "infants come into being differently according to whether the conditions are favourable or unfavourable" (p. 43). A key point is that while the infant's inherited potential is a fact, this potential can only develop when linked to maternal care. Where dependence is adequately met, the child achieves healthy interpersonal relationships and is resilient enough to deal with personal conflict. Mitchell (1988) cites Bion's (1957) characterisation of the mother's holding functions in relation to the infant's inchoate experience, using the metaphor of the "container".

Klein (1987) considers that the primitive self is a sensory experience not a conceptual one. Before the differentiation of "me" and "not me" mother and infant are one. The baby has to (e)merge, to cease to merge, and as the baby (e)merges so does the mother with body imagery seen as the forerunner of self-imagery. This conceptualisation has correlations with the formulations of Bick (1968) and Tustin (1972, 1981, 1984) who viewed the infant's skin as a container binding together the most primitive parts of self and differentiating "me" from "not me". This is the container then for the rudimentary self prior to the development of an internally felt sense of self. Bick considered it to be observable in relation to dependence and separation in the transference, viewing the stage of primal splitting and idealisation as resting on a previous containment of self and object by their individual "skins". Tustin (1972) explores the infant's experience of the mother as skin, container, and organiser, considering that the psychological skin formation occurs when the infant has internalised nurture. Winnicott (1965b/1984) would recognise this conceptualisation as he highlights the boundary of the skin as the identifier of "me" and "not me", a construction that Bick (1968) also placed upon the skin as representative of that boundary. Winnicott considered that ego development starts from absolute dependence on the mother for support. The strength of the ego is dependent on the mother's ability to meet the absolute dependency of the infant. The origin of the word "*infans*" means "not talking", and because of this pre-verbal state the infant is dependent on maternal empathy rather than understanding or on what can be verbally expressed.

Maturational developments depend on environmental provision. The facilitating environment makes possible the steady progress of maturational process. The environment does not make the child, but allows the child to develop up to its potential.

Winnicott (1960, p. 89) describes the early stages of emotional growth:

• The individual inherits a maturational process which meets with a facilitating environment which is adapted to the changing needs of the individual.
• The individual proceeds from absolute dependence to relative dependence going towards independence. In health, development takes place at the appropriate pace.
• The facilitating environment—described as holding, moving into handling and then to object presenting.
• In this environment the individual undergoes development—integrating towards in-dwelling and then object relating.

In absolute dependence, where the mother supplies the auxiliary-function, the infant has not separated out the "not me" from the "me", seeing that the mother's "primary maternal preoccupation" enables her to know about her infant's earliest expectations and needs, and makes her personally satisfied in so far as the infant is at ease through it, the mother knows how to hold her infant and the baby can then start existing and not purely reacting (Winnicott, 1974, p. 341).

The "true self" is its own source of action, a notion which is closely linked to the philosophical theory of the transcendental ego. This is the radically anti-deterministic view that the person has within him or her, a source that cannot be explained by antecedents alone. Freedom then is the capacity to act from this source. Winnicott's theory is that the mother, through her spontaneous responses, is able to bring this source of creative activity to birth (Symington, 1986).

The self-regulating process between infant and mother is described by Lewis (2004, p. 5):

> The parent or caretaker is the auxiliary ego for the infant during
> its prolonged period of total dependence. The parent senses the

inner needs of the infant and gratifies them; the parent is the buffer between the external world and the infant. Sudden noise, temperature change, positional change are avoided or tempered by a reasonably attuned parent.

"Reasonably attuned" covers a broad spectrum: there is a tremendous range of what constitutes adequate empathy as a particular mother and infant get to know each other. This question of the parent as auxiliary ego is well covered in the literature of ego psychology. The parent is not just gratifying the infant: she or he is really helping it to organise itself. This positive and specific function of helping the infant to control and modulate its movement and feeling is taken for granted in a reasonably healthy mother/infant dyad. The biological aspect of this relationship is addressed by Bowlby's (1969) theory of attachment. Attachment theory recognises the search for relationship for protection and support. An infant seeking proximity is seen as a response to a distinct biological motivational system involving intense emotion. Bowlby and subsequent attachment theorists consider that the patterns of affectional bonds occurring throughout life depend on the way that their attachment was formed in infancy.

I will now explore what happens from this construction of infant development when an ideal attachment bond does not develop and when an ideal facilitating environment is not available.

## Failure of the facilitating environment

Winnicott's (1988, p. 131) formulation of infant development identifies that in the earliest stage of development disturbing happenings are unable to be experienced or integrated by the infant because they "have not yet reached a stage where there is a place to see from". Tarantelli (2003, p. 916) cites Blanchot's (1986, p. 28) identification of the same process as "a non-experience [...] which [...] cannot be forgotten because it has always already fallen outside memory". Little (1990), in giving her personal record of her analysis with Winnicott, describes her regressive return to disorganisation and anxiety that she experienced during her therapy, clearly outlining the infantile roots of this experience. She concurs with Winnicott's assertion that environmental provision is necessary to manage these experiences within the therapeutic relationship. Erskine (2007) also recognises the impact of pre-verbal trauma, whether acute or cumulative, on the individual which may not be available to consciousness because of the pre-verbal origins, yet surfaces at points, usually times of stress, throughout adult life.

Lewis (2004) asserts that parents with their own unmet developmental needs can fail to help their infant to develop self-regulation. He describes dissonance being laid down in the cells, autonomic nervous system, and energy centres of the infant. He identifies this dissonance as the basis of falling anxiety and premature ego development which from a relational and developmental perspective could be formulated as a fear of letting go, and a split into thinking to avoid feeling. This has emerged in client work when the client experiences a desire to let go of control and "rest" with the therapist in order to experience dependence. When this emerges in therapy a fear of falling, or of being dropped, can be manifested. For me as a client this manifested as a fear that my therapist couldn't "hold" me. Bion (1962, p. 116) posits that where the mother is an inadequate container for the child's indigestible feelings he remains in a state of "nameless dread". This could then be seen to lead to psychopathology, where it may remain to re-emerge in adulthood.

The argument that the ruptured strivings for human contact in infancy can be manifested in adulthood and in the therapeutic relationship is constructed by Hedges (1994b, pp. 5–6). He identifies this as the continued search for the lost mother of infancy, the empty place where the needed love and acceptance were never received, which has left "its own definite and indelible mark on personality". This "living record of failed connection" leaves them searching for a relationship to fulfil the need and complete them, a stance taken by both Freud, (1905d) and Van Sweden (1995). This search for that lost mother of infancy then continues into adult life and is the premise of this study.

When infantile trauma re-emerges into the life of the adult client it can be very frightening and can be described as chronic anxiety or panic attack. Such an experience was described to me as:

> [...] triggering a very scared child inside of me [...] and from that place of scare, you know, completely losing touch with what was happening in the moment, and re-experiencing quite strong emotions, that I couldn't put words to, or understand or explain, and often quite strong physical reactions, like my arm shaking and not knowing why my arm was shaking, or my leg twitching up and down for [...] my body was remembering, I would realise that my

body was remembering things that I didn't know what they were.
[...]

Bodily and psychosomatic manifestations are interpreted by some theorists as residue of traumatic experience. Hedges (1994a, 1994b) considers that infantile emotional pain can be ascribed to various aspects of the body, and trauma theorists such as Solomon and Seigel (2003); Etherington (2003); and Ogden et al. (2006) recognise the connection between the body and traumatic experiences. This body/mind connection in infancy is identified in Winnicott's (1958b/1984) construction of the infant's developing mind, seeing the infant experiencing from a body/mind perspective where experiencing is both "think" and "feel". It is also important to identify the essential role of the body in dyadic regulation (Ogden et al., 2006). Based on his experience with mothers and their infants Winnicott theorised about the development of the mind from the psyche–soma (the whole of a person, mind and body), seeing that the early psyche–soma proceeds in its development "provided its continuity of being is not disturbed, in other words for the healthy development of the early psyche–soma there is a need for a perfect environment". This is considered to be an absolute need whereby the environment adapts to the needs of the infant and when there is a failure to adapt the infant "must react", so disturbing its development. Initially these needs are physical, but eventually become emotional, psychological, and social. Over time, if the infant's needs have been adapted to sufficiently, the infant's mental activity becomes able to allow for any deficiencies.

It is important that the initial perfect adaptation of the caregiver to the infant should become a graduated failure of adaptation according to the infant's capacity to allow for it by mental activity or understanding. Winnicott (1949) considered psychosis as "an environmental deficiency disease", and that when the infant's environment is not responsive to its needs then there can "develop an opposition between the mind and the psyche–soma" whereby the infant starts to care for itself in ways which should be the function of the environment, thus Winnicott considers that the infant prematurely takes over this function, placing a strain on "mental functioning" and "self disorder" (Winnicott, 1965b/1984, p. 56). The infant's self, identified as "inherited potential which is experiencing a continuity of being" known as the "true self" (Winnicott, 1960, p. 280) which begins to have life through the strength given to the infant's weak ego by the mother's implementation of the infant's omnipotent expressions (p. 145). This means that the mother's preoccupation, a sort of sensitive attunement, with the infant and its needs, enable it to develop a sense of its own continuity over time, as Winnicott says, a sense of "going on being".

The mother's implementation of the needs of the infant results in the development of a sense of "I-ness" which will become the "true self". He considers that the holding environment has the function of reducing the number of impingements to which the infant must react, and must provide for physiological needs. As physiology and psychology have not yet become distinct the environmental provision should be reliable, but not in a mechanical way, being based on the mother's empathy and attunement and therefore adaptive to the needs of the infant. Holding protects from physiological insult, takes account of the infant's skin sensitivity to touch, temperature, auditory sensitivity, visual sensitivity, sensitivity to falling, and of the infant's lack of knowledge of the existence of anything other than the self. It follows the minute changes of the infant's growth and development. Holding includes especially the physical holding of the infant which is a form of loving, maybe the only way that the mother can show the infant her love. The basis for instinctual satisfaction and for object relationships is the handling and the general management and care of the infant. Symington (1986, p. 313) identifies that, from Winnicott's perspective, if mother has not responded to her baby appropriately it puts up a protective screen to protect the "true self". The primitive fears of invasion, annihilation, and breaking to pieces are felt. The "true self" does not become a living reality unless the mother repeatedly meets and affirms it. From this perspective, the mental health of the individual in the sense of freedom from psychosis or liability to psychosis is laid down by this maternal care, "It is in the years of one and five that the foundations of mental health are laid and here too, is to be found the nucleus of psychoneurosis" (Winnicott, 1958b/1984, p. 7).

The early development of the infant is described by Hedges (1994b) as the "organising experience", referring to the process occurring within the infant within the first few months of life, maybe even in the womb. This description has also been used by Yorke (1986) and by Stolorow and Atwood (1992) to designate a state of psychological organisation. When the infant fails to organise mental activity because of the absence of a present and attuned mother, it organises around aspects of itself, becoming aversive to contact with the primary nurturing object, that is, the infant fails to attach to a mother who is unavailable. This phenomenon is referred to by Grotstein (1994) as an early massive dissociation of the personality, and he quotes a variety of other theorists describing this period as "infantile catastrophe" (Bion, 1962, 1963), "failure to go on being" (Winnicott, 1952/1984), "annihilation anxiety" (Mahler, 1952, 1958, 1968, 1972) and "black hole anxiety" (Tustin, 1966, 1972) and (Grotstein, 1990). He also describes this as Balint's "basic fault" (1968). Fosha (2003, pp. 227–228) recognises that fear constricts the range of tolerance and exploration of emotion. In the absence of such "dyadically constructed safety", energy will be devoted to defence mechanisms to enable the infant to psychologically survive. Adams (2006) identifies the primitive nature of the defences used by such clients. In her 2009 work she identifies how, in primitive ego states, terror of intimacy and the need for human contact in dichotomy can result in the experience of annihilation anxiety and dissociation.

The concept of the "false self" (Winnicott, 1965a/1984) can be seen as such a defence mechanism, where the vulnerable "true self", because of the risk of annihilation, is split off, sequestered and protected by the "false self". The "false self" hides the "true self" by complying with the environmental demands, and in extreme circumstances may completely isolate the "true self". Splitting is a complex subject, and as such I am limiting it in this book to my understanding of splitting which relates largely to Winnicott's meaning, where spontaneous and creative aspects of self are split-off or isolated from the rest of the personality. This isolation of an aspect of self could also be seen as dissociation, a defence mechanism of primitive origin.

Guntrip (1971, p. 172) describes what he sees as splitting of the ego: "Here, in this complex pattern of ego-splitting or loss of primary psychic unity, with all the weakness and internal conflict it involves, is the root cause of personality disorders in later life: and the most vulnerable part of the self is the most hidden part, cut off from all human relationships in the depths of the unconscious." According to Klein (1987) Guntrip has developed this construct through lack of knowledge of the development of the infant, basing his understanding only on what he saw of adults in the consulting room. Klein considers that this led to Guntrip misunderstanding ego development.

The splitting off of aspects of the self in early infancy could be seen to result in "walled off" separate self states, which are thus avoided in order to maintain functionality, and to manage adaptation to the demands of the environment. This self state can also be retreated into in regression. An increased understanding of infantile development has enabled increased understanding of this early process.

## Attachment

In his 1988 work Bowlby described the applications of attachment theory developed during his previous writings (1969/1982, 1973, 1980). He propounded a model of the development of the attachment bond between infant and primary caregiver, seeing the infant leading the relationship, and the mother/caregiver sensitively responding. The mother's response to the infant's cues (her attunement) leads the infant to adapt either towards, or away from, cooperation with her. Those infants receiving attentive loving care will view themselves as loveable, developing secure attachment behaviours while those whose comfort-seeking behaviour is dismissed or rejected will see themselves as unlovable and will develop insecure attachment behaviours.

From an attachment theory perspective chronic misattuned dyadic interactions can result in disorders of attachment. Attachment theory describes the nature of significant relationships between humans from their development in infancy through to later life (Bowlby, 1969).

## Trauma and cumulative trauma

Having explored the results of environmental failure upon the developing infant it is evident to me from this construction of human development that where provision fails and deprivation results, trauma could be experienced by the infant. Winnicott (1958b/1984) described maternal failures as "impingements" upon the infant's experience, affecting its sense of "going on being". He sees that frequent and serious impingements can lead to failure to develop a sense of being real and a fear of annihilation with most impingements occurring because of misattunement between mother and baby. In Winnicott's view, during infancy the ego is too immature to manage the "primitive agony" of serious and frequent impingement leading to the development of a "false self" defence and "self disorder" (1989, p. 91). He coined the term "false self" to describe a defensive organisation in which the protective functions of the mother, which are unavailable to the infant because of misattunement, are instead taken over by an aspect of self. The taking over of this function allows the infant to adapt to the environment whilst protecting and hiding the source of personal impulses, viewed as the "true self". The "true self" then could become sequestered to avoid the risk of annihilation when impingements are too severe and too frequent. While being protected by the "false self", opportunities for "true self" living were limited by the actions of the "false self". He considered that the "true self" was the source of spontaneity and real impulse, and for this aspect of self to function at its fullest someone else would need to take over once again functions which defend the "true self" (we will see later that this role is within the domain of the therapist). In the regression the client returns to a developmental phase which is incomplete, and this has previously been managed by the development of defences to compensate for this incompleteness.

Trauma can take the form of easily identifiable events, such as abuse or physical neglect, but also can involve repeated less discrete but more pervasive accumulations of misattunements which are traumatising to the young infant who does not have the psychological reserves with which to manage overwhelming and painful emotions. This is known by some theorists as cumulative trauma. The concept of cumulative trauma is identified by Khan (1963) as resulting from the lack of fit between child and parent, and as a specific traumatic childhood experience based on continuous environmental failure (misattunements) from a caretaker in infancy (Lourie, 1996), leading to psychopathology. Fosha (2003, p. 226) also recognises the impact of cumulative trauma "the sequelae of trauma and neglect not only become evident in the dramatic disturbances of PTSD, but also make themselves known and felt in the havoc wreaked on social relationships and the devastating ruin of a baseline of well-being". Lourie (1996) sees the result of these failures as having an impact on the child's developing relationships into adulthood with both themselves and others. To manage these feelings requires the development of defences, initially to protect against the effects of further failures. She considers these defences from the perspective of bodily armour which was donned in infancy and remains so into adulthood.

Hurvich (2000, p. 82) quotes Rothstein (1983) regarding the unconscious presence of the early traumas of infancy, "the primal traumas and therefore the primal danger situations are derived from pre-verbal memory traces of experiences of mounting tension that never become conscious in the true sense and are in a state of primary repression. The infantile ego's experience of these primal traumas is influenced by its 'basic core' (Weil, 1970) and by the quality of its caregiving environment". Hurvich (2000) also acknowledges the mother's role as the protector against over-stimulation, citing among others Khan (1963), Searles (1965), and Winnicott (1958b/1984). Fosha (2003) identifies that the receipt of empathically attuned caregiving results in the child experiencing himself as an individual, enabling him to modulate emotion, to have flexible responses and to have resilience. Empathically attuned care, which is ideal in the mother/infant relationship, can be supplied in the therapeutic relationship with dyadic affective processes of attunement, empathy and repair. She considers that "the processing of emotional experience solidifies, rather than taxes and erodes, the attachment bond".

When the facilitating environment does not appropriately match the needs of the infant, the resulting psychic disturbance is described by Balint (1968, pp. 19–22) as "the basic fault". He considers that this fault which develops in infancy can remain for the whole of a person's life "it is a fault, something wrong in the mind, a kind of deficiency which must be put right. It is not something dammed up for which a better outlet must be found, but something missing". His theory of "new beginnings" required the patient to be capable of regression, that is, a return to the area of the "basic fault" in order to re-emerge with the capacity for a mature object relationship. Winterson (2011, p. 145) identifies that "the past is so hard to shift. It comes with us like a chaperone, standing between us and the newness of the present—the new chance".

Winnicott conceptualised similar experiences in his 1974 paper entitled "Fear of breakdown" where he described the ego's inability to encompass intense emotional experiences, a view with which Erskine (2007) concurs. Psychosis is seen as "the defensive organisation designed to protect the self" resulting from failures in the infant care process. He described the infant in a place of psychotic anxiety with feelings of annihilation, going to pieces, falling for ever, having no relation to the body, having no orientation in the world, and complete isolation without means of communication. In his view, these horrors surface in later life as psychotic or borderline-state anxieties in which one's very being seems threatened. Rather than its present-day association with schizophrenia, psychosis is used in its original sense to denote a loss of contact with reality, strange experiences and a sense that personality is fragmented or dislocated in some way. One of my research participants describes such an experience:

> [...] to the regression that I experienced as being in such a deep, dark place that it was, it still is, quite hard to talk about it [...] I built myself a couch on the couch, and got a blanket and for about two to three days just stayed in a crazy place [...] I was in and out of consciousness all the time [...] I felt feverish, sick. [...]

This complete disorganisation of the self is described by Winnicott (1974) as the "unthinkable state of affairs that underlies the defence organisation" (1974). This psychotic anxiety concerns survival and identity, and relates to the earliest experiences of the infant as described by this participant:

> [...] in the most vulnerable place, not being able to understand it and not have words for the experience, really, so it becomes like a psychotic experience, because you can't, you can't, don't have a frame for it. [...]

Little (1990) described such experiences as resulting from pockets of psychosis which can be experienced in the regression to dependence process, as in her 1981 quotation from Santayana (1921) "the suppressed madness in a sane man". When clients are in this phase they may be considered to be experiencing the terror and rage of early maternal failure, and the therapist's task is to provide a holding environment to allow the experience and expression of these emotions. Winnicott describes "unthinkable" or "archaic" anxiety being aroused by trauma "against which an individual has no organised defence, so that a confusional state supervenes". It can be experienced as annihilation, total destruction, falling forever, being isolated through having no means of communication, being unconnected to the body, or being lost in space (Winnicott, 1958b/1984, 1965b/1984). Integration can then be promoted in an environment where needs can be acknowledged, validated and appropriately met. He identified how the transference relationship becomes real for the client, "In so far as the patient is regressed (for a moment or for an hour, or over a long period of time) the couch *is* the analyst, the pillows *are* breasts, the analyst *is* the mother at a certain past era" so recognising this psychotic aspect of the regression (1984, p. 288).

Little (1990, p. 83) considers that the value of regression to dependence is identified thus "it is a means by which areas where psychotic anxieties predominate can be explored, early experiences uncovered, and underlying delusional ideas recognised and resolved, via the transference/countertransference partnership of analyst and analysand, in both positive and negative phases". In a conversation with the author Richard Erskine, he described to me how he views clients' regression as a need "to tell their story at the emotional, physiological level of the narrative", seeing it as a form of non-verbal early communication of those neglectful and traumatic experiences.

Clients frequently present with chronic anxiety as the motivation for attending therapy. This anxiety is often spilling out into every part of their life, at times reaching its culmination in chronic panic attacks, whereby the fear has been described to me as of death, collapse and/or annihilation. Cognitive therapies aim to change thinking about these outcomes, but in my experience these fears appear again in a slightly different form. It seems clear to me that whilst short-term therapy for these issues may address symptoms it does not holistically address a person's life issues.

In facilitating clients to revisit early developmental stages clients inevitably re-experience any psychological trauma which occurred as a result of an environmental deficit. This can be a frightening experience which cannot be articulated because it is of pre-verbal origin as described by some of my participants:

> I couldn't find the language though I was in terror at times though I couldn't [...] move it in any way forward.
> [...] it was utterly [...] and all consuming.
> And I know I knew, but I didn't have the language for it [...].
> [...] of regressing to a kind of wordless state.
> [...] helping me make the history and not lose the thread with me, and it was all on this, on the regressive pre-verbal, really pre-verbal, you know we're talking about early [...] we're talking the first few months, your birth to the first few months.

In similar vein, Laing (1960, p. 99) described this psychosis as "simply the sudden removal of the veil of the false-self which had been serving to maintain an outer behavioural normality that may, long ago, have failed to be any reflection of the state of affairs in the secret self".

Within the therapeutic regression to dependency process the regressive pull is in the interest of progression, i.e., for the individual to master that incomplete developmental phase. Kohut (1977, p. 178) identified the single "original development tendency" which is reactivated in the therapy, allowing the client to search for the developmentally needed, reparative relationship.

## Regression ...

*The Shorter Oxford Dictionary*'s (1983) definition of regression is "a return to a subject: the action of returning to or towards the place or point of departure: return to or into a state or condition: reversion to a less developed form". The term "regression" can refer to experiences of regression or shock occurring spontaneously in a client's life, or spontaneously within the therapeutic relationship which the therapist has not facilitated, but should respond to. It can also refer to the regression occurring as a result of the therapist's facilitation in order to allow the client to connect with earlier developmental aspects of their experience for healing purposes (Clarkson, 2003).

Regression is a well-documented experience in therapy (Balint, 1968; Bollas, 1987; Erskine, 1998). I would view regression occurring in everyday life in some cases, for example, individuals returning to study in later life may both remember and affectively experience feelings as if they were children in school once more, likewise a job interview can bring with it the experience as if the individual is back in the headmaster's office, and attending a party can reconfigure the experience of being on the playground. Clients can bring into therapy stories of difficult experiences in their everyday life of which they have no understanding. They bring with them such experiences for exploration and also bring with them their conscious or unconscious representations of historic stories that can re-emerge in the therapy room in differing ways. Many therapists will work with these stories to express affect, to understand their meaning, offering empathy and support.

In the therapeutic setting the client's history can become re-enacted, allowing for the possibility of a different experience and so providing the opportunity for relational repair where the client can experience both emotional and physiological effects. If managed correctly the client can feel understood, supported and often healed by the interaction between themselves and the therapist, and some new insight may be gained from this revisit which reframes the experience through the eyes of an adult. So, for example, an individual might have experienced physical or sexual abuse as a child and have felt blamed and shamed by themselves and others. Having viewed this with an empathic other, the support and concern that was not available at the time of the original incident(s) can be offered by the therapist.

This conceptualisation of regression considers that the client's need is to experience the developmental stage prior to that in which ego damage occurred in order to offer repair, and progress into later ego development (Van Sweden, 1995, p. 197). He quotes Winnicott's view of regression within the therapeutic relationship: "The patient regresses because of a new environmental provision which allows of dependence." "The regression represents the [...] individual's hope that certain aspects of the environment which failed originally may be re-lived, with the environment this time succeeding instead of failing" (Winnicott, 1989, p. 128).

## ... to dependence

"Regression is a flight backwards in search of security and a chance for a new start. But regression becomes an illness in the absence of any therapeutic person to regress with and to" (Guntrip, 1969, p. 86). He is describing the needed regression to dependence which is at the heart of this book.

The way that the concept of dependency within psychotherapy is viewed by some theorists is highlighted by Weiss (2002). He explains that some theorists writing on dependence tend to see it as pathological, and that this stems from the idea that dependency is something to "get over" in order to become truly independent. He cites Guntrip's (1969) recognition of mature dependency as "what makes the experience of independence possible, and that independence without a mature dependence is only pseudo independence", which Weiss sees as self-sufficiency (Weiss, 2002, p. 8). This concept suggests that independence naturally emerges through satisfactory resolution of dependency needs. Weiss highlights that therapists may respond from three potential positions: a) they may withhold gratification of dependency needs; b) they may attempt to respond literally; or c) symbolically. Their response will depend upon their theoretical understanding of the process (p. 11). He also considers that "the more wounded the patient the more likely he is to experience his needs in literal rather than symbolic terms", which echoes Winnicott's understanding of the loss of the "as if" within the transference (1958b/1984).

Some clients enter therapy with obvious dependency issues, some clients are so extremely independent that they cannot acknowledge any need of another and present with an extreme self-reliance and almost pathological independence. In either circumstance the issue emerges from an environment where appropriate dependency does not develop, but remains in the psyche and in adult relationships as a searched for relationship or as a confusing aversion to such relationships. Guntrip (1969, pp. 85–86) recognises that this process usually takes a long time before the patient can reveal the passively dependent ego because of the anti-libidinal defence of independence. This means that when the client understands and accepts the regressive process they are able to allow it, and "find security for their regressed ego in the psychotherapeutic relationship".

Steele et al. (2001) identify an evidence base which demonstrates that dependency increases where there are insecure attachments which developed in traumatic parental environments. Clients with these attachment styles can present with dependency issues which can be extreme and contradictory. They describe this traumatically induced dependency as a "manifestation of the attachment emotional system" but also "closely related to a defence" that is the struggle of the client to stay with the other, to cling on demonstrates the dependency relationship but also defends against loss of the other. Bornstein (1993) notes that every theory of personality includes a conceptual model of dependency, that is, a philosophical/theoretical understanding of the presence of dependency in adulthood. Humanists and behaviourists see dependency as a defensive behaviour resulting from a failure to self-actualise, while the psychodynamic view links dependency to events in the oral period, linking personality development to feeding, Freud (1905d). The psychodynamic view of "fixation" means that conflicts which are unresolved remain fixated into adulthood, for example, someone who is orally fixated may remain inappropriately dependent into adulthood and manifest oral need for food, smoking, etc. In psychoanalytic theory oral fixation is seen on a continuum. This is considered to be out of awareness by repression, denial, and other ego defences. Bornstein (1993) also notes that these defences keep dependency needs out of awareness unless under extreme regression. Steele et al. (2001)

also offer insights from Akhtar (1999) regarding the difference between wishes and needs, a frustrated wish for another to depend on to avoid the pain of mourning what didn't happen in infancy may lead to an internal shift in the dynamics of the client, whereas a frustrated need for dependency may lead to a fragmentation of the self. This resonates with Balint's (1968) benign or malignant regression.

Regression is seen by Balint (1968) as a demand for a certain kind of relationship, namely the early relationship into dependency, seeing that this need occurs when there is a mismatch between the infant's needs and the environmental provision. He considers that an individual develops more or less normally to the point when he experiences trauma, from that point on any further development is fundamentally affected by the method chosen to cope with the effects of that particular trauma. These effects are the defences developed by the infant to enable the primitive ego to survive the trauma, and are described more fully in the chapter on Terror. The aim of facilitating regression to dependence then is to relationally re-experience with the client their development prior to the time when the trauma had occurred, thus allowing the possibility for undoing the primitive defences. In his foreword to Hedges' work Grotstein (1994a, p. xxi) posits that "all emotional illnesses spring from failures or disorders of bonding and/or attachment in some measure". The task of psychotherapy is then "to help establish anew, or to restore the conduit of attachment and bonding". Van Sweden (1995) describes regression to dependence as a "second opportunity for ego integration and developmental progression", an opportunity which had been unavailable to clients who have experienced maternal deprivation in early life, thus leaving lacunae in their ego integration which then impacts their later relational capacity.

The object relations movement and the attachment theorists emphasise the infant/caretaker relationship where the infant is seen as appropriately dependent on the mother, but de-emphasise practical oral activities seeing the actual relationship between mother and infant as a dependent one from an emotional perspective, and rather than physical deprivation of the breast emotional deprivation being the precursor of dependant personality traits. I would suggest that both biological dependency needs and emotional dependency needs have some correlation in the development of dependent personality traits and subsequently can become a factor in their repair. This work does not consider specifically or in detail those with dependent personality traits, whereby help is sought from anyone who seems able to provide it, but rather addresses those dependency needs which are related to relationship and attachment, where the dependency is focused upon a particular individual for support, attention and reliability. Steele et al. (2001) note that dependency increases in insecure attachment relationships where there is trauma or neglect. So we can conclude from these relationship focus models that environmental failure in the normal developmental period where dependency is appropriate, results in a potentially life-long search, either consciously or unconsciously for that solid, reliable, transformative other who can bond with the individual and offer the potential for that individual to grow through dependency into the relational interdependency of adulthood. Steele et al. consider that Bornstein and Bowen (1995) clearly link dependency with attempts to develop a secure attachment relationship. In integrative psychotherapy the aim is to develop an inter-dependence whereby individuals are supported by trusted persons whose help they can access when in need.

The process of regression offers a chance to re-visit previous developmental stages and learn new ways of relating. The regression is not a regression back to something that was once there but became lost, but rather to a developmental epoch where something was needed but never existed. Bromberg (1991, pp. 416–417) recognises the need and the value of regression for some patients "[...] the deeper the regression that can be safely allowed by the patient, the richer the experience and the greater its reverberation on the total organization of the self."

## Regression and progression

Balint (1959) considered that making a "new beginning" meant going back—regression, to something "primitive" to a point before the faulty development started, and finding a new way of relating—progression. Winnicott (1958b/1984), Balint (1968), and Van Sweden (1965) are among the theorists who view this return in terms of a therapeutic experience and a theoretical concept. The process of regression to dependence aims to treat clients whose psychological damage relates to early emotional development prior to the development of self (Winnicott, 1958b/1984, p. 280). He recognised in these clients the "very early development of a False Self [and, in order] for treatment to be effective, there had to be a regression in search of the True Self". Given this premise then treatment involving regression to a state prior to the development of the "false self" is appropriate.

Van Sweden (1995, p. 210) recognises the paradox of the regression to dependence process:

> Paradoxically, the way to progress is to regress; in this case, further developmental progression can only occur through the regression-to-dependence process. The greatest reward of this progress is that the analysand is finally able to relinquish a life of futility and hope-lessness and to move toward the creation of a new life that is emotionally rich, full of vitality and hope.

This concurs with Winnicott's (1963a) thinking. These dependency needs, when revived in the therapeutic relationship, offer the opportunity for a corrective experience and also an opportunity to understand them from an adult perspective, rather than helplessly as a child would.

This chapter has identified the importance of regression to dependence and how this can result in progression for the client. It is important to mention however that when the therapeutic relationship becomes "significant" the regressive processes which occur as a result of the transference can result in the re-experiencing of frightening feelings and their subsequent defences. This process is developed further in the chapter on Terror.

## Conclusion

Within this chapter I have identified the experiences of participants which relate to the concept of regression to early developmental stages. Having explored theories relating to infant development I have identified how failures in an infant's early environment can result in relational difficulties and trauma, and the effects upon attachment patterns which then may continue into adult life. Unconscious processes have been identified as being present in the therapeutic relationship, and viewed as transference enactments which re-configure aspects of the client's early relational history. I have described my understanding of regression and regression to dependence, and identified the psychological hope that regression can result in the client being able to move on; to progress. "It is as if there is an expectation that favourable conditions may arise justifying regression and offering a new chance for forward development, that which was rendered impossible or difficult initially by environmental failure" (Winnicott, 1958a/1984, p. 281).

When the interaction between caregiver and infant is placed at the centre of developmental theory and the therapeutic relationship is formulated as a replication of the original infant/caregiver relationship because of its dyadic nature, and its intense focus on the client and hypnotic quality, then the potential for relational repair becomes possible. This repair can span a wide spectrum of therapeutic interventions, from the offering of a listening and non-judgmental space for a client to explore issues which are currently troubling, to a regression to, and re-experiencing of, traumatic events in early life. In a facilitative relationship these traumatic events can be identified, and a narrative of the client's experience can emerge. Erskine (1998) views these aspects of experience as "a form of non-verbal early communication of those neglectful and traumatic experiences". This view of the relational and communicative aspects of regression echoes Balint's (1968) view. Bromberg (1991, p. 416) considered that: "Therapeutic regression refers to the raw states of cognitive disequilibrium allowed by an analytic patient as part of the progressive self-perpetuating restructuring of the self and object representations."

Winterson (2011, p. 172) writes about the consequences of her dysfunctional childhood:

> This is the most dangerous work you can do. It is like bomb disposal but you are the bomb. That's the problem—the awful thing is you. It may be split off and living malevolently at the bottom of the garden, but it is sharing your blood and eating your food. Mess this up, and you will go down with the creature.

Flanders Dunbar (1947, p. 45) had formulated such experiences thus:

> [...] the delayed-action mines of childhood, planted either in shock of some single incident or in the steady friction of a conflict between mind and environment. Once these mines have been planted, they may become covered over with a thick, hard crust of oblivion, but they never cease to be dangerous unless the fuses can be drawn.

It is my belief that regression to dependency occurring and facilitated within the therapeutic relationship is the process by which the mines are defused.

For a time in my personal therapy I became aware of an aspect of me that felt dead. I could see it as an aspect of my true self, or a sequestered infantile aspect of me. I felt as though I was taking a dead baby to therapy with me, and I had many dreams about carrying a dead infant in a bag. These dreams developed over a period of time, so that initially the baby was dead, then it was barely alive, but I kept leaving it outside the therapist's door where it would become frozen, until eventually it came into the room. I viewed this as a development in my ability to re-integrate a split. In almost every way I was describing what I saw as the existence of the split-off, inert, infant ego. In Winnicott's (1958b/1984) view this split-off infant ego results from disruptions or deficits in caregiving in infancy. In other words, this had constituted too much impingement upon myself as an infant and had made this splitting-off necessary. Splitting is seen as an early defence to wall off experiences which are impossible for the infant to contain so that it can keep pain away from itself and continue to function. Over time, my therapy sessions needed to increase in frequency to contain my increasing levels of disturbance which included manifestations of psychotic anxiety during the sessions. These were always well contained and eventually my terror of my own "craziness" was diminished by my therapist's acceptance and management of my behaviour. Throughout this period there was movement both towards intimacy and flight from it, but I gradually allowed my infancy needs to emerge and begin to be met despite my shame about them. These experiences then, rather than being unique or idiosyncratic, have turned out to represent a valuable source of insight in working with my clients. Careful reflection on their own experiences like this can enhance the empathic reach of the therapist in assisting clients with their troubles.

Kohut (1977, p. 178) considers that a person's strength depends on the organising and integrating processes. Where these are split off and inaccessible a person may be lacking in integration without a reliable and intelligent ego able to work through the normal analytic process using words. Psychotherapy provides a supportive environment "until such time as their nuclear self becomes consolidated". In the next chapter I will explore the sort of supportive environment which may be seen to address these issues, and some theories which recognise and respond to these symptoms, offering comments and suggestions for the therapeutic response.

# CHAPTER THREE

# Shame in regression to dependence

I couldn't own my own skin, you know, shame just for existing, shame, shame for feeling, shame for whatever feeling, you know the messages in my childhood were, "don't feel, just don't", so [...] don't need [...] "don't exist". (Extract from research data)

## Introduction

The above description of shame from one of my research participants links their experience with childhood messages. Whilst shame is a normal human emotion it is the destructive aspect of shame that is frequently present within the psychotherapeutic encounter and particularly within the regression to dependence process. Shame is a relational wounding which particularly impacts the therapeutic work. Shame can be a block to progression, particularly affecting the client's ability to identify and articulate their needs. Brenne Brown (2010, p. 26) identifies the injurious role that shame can play, "Shame, blame, disrespect, betrayal, and the withholding of affection damage the roots from which love grows. Love can only survive these injuries if they are acknowledged, healed and rare." It is part of the therapeutic task to acknowledge and offer a relational healing of these injuries.

In this chapter I will consider the role of shame, its development in infancy and the potential for repair through the therapeutic relationship.

## Shame as normal human emotion, or as a destructive force

Shame has been recognised "since antiquity" (Gilbert & Andrews, 1988), and there are powerful words used to describe the feeling of shame which emerge from poetic and theological imagery, linking the biblical description of Adam's sin and the resulting experiences of shame when separated from God, or the dualistic view of good or evil where to sin results in the ultimate punishment of Hell. Evans (1994) sees shame in this way, calling the experience of shame "a descent into Hell". Kaufman (1992) cites Tomkins' (1962, 1963) view of shame as "a sickness of the soul", and Lewis (1987, p. 95) describes shame as "a momentary 'destruction' of the self in acute denigration". Bradshaw (1988) cites Kaufman's term of "internal shame spirals", where shame feelings "flow in a circle, endlessly triggering each other" (ibid., p. 60).

Kaufman (1994) uses Schneider's (1977) identification of the word "shame" as having its origin in two words with opposite meanings— "cover" and "exposure", leading him to consider shame as a regulative principle. He then identifies normative (healthy) shame leading to self-experience and self-exposure, and dysregulative (toxic) shame involving inhibition or exposure.

The feeling of shame belongs within humanity, identifying limits and boundaries of the self and others, helping individuals to know their need of others (Bradshaw, 1988). The work in regression to dependence has its focus in the early stages of the client's infancy experience; it is here that shame is considered to develop. Erikson (1950) places shame as a stage of psycho-social development where, based upon the environmental response, the infant learns a self position of shame or acceptance. When the infant does not see its own acceptability in its mother's eyes, but sees instead disapproval, disgust or disdain, shame as an identity forms. If the mother herself has been looked at in infancy with non-acceptance, this may be the only look she is able to give to the infant, and the intergenerational transmission of shame continues. Nathanson (1987, 1992) considers shame to have been an ignored emotion, having a hidden nature, and an evolutionary connection. He describes the shame process, physiologically and psychologically; a position held by other theorists such as Bradshaw (1988), Lansky (1994), Erskine (1995), and Shaw (1998).

Bradshaw (1988) identifies "the interpersonal bridge" which is an emotional bond formed between child and caretaker, and represents the significance of the other to the child. Gestalt therapists Perls, Hefferline, and Goodman (1951) view the self as created at the contact-boundary between the self and the environment, and that the self is a system of awareness at the boundary between self and other. Erikson (1950) cites shame in the second stage of psychosocial development concerning the development of this bond of the interpersonal bridge between self and other; with the establishment of this significant relationship in early infancy comes the recognition of the importance of the relationship and with it the potential for shame.

## Shame as relational wounding

In the infant's early environment, it's significant others show it what is acceptable, either explicitly or implicitly. This can be demonstrated to the infant verbally or non-verbally, so when the infant spontaneously takes action, needs, feels, thinks, looks like, the way in which they move can be met with approval or disapproval within their environment. In healthy development the child needs to learn that his developing autonomy will not destroy the interpersonal bridge. From this position the other's approval or disapproval has profound importance for the infant and can be part of a normal socialisation process or can result in psychopathology, thereby constricting the self-development and leaving the infant with a negative reaction to themselves. Bradshaw (1988) considers that when the child's parents are shame-based they are only able to focus on their own need and, therefore, are unable to address the child's need when it clashes with the parent's need. The child grows up and develops, but underneath still remains the neglected child with "a hole in the soul" (Tomkins, 1962, 1963), which is unable to be filled within adult to adult relationships, because it is the needs of the archaic infant, present in the adult, which are yearned for.

Shame is a normal human emotion and can be healthy, when the infant experiences his own limits, or can be experienced as toxic:

> Shame as a healthy human emotion can be transformed into shame
> as a state of being. As a state of being, shame takes over one's whole

identity. To have shame as an identity is to believe that one's very being is flawed, that one is defective as a human being. Once shame is transformed into an identity, it becomes toxic and dehumanising.

Shame carries with it feelings of being defective, unlovable, dirty, and can be based on any aspect of a person. This sense of being shameful develops over the years and the infant is unable to internalise a sense of himself/herself as loved and respected (Bradshaw, 1988, p. vii). This situation can arise as a result of a lack of empathy, misattunement and cumulative trauma, and, of course, in all other types of abuse (Bradshaw, 1988; Erskine, 1995). Shame is a relational rupture caused by humiliation, criticism, putting someone down, and diminishing them. This situation is widely known as "toxic shame", a term primarily emerging from Transactional Analysis (Stewart & Joines, 1987).

## The consequences of destructive shame

Because of the central role played by shame in social and self development, when it becomes a state of being, taking over the whole identity, it can result in the development of feelings of inadequacy and worthlessness resulting in poor functioning and emotional distress, feelings of isolation because of difficulty in relating to others, and ultimately lead to psychopathology (Lewis, 1971), affecting the ability to trust oneself and one's own judgement, feelings, needs or desires. When an infant has experienced non-acceptance of itself frequently and over a relatively long period of time, the experience of shame is internalised and the self and all the expressions of that self feel shameful.

Solomon and Siegel (2003) consider that early exposure to shame and humiliation are, frequent accompaniments to early child abuse. Fosha (2002) identifies fear and shame arising when the response of the attachment figure to the child's affective experience is traumatic. When there is no repair of this trauma the child experiences emotional overwhelm, loss of self and lack of safety in the emotional environment. These affects are pathogenic and can therefore be experienced by the individual who is alone.

The experiencing of fear and shame (which are normal emotional responses to external situations) are problematic when they are generated by the attachment figure itself, "when shame and fear are elicited by disruptive experiences with attachment figures *and* cannot be dyadicly repaired, individuals find themselves alone, emotionally overwhelmed, unable to be real and unable to count on the safety of the emotional environment. Highly aversive, the hallmark of *the pathogenic affects* is that they are experienced by an individual who is alone, as the affect-regulating attachment relationship has collapsed" (Solomon & Siegel, 2003, p. 242). Fosha (2002), cited in Soloman and Siegel (2003), identified fear and shame as pathogenic affects arising when the attachment figure's response is disturbing and disruptive.

There is general agreement that shame follows some kind of exposure which reveals a vulnerable side of self. Wurmser (1987) summarises what we are most ashamed of, the main points being; I am weak and a failure; I am dirty, messy and disgusting; I am defective, physically or mentally. All of these views contribute to the sense of being wrong and feeling wrong. This non-acceptance, which begins as an external experience, becomes internalised as part of the self.

The connection between being seen and shame is made by Wright (1991) who also acknowledges that shame can occur in isolation when both aspects of self and other are intrapsychically experienced. He quotes from Lynd (1958) that "shame forces into awareness some aspect of one's self that one had not realised". Clients often experience buried needs and thus feel shame as they come into awareness during therapy, but ultimately the experience of shame can increase self-awareness and understanding of one's own needs and identity. He argues that shame begins in the experience of being seen by the other and the realisation that the other can see things about us that we may not be aware of. The experience of shame, then, occurs when one's awareness of one's self shifts from the embodied experience to a perceived objective view of one's self. He also quotes from Sartre (1957) writing about the threat of the other, and the other's objectively defining of the self. Wright sees that the threat of attack by the other is a threat to annihilate the subjective self, by becoming an object of the other in their subjective world.

## The development of the "false self"

If an aspect of self is deemed unacceptable within the family system, then it may be disowned and so, when it is subsequently experienced, it brings feelings of shame with it. As feelings, needs and drives become bound up with shame, these disowned aspects result in  from self (Bradshaw, 1988 p. 13). This results in objectification of aspects of self, when eyes are "inward, watching and scrutinising every minute detail of behaviour". The following participant describes her shame for having needs in her therapy:

> I think at the beginning it was definitely enormous, the shame, just embarrassment and thinking, "I shouldn't be here, I shouldn't need to be held, I shouldn't need all of this".

Bradshaw (1988, p. 14) uses Winnicott's concept of the "false self" to describe a carapace which covers the vulnerable and shamed "true self". The concept "false self" is a misnomer as Winnicott's concept is better described as "an incomplete self" as it is missing the completing aspect of the "true self". He sees the creation of the "false self" as an escape from exposure, developed to cover up a "deep sense of self-rupture, the hole in their soul". He recognises the hiding nature of toxic shame, seeing its development when the unexpected exposure of vulnerability occurs before the child has their ego boundaries for protection (p. 14).

In Winnicott's (1967) construction of the development of self in infancy he identifies the mother's face as the child's first mirror, thus, if the child sees the mother's expression of disapproval, disgust, disdain then the child will ascribe these characteristics to the developing self, which includes the infant's needs, likes, dislikes, looks, shape, feelings; the entirety of its being. He considers that, to look creatively at the world, the infant must first of all have been seen and internalised that experience. The infant depends on the mother's facial expressions when looking at her to establish its own sense of self. Jacobs (1988) identifies that Erikson (1950) associates shame with the inability to perform tasks and a self image of being immature. Jacobs differentiates this from shame associated with damage to the self. Infants are dependent upon their caretakers for their needs to be met. When needs for dependency, physical contact, mirroring, empathy, and any other need have been neglected by the caretaker these needs themselves can become a source of shame, for example, where physical contact has been experienced as shameful in childhood the individual in adult life is shamed both by physical contact itself and the need for it. This is demonstrated in the words of a research participant, who recognises that shame issues around touch link back to issues around touch with his mother:

I think it stirred up intense shame issues for me, which go right
back to my early childhood, and I think … rejection to do with
touch with my own mother […] and issues that […] clearly got
caught up with it all […]

A sense of personal value is lost when children are given the message
by their parents/caregiver that their needs are not important. When this
need deprivation is experienced, the child's awareness of their needs
can be lost to them. Bradshaw (1988) considers that "our families are
where we first learn about ourselves" where our "significant relationships are our source relationships" and the learning about ourselves
and our relationships from these sources is taken into adult relationships (1988, p. 29). Josselson (1992, p. 117) identifies shame as resulting
from "putting forward some valued part of ourselves and seeing revulsion in another's eyes". When this revulsion or non-acceptance is seen
in the mother's eyes in infancy the effects upon the developing personality can be devastating. Erskine (1995) recognises that when a client
has internalised a sense of shame in childhood they can adopt a belief
that "there's something wrong with me" which Erskine sees as a confluence with those who have shamed them. He describes this as consisting
of "a child's defensive transposition of sadness and fear, a disavowal
and retroflection of anger at not being treated respectfully, and a fixated
diminished self-concept in confluence with the introjected criticism"
(Erskine, 1995, p. 5).

Shaw (1998) considered that there appear to be two types of shame
response; an innate biologically driven affect, and an internalised
response within relationship. The biological affect is triggered in the
here-and-now environment, "relational shame" can occur within relationship or when one is alone in relationship with one's self.

Kaufman (1992, 1993) sees shame as intrapsychically internalised,
and the striving for perfection as a defensive strategy against shame
and the pursuit of power as an attempt to cover the sense of defectiveness that accompanies shame. As someone increases their power, their
vulnerability increases because shame travels down the dominance
hierarchy. Lewis (1987) identifies narcissism as a defence against self-
hatred caused by shame. Bradshaw (1988) sees the striving for power
and control as avoiding shame and vulnerability. In disowning the
shamed self we are driven outside the self; we then objectify the self

and see ourselves as defective. As with Kaufman, pursuit of power and control is seen as a compensation for this sense of defectiveness.

A number of theorists recognise the reduction in functionality as being part of the shame process, for example, Nathanson (1987) cites Darwin on shame, "persons in this condition lose their presence of mind and utter singularly inappropriate remarks" (1872/1979, p. 332). Kalsched (1996) cites McDougall's (1989) term "alexithymia"—having no words for feelings. Shaw (1998) also recognises the wordless component of shame placing the experience of shame in the pre-verbal, quoting from Kaufman (1993) that "shame begins as a largely wordless experience". Shaw makes a comparison between Kohut's (1977) "nameless shame" and Tomkins (1962, 1963) naming of the affects of shame. Erskine (1995) identifies how there can be no language of emotion, "When there has been a lack of attunement, acknowledgement, or validation of needs or feelings within the family or school system, the client may have no language of relationship with which to communicate about his or her affects and needs" (Basch, 1985; Tustin, 1986).

Relational shame is of significance when working with regression to dependence because as clients regress within the therapeutic relationship they re-experience their vulnerability and dependence on the other. They will therefore experience the shame that is within, finding their needs and vulnerabilities shameful and expecting, in the transference relationship, that the therapist will also find them shameful.

## Shame and the therapeutic relationship

Therapists working from a relational/developmental perspective identify extreme shame reactions as emerging from early infancy and childhood, so would also expect that shame would be experienced in clients who are revisiting these early developmental phases. The source of these present experiences of shame is sited in the client's past history, the history of their early relational experiences. Wilkinson (2010) describes early relational trauma and its effects as "the old present".

Jacobs (1995, p. 87) recognises the potentially shame-invoking elements of the therapeutic setting when the client is shame based, seeing that:

> [...] such a patient will likely be exquisitely sensitive to the signs of the differential, easily wounded by its emergence, and assimilate

it readily into a fixed belief that this difference is a confirmation of his unworthiness and of the therapist's understandable distaste for him and his needs.

It is important to note that in society, and in the client population, such experiences may be described differently; as shyness, social anxiety, and social phobia. Shame and guilt are two major forms of negative reaction to one's self. Shame is the feeling that "I am not ok", guilt is the feeling of having done something bad. Shame as an experience in therapy is common and yet often not identified or acknowledged, as the therapist may easily be caught up in the shame process. The experience of shame is frequently accompanied by the need to cover up or hide. In the therapeutic relationship the client may not identify this, but if recognised by the therapist the experience and effects of shame can be brought into the client's awareness, so that over time the shame reaction can become moderated. The experience of shame in a shame prone person can feel very natural and therefore is not identified as an issue in its own right. A person experiencing shame may find speech and articulation difficult when viewing shame through a developmental lens because of its developmental positioning in early infancy. Because of the development of shame in early infancy shame feelings are often not in verbal awareness, existing only on a feeling and embodied level. The anguish of shame and the defences of despair and paranoia can lead to the loss of an aspect of the self which is needed for intimacy. This can result in feelings of emptiness and may be presented at assessment by the client even though the external features of their life appear to be fulfilling.

The power of the therapist in shame bound clients can be experienced as if it were the shaming parent that the client grew up in contact with. Sometimes therapy can replay these past experiences and the client resorts to learned defences against feeling wrong and bad, an experience described by a research participant:

> It was explicit, that she clearly said that we couldn't work if I didn't take more responsibility, and that she was angry with me for not coming, not being there, and I think I then became the compliant child then and did, and was the good girl and did everything she wanted me to do, I came out the right door, did all the things she wanted me to do, so it felt like it repeated the pattern of [...]

cos that's how it would have been with my mum, that I couldn't
tolerate her reaction to my being lost, so I was compliant then. [...]

Josselson (1992) considers that the extreme of shame is the experience
of annihilation, if "I" am not seen, "I" cease to exist, and fragmentation
occurs. Seeing acceptance in the eyes of others is essential to the development of a healthy self. When shame is understood and acknowledged
by the therapist it can allow the client to work through their experience
and develop a reparative relationship which allows the client to start to
develop an identity which is not shame bound and "wrong".

Even when the therapist is accepting and non-shaming, archaic
shame does not just disappear, and can impact the work at any point.
From my own experience, both personally and professionally, even
when the shame process is identified sufficiently well to enable the client to allow regressive needs to surface, shame is still present within
the work and can surface with renewed vigour when there has been a
break in the relationship for holidays or illness, and also when the client
is about to make a new leap forward in the development of the relationship, that is, when the client is about to risk exposure of self, or of needs
of the self, by identifying them to the therapist, shame can emerge,
preventing such exposure and resulting in the client remaining silent.
One of my research participants recognised another aspect of shame as
it emerges in the regression to dependence process. He considers that
helping the client to work through shame enables the client to assess
the therapist's commitment and capacity to hold the regressive process:

> I have to pass this enacted slow test of working through this shame,
> before I have earned the right to be their partner in regressive work.

## Interpersonal reparation

Enquiry into the phenomenological experience and uniqueness of each
individual client will increase understanding of shame for both therapist and client "the therapeutic processes of attunement and involvement acknowledge the difficulty in revealing the inner confusion and
struggles, value the desperate attempt at self-support and coping, and
simultaneously provide a sense of the therapist's presence" (Erskine,
1995, p. 114; Evans, 1994). Kalsched (1996) identifies that therapist self-
disclosure in the face of the client's shame can result in an experience of

shared humanity, so enabling the client to experience her vulnerability with reduced shame.

Working with empathy and attunement is essential for developmental repair. This enables the therapist to identify the client's experiencing of shame. When clients do successfully bring to light their shameful feelings the quality of the therapist's presence and empathy can be a healing experience. If the therapist is able to share a personal but processed shame issue it can give the client a shared experience of the humanity of both parties, seeing shame as present in all humanity rather than solely an experience about themselves. The therapist's response to the client's shame should be empathic, compassionate, and pro-active, helping the client to overcome their shame by initiating actions determined by knowledge of the client, their ego state and empathic attunement. This "attunement occurs in the therapist's honouring of the client's developmental level of coping with shame and the absence of any defining or categorising of the client's fantasies, motivations, or behaviour. Attunement also involves sensitively communicating to the client that the therapist is aware of the inner struggles; that he or she is not all alone in the sadness at not having been accepted as one is, and in the fear of loss of relationship because of whom one is" (Erskine, 1995, p. 8). Premature confrontation, emphasis on emotional expression, excessive focus on aggression, or emphasis only on the here-and-now may cause shame to be experienced by the client. The genuine enquiry into the other's experience, motivation, self-definition, and the way they make meaning avoids the potential for shame and so enhances interpersonal contact. Erskine (1995, p. 109) considers that "when the sense of shame has become fixated it represents an intrapsychic conflict". Clark (1993, p. 52) also recognises the necessity of empathic transactions to diffuse shame identifying the potential interpersonal transmission of shame. She recommends that when therapists fall into the client's shame process "the only way to get out successfully is to use their theory as a ladder to let them out so that they can once again be of some use to the client".

Erskine (1995) identifies the unconscious hope in the client that the caregiver will heal the relational breach. The therapist's task is validation, normalisation, acknowledgement, and presence through which the shame can be diffused.

As in the infancy relationship when the therapist becomes a significant other there is a potential for shame to occur. Lewis (1971) has recognised that "when the therapist failed to recognise the patient's feeling of shame, the patient's problems were prolonged or worsened. When the therapist recognised the shame and helped the patient to deal with it, the treatment was shorter" (cited in Bradshaw, 1988, p. 239).

## Shame binds

When clients' childhood dependency needs have been met with derision, or denied, they can experience a self-attack upon their neediness, considering that this archaic defensive system comes into play as a result of unbearable childhood trauma (Kalsched, 1996, p. 23). In therapy then the client experiences extreme feelings of shame for need which initially may be held out of awareness as a defensive protection. Bradshaw (1988, p. 55) terms shame as the master emotion, because as it is internalised all other emotions are bound by shame. He also considers that the emotional neglect of developmental dependency needs constitutes abandonment.

Feelings of shame for needs are a common experience. Bradshaw (1988) identifies that in toxic shame, feelings, needs, and drives become bound up with shame. This means that any feeling, need or drive is accompanied by shame. "When these are bound by shame, you are shamed to the core" (1988, p. 12). Kalsched (1996, p. 24) describes vulnerable longings, which, when experienced, serve as warnings to the client's psyche of potential re-traumatisation, so a splitting occurs to separate feeling from affect. One of my research participants describes the re-emergence of her experiences in the therapeutic relationship:

> [...] the terror was also about feeling shamed around needing, feeling shamed about wanting and needing of her, and that I couldn't do it all for myself, and that I couldn't be full without needing of her.

Bradshaw (1988) describes these negative shaming, self-deprecating voices which dwell in a shame based person, that is, a person for whom shame has become an aspect of personality, telling them that they are unlovable, worthless, and bad and may be experienced either consciously or unconsciously. He considers that these voices originally keep the child "bad" and the parent "good", thus maintaining the bond between infant and parent. In adult life these critical internal voices can remain, essentially shaming the individual in the same ways in which they were implicitly or explicitly shamed in infancy, but in reality the consequences of these voices are that the individual avoids external shaming because the internal shaming prevents exposure, and that because of this shame flourishes in secret and the spontaneous expression of the individual is blocked. Wurmser (1981) points to the shame-based person's core feeling of unlovability. He describes shame using Freud's words as being "the fear of the super-ego".

For the therapist the demand for perfectionism from oneself as a defence against shame (Bradshaw, 1988) can mean that the therapist attempts to "get it right" in order to avoid shame. This results in a movement away from the relationship with the client and an attempt to be "something that I am not" at the moment, thus presenting a false self rather than real self engagement (Winnicott, 1965a/1984). To recover from toxic shame the individual must come out of hiding. Bradshaw (1988, p. 115) offers some suggestions for the client to combat toxic shame: sharing feelings with significant others, re-establishing an interpersonal bridge with another who is non-shaming, recognising the reality of his story and associated affect, recognition and re-integration of split-off parts. By holding attitudes of love, compassion and acceptance the therapist is able to provide a buffer against shame.

One of my research participants identified the reparation in her personal therapy:

> Well, first of all there was fun, there was never much fun in my childhood, there was fun in the therapy as well as the other stuff, and there was also laughter which was really important to me, and there was just a real sense of affectionate engagement which was really important, and a welcoming, welcoming me into the room which was very important, and for me you know, 'cos I'd got, I had so many kind of quite powerful, strong, dependant/independent kind of [...] to offer that was huge for me, really [...] it really takes me a lot to trust, it did in those days, to trust anybody, so working with those trust issues, welcoming me in [...] to if I'd done paintings or poems I was first greeted with real interest, you know, in what I'd got to say, and no big deal about tears, you know that, that was really important as well. [...]

## Metaphor and shame

Metaphor is frequently used as a therapeutic intervention. When working with shame processes the use of metaphor, either one that the client introduces or one introduced by the therapist, can help to titrate shame. Metaphor allows the therapeutic interaction to move into the third person and out of the here-and-now relationship with the therapist. In this way the client can engage some objectivity and talk "about" rather than "be in" the experience. This movement away from subjective experiencing can help to alleviate some shame and allow the client to talk about subjects which they consider shameful from a "once removed" place. Loue (2008) sees the use of metaphor as a way of enabling the client to externalise what is seen as "the problem". She considers that in working with metaphor we give the client permission to explore their thoughts, feelings, behaviours, ideas and fantasies. Such permission in itself can be shame-reducing, but from my experience, personally and professionally, the use of metaphor and stories enables the client to initially broach and consider issues which may be too shameful to own, but through the use of story they are able to assess the therapist's response, and to explore thoughts and feelings which may eventually become owned and accepted. Zeig (1980) identifies how the use of metaphor can desensitise clients against fears; I would include shame in this. This "stepped" process facilitates the titration of shame.

Tompkins et al. (2005, p. 2) recognise that "clients will often switch to metaphor whenever they need to [...] talk about something obliquely". They recognise that some experiences are too difficult to talk about in other ways. Clark (1993) describes how initially the client has the belief that the therapist sees some aspect of them as shameful, so using metaphor enables the client to test out the therapist's responses to the issue before owning it, so lessening the risk of shame. The field of play therapy recognises the developmental processes that children transition. Working with symbolisation allows children to tell their story. This initially symbolic story becomes languaged through the therapy, and then will begin to take over from symbols. Using metaphor engages with this developmental process and the symbolic emerges to become language which can then be shared and worked through with the therapist.

## Conclusion

In this chapter I have highlighted the presence and development of shame in infancy. The impact of shame, carried into adult life, can then emerge in the therapeutic relationship, where resolution and repair can be offered to address the toxic aspects of shame.

Throughout this chapter I have identified the relevance of an understanding of shame when working with pre-verbal processes. If it is accepted that shame for being, destructive or toxic shame, develops in the pre-verbal experience, then when working with clients in the regressive phases of their therapy its emergence would be expected. If therapists and clients recognise the origin of shame bound needs, feelings and behaviours the therapist can seek to normalise and validate these feelings both in the there-and-then and in the here-and-now, and clients can view these previously shaming aspects with compassion and understanding, thereby reducing shame. By formulating and naming these experiences as related to shame, both therapist and client, having a shared understanding, now have a way to move forward; the issue has become actionable.

Feelings of shame result in vulnerable aspects of self being hidden, therefore it may not be evident to the therapist, especially when their own shame issues remain unaddressed. It takes bravery as a therapist to feel shame, even if countertransferentially (that is, the client's disowned or disavowed shame) yet still bring it into the therapeutic arena. Maroda (1991, p. 65) advocates for therapists' self awareness—"a level of expertise can only be as great as our level of self awareness and our capacity to bear being seen realistically by others". Evans (1994, p. 107) considers this to be particularly true when working with shame processes. He supports the view that it is necessary for therapists to face their own "enemy within" in order to facilitate the client's self-awareness. He considers that in facing the enemy within he has diminished the enemy's power, "I am no longer ashamed of being ashamed". Jacobs (1995, p. 90) considers that therapy can offer resolution for internalised shame:

> [...] thus, the most basic shaming self-statement "I am unfit for human company", has the most potential for resolution by paying close attention to the vicissitudes of shame between the therapist and the patient. In my opinion, the resolution of internalised shame is one of the greatest gifts we can offer to patients as they work to transform their contacting and their lives.

I consider that addressing such toxic shame is an important task of therapy, which once addressed leaves the client with more freedom to reveal their story in a meaningful way, allowing the therapist to appropriately respond in a reparative way.

# CHAPTER FOUR

# Terror: a sickness of spirit

> I saw this huge, huge, great black lake and distant mountains, and the thought was at that moment, "f**k, that's my source" and the dread of that, the horror of it was just completely overwhelming in that moment, like it was a big, black, bleak, cold lake, where I didn't even know if things survived [...].

Here my participant was describing the terror she perceives at her "core". Kierkegaard (1849) seems to identify a similar experience: "This man is going about and carrying a sickness of the spirit which only rarely and in glimpses, by and with a dread which to him is inexplicable, gives evidence of its presence within."

## Introduction

This quotation described my experience at the start of personal psychotherapy and echoes what I have seen in some of my clients. This life or death theme may seem unexpected in a work that relates to the early infancy period, however, pregnancy, birth, and early infancy are times when the balance between life and death is most easily tipped. I can identify with these concepts from my own experience as I recognise them as the source from which my anxiety flowed. Kierkegaard (1849) sees this "sickness unto death" as despair and through this the self is lost. The threat of the loss of self in infancy results from external pressures which are beyond the capacity of the infant to manage and have to be isolated from the developing ego to enable psychological survival, this isolated "presence within", the threat of loss of self, is then carried into adulthood to emerge as anxiety, despair and dread. Neuroscience demonstrates the importance of the attachment relationship with the caretaker to the development of the brain. During the data analysis phase of my research I identified with the experiences of terror described to me by my participants. This again reminded me of my own experience of the confusing emergence of my "sickness of spirit" which would surface at times of stress and anxiety, and of the fear of falling into the source of my dread, the loss of self, which various theorists have identified in different ways. I saw that to find self was life, to lose self was death, and that terror was present when the scales were perceived to be tipping towards death.

This is a recognisable theme; I am reminded of Steinbeck's (1952, p. 132) words "who in his mind has not probed the black water?" Some clients enter therapy having had experiences such as the one described above. They function well most of the time, but live with the fear of panic or of overwhelm which can develop, seemingly from out of the blue. Prior to entering therapy myself, I was high functioning, caring for my children and in a responsible job, and many of my acquaintances would have been unaware of the fear that lived beneath my surface. I was always afraid that it would surface in the form of a panic attack, and sometimes it did. I expended vast amounts of energy in attempting to contain it. Had I sought medical help at this time I may have been prescribed medication for panic disorder; instead I chose the therapy route. Adams (2009, p. 132) notes that clients "oscillate between feeling just fine, and then inexplicably falling apart."

One of my participants describes her experience:

> I've felt mad, mad and crazy [...] images of something just out of
> my sight lines, there would be something there that was hostile,
> just there, just there, but I could never catch it, and it was quite
> crazy—making. [...]

Little (1990, pp. 32, 42–43), in her account of her analysis with Winnicott, describes the infantile and childhood roots of her difficulties. As an adult she sought psychotherapy and identified a number of difficulties; "apologising for existence, profound disturbance, fear of annihilation with a deep sense of longing, panic, fear of destruction, being bodily dismembered, driven irretrievably insane, wiped out, abandoned, relationship difficulties and terror".

In this chapter excerpts from my research data illustrate the concepts for discussion. My participants have shared both their personal experiences as clients, and also their understanding and experiences as therapists. I will explore some theoretical concepts to provide a rationale for these experiences, looking at the development of primitive defences in relation to trauma, and how the therapist, the client and the therapeutic relationship may transform these experiences.

## Terror in infancy—terror in therapy

Some of my participants have acknowledged the experience of terror as part of their presenting issues on entering therapy. Others would only recognise and name these feelings subsequent to entering into the therapeutic relationship and beginning to re-experience a significant relationship which has the same depth and quality as the infant/caretaker relationship. The development of this new relationship and the regressive process occurring during therapy can then stimulate the client to re-experience the cumulative trauma of their infancy, and the subsequent defences arising because of fears of the re-emergence of dependency which had originally failed. This is known as juxtaposition which "occurs when there is, for the client, a marked contrast between what is provided in the therapeutic relationship and what was needed and longed for but not provided in previous relationships" (Erskine et al., 1999, pp. 151–152). Hedges (1994b) considers that such experiences and fears are always present when working with pre-verbal processes because the primordial terrors of life or death which he sees, (as does Winnicott, 1974), as being present at the beginning of life, have not been soothed or mediated in infancy and are now dysregulating, to re-emerge in the regression. In order to manage these primordial terrors in infancy individuals develop means of protection against these terrors.

Defence mechanisms can be categorised based upon how basic or primitive they are. Primitive defences are largely unconscious and may include aspects of denial, regression, acting out, dissociation, and projection. Later in the chapter I will discuss these defences in greater detail using Winnicott's description and understanding of them. Kalsched (1996) offers insight into the development of primitive defences in individuals who have suffered early infantile trauma. He identifies the division that forms within themselves, describing how their original protector against further abuse in infancy also takes on a persecutory role and becomes part of a perpetual, internal re-traumatisation. He describes how these primitive defences allow the individual who has experienced unbearable pain to continue with an external life, and how this can result in a disconnection between earlier traumatic experiences and current life. However, the "psychological sequelae of the trauma continue to haunt the inner world" (p. 13). Siegel (2015) identifies the experience of trauma as resulting in a lack of integration in brain functioning.

A research participant describes her understanding of the core primitive developmental aspects of her regression:

> This was a real developmental stuff about separation, identity, about coming into the world, about that survival [...] that is the memory that most comes to mind.

In considering the mother as the repository for indigestible feelings which are made digestible and returned to the infant in a palatable form, Bion (1962, p. 116) posits that where the mother is an inadequate container the child remains in a state of "nameless dread". This failure to contain anxieties can then lead to pathology, remaining into adulthood to re-emerge. Winnicott uses the terms "unthinkable anxiety" (1952) and "fear of breakdown" (1974) to describe what he views as a response to happenings in early infancy where the baby's psychological immaturity keeps it perpetually on the edge of "unthinkable anxiety" which is normally kept away from the infant's being, and is regulated by the mother's holding function. Other theorists have similar ways of thinking about such processes experienced by clients, using terms such as "psychotic anxiety" (Klein, 1935), "annihilation anxiety" (Hurvich, 1989), and "pre-verbal anxieties" (Symington & Symington, 1996). People who have these experiences will find various different ways of describing them, but terror seems to be present in all of them. Theories of traumatology have some information to offer regarding the symptomology of the experiences, while some aspects of Jungian thought help to offer insight into the more hidden aspects of the psyche.

In the excerpts below the participant describes her experience of a fear that she couldn't understand at the time, which was not engendered by her current life circumstances, but which would emerge unbidden. She also identifies the vulnerability and the inability to articulate the experience:

> [...] that nameless dread of [...] that I can still feel sometimes [...] there'll be a surge of something [...] an anxiety which has no reason nor rhyme nor even a shape, it's just terror or anxiety [...].
>
> [...] there was this thing in the water with, like a Moray eel that was all teeth and mouth and threat [...] the two images together were really aversive, and quite terrifying [...] levels of terror were quite huge. [...]

Adams (2006, p. 143) describes some patients as carrying:

> [...] anxiety and a vague sense of dread [...] struggling to overcome shock: shocking disappointments, shocking abandonments, shocking betrayals, shocking reversals in health and fortune. The substate of shock lives in their brains and bodies as a shadow imprint of their earliest experiences.

In this quotation Adams makes a link between the experience of dread and shock that she describes and the infant experiences of the patient. She acknowledges the importance of the therapeutic relationship in providing support and regulation to the client when they re-experience these frightening episodes. One of my research participants identifies her understanding of clients who have experienced early relational deficit:

> I would say they all had a developmental need [...] it was a relational need and a safe containment. All of them have not had physical holding, or safe physical holding as children [...] and I feel that they have reached the point of utter despair [...] not necessarily suicidality, but that feeling that they are just going to completely collapse [...] or not being able to cope at all [...] for the client I think they need to know that I'm gonna be there consistently [...] and

because of their own fear of collapse they need to somehow trust
me sufficiently to hold them, psychologically [...] I think if they are
afraid of falling apart they need to know that somebody will stop
that happening [...].

[when] clients come into therapy they may well be in a regressed
state, so [...] they've got limited kind of resources, or something
has pushed them back into a place [...] that's familiar, but they can't
escape from.

I have previously discussed the contention of many psychotherapists
that from the nascent period up to the age of five character styles and
defences develop which are carried into adult life. This means that the
early experiences of human beings leave their mark upon the psyche
of the individual. If this is the case then, what happens in early infancy
is of critical importance when trying to understand the ways of being
of adult clients. We have already seen how the environment that the
infant is born into is of key importance to its development therefore the
caregiver/infant relationship is pivotal to the successful (or otherwise)
development of the infant. Caregiver/infant relationships all vary in
their quality and style, the key issue seems to be that the environment
that the infant is born into should take account of the needs of the infant.
If this occurs the infant will move from an unintegrated, unformed self
to the development of a sense of self and self-identity. When an ideal
facilitating environment is not available Borgogno and Vigna-Taglianti
(2008) would see this as causal of pre-verbal trauma because of the
potential for damage occurring to the ego as it is developing. Tustin
(1994) also recognises the disruption to the infant's development resulting from a stress caused by discord which she considers develops into
"an agony of consciousness beyond their capacity to tolerate or to pattern" (1994, p. 192).

In the earliest stage of development some theorists consider that disturbing happenings are unable to be experienced or integrated by the
infant because they "have not yet reached a stage where there is a place
to see from" (Winnicott, 1988, p. 131). As the infant has not yet identified its self it is unable to experience happenings from a place of self.
Tarantelli (2003, p. 916) cites Blanchot's (1986, p. 28) identification of
the same process as "a non-experience [...] which [...] cannot be forgotten because it has always already fallen outside memory". Kalsched
(1996) understands that the young infant oscillates between painful,

uncomfortable feeling states and satisfied, comfortable feeling states. The mother's empathy is required through empathic responses, comfort, and naming of states by which emotional homeostasis is restored, ultimately resulting in the development in the infant's psyche of the ability to contain internal affect. Little (1990) describes her regressive return to disorganisation and anxiety that she experienced during her therapy, clearly outlining the infantile roots of this experience. She concurs with Winnicott's belief that environmental provision is necessary to manage these experiences within the therapeutic relationship. Without this environmental provision in infancy, anxieties concerning existence, survival and identity can remain, and emerge as feelings of "inexplicable dread" within the psyche, emerging in times of stress, distress and in regression.

A mother's repeated lack of atttunement has painful consequences for the infant, as described below by one of my participants, who goes on to describe the effect of touch in her therapy:

> It was inappropriate touch [...] possibly quite violent or scary touch, my mother was quite rough and didn't appreciate [...] and I was, as a child, very colicky as a baby and had a lot of eczema, so that touch would be painful and irritating, so it was never soothing, so the therapeutic touch was like [...] I remember it now, it was just so [...] it wasn't invasive, it was just like warm electricity going through me [...] it brought tears to my eyes because it was soothing.

Clients who have apparently experienced early mishandling or other misattunement may present for therapy with a desperate need for relationship yet have a real fear of it, and they may fear touch and intimacy generally. Erskine (2007) would consider the above experience as an example of the impact of pre-verbal trauma. Such trauma, whether acute or cumulative, can be largely unconscious because of its pre-verbal origins, leaving the client without knowledge of their story, and an inability to understand the experiences and feelings occurring in their daily lives.

Writing from a body psychotherapy perspective, Lewis (2004) identifies the shock that the infant feels upon experiencing sufficiently unempathic parental holding and handling in early life. He describes his construct of cephalic shock which develops when the infant experiences dissonance due to unempathic parental handling in the early months of life. Thrown back upon an immature nervous system, the infant will have to find a way to *hold on, hold together, and hold against* the parent, who cannot provide it with auxiliary ego (i.e., to fight gravity prematurely and unnaturally). The dissonant handling creates a chronic state of disequilibrium or shock. He associates this with the "false self" of Winnicott considering that the absence of empathic holding leads to Winnicott's (1965b/1984) "unthinkable anxieties". Lewis (1981) describes the Moro reflex (startle reflex) occurring when the infant experiences a change in its equilibrium. He argues that rough mishandling "creates a chronic state of disequilibrium or shock […] that is far beyond the shock that the infant can discharge via the Moro reflex" (Lewis, 1981, p. 8) and is therefore experienced as annihilatory. Little (1990, p. 88) also recognises this phenomenon occurring with her adult clients, "There is the risk of repeated annihilation by stimuli to which the client may have to react to physically (startle reflex)." Before I became a client in psychotherapy, I was aware of my pronounced startle reaction. I would be completely dysregulated by a loud noise, for example, and would often cry. I have also witnessed this reaction in my clients who have had a lack of a soothing and containing other in their infancy. Some clients enter therapy recognising that they are "jumpy", others find that as the regression develops they can be easily startled by sudden noise or unexpected events. These clients may also present with an overt or covert fear of annihilation.

Balint's (1968) way of understanding patients with a high level of psychic disturbance coins the phrase "the basic fault" which he considers occurs in early infancy when the needs of the infant are not appropriately matched by the facilitating environment. He recognises that this fault which develops in infancy can remain for the whole of a person's life "it is a fault, something wrong in the mind, a kind of deficiency which must be put right. It is not something dammed up for which a better outlet must be found, but something missing either now, or perhaps for almost the whole of the patient's life" (Balint, 1968, pp. 19–22). He is making the case for the possibility of a reparative relationship between therapist and client.

My participants, through the descriptions of their experiences, led me in the direction of theories which seemed to inform, and illuminate my understanding. Winnicott's writings were important in this understanding.

## Annihilation anxiety

Winnicott uses the word "impingements" to describe happenings which disturb the "going on being" of the infant. These happenings are seen as a failure in the facilitating environment to protect the infant from disturbance by the external world. When such impingements occur the infant must react and this is seen by Winnicott as "resulting in annihilation of personal being" (1965b/1984, p. 47) as in the loss of self, resulting in the death of self. This threat of annihilation can then be seen as the source of the terror which is experienced by clients who have not had a protective, attuning and available caregiver, able to shield and support their developing self.

The sense of being balanced between life and death and the threat of annihilation, is described by my participant:

> [The loss of] my own identity, which was like a battle for my own
> life really, it was a life and death [...] quite a profound experience.

In describing experiences in her adult life, she also tells the story of her early life. These types of experiences are seen by theorists as emerging from the re-experiencing of an early infantile occurrence in later psychological states. Little (1990), writing about regression, recognises that in inchoate development the infant is dependent and at birth integration has only begun and survival is not a certainty. Because at this stage of infancy there is seen to be no integration then there can be no organised defence against unwanted stimuli from the environment. She identifies a confusional state which is experienced as annihilation and that this "annihilation anxiety" will persist unless supported by "an environment which is capable of meeting all needs [which] can ensure survival and promote integration" (Little, 1990, p. 87). Winnicott (1984, p. 47) places this early anxiety as against annihilation, the threat of loss of being, loss of self. The dictionary gives a literal definition of "annihilation" as "to make into nothing", so simply ceasing to be.

If there are infrequent and minor impingements, these do not interrupt the development of the continuity of being. Too many impingements threaten the development of that continuity of being, because instead of engaging in the process of developing potential the child (and the client) must instead deal with their environment. The task, then, of the holding environment is to reduce and minimise the number of impingements which result in loss of continuity of being by the infant having to react rather than just be. Secure attachment supports the growth of neural integration within the brain, lack of such integration leads to chaos or rigidity (Siegel, 2015). Winnicott (1984) describes the more acute deprivations of infancy as "primitive agonies", a nameless dread associated with the threatened dissolution of a coherent self. "To experience such anxiety threatens the total annihilation of the human personality, the destruction of the personal spirit" (Kalsched, 1996, p. 1). This results in the development of primitive defences which cause psychopathology because of their primitive nature. It is viewed that this trauma is a break in the continuity of "going on being" and the primitive defences organise to prevent a repetition of "unthinkable anxiety" or a "return to the acute confusional state that belongs to disintegration of nascent ego structure" (Winnicott, 1971, p. 97). These defences though, later become the relational problems that clients bring to therapy. Adams (2009, p. 139) considers that the experience of annihilation anxiety and dissociation is not confined to those who have experienced overt trauma or abuse. She attributes work in depth therapy to revelations of covert primitive ego states which exist in parallel with mature functioning. She describes the dichotomy, terror of intimacy and a need for human contact as "intense waves of feelings" and "sensations such as sinking, falling, exploding", when caught within a primitive state of mind.

Winnicott's earlier paper (1974), describes patients in therapy as experiencing a powerful "fear of breakdown", which he sees as the sequelae of infantile "primitive agonies". He considers that the adult client's fear of the breakdown which they believe is about to happen is actually the fear of a breakdown that has already been experienced in infancy. "It is the fear of the original agony which caused the defence organisation." Although viewing this "fear of breakdown" as being related to the individual's past experiences, he also considers "there must be expected a common denominator of the same fear, indicating the existence of universal phenomena" (Winnicott, 1974, p. 88). He asserts that his theory of the fear of breakdown can be generalised to the fear of death, seeing that it is the death that happened but was not experienced that is being feared.

> Death looked at in this way as something that happened to the patient, but which the patient was not mature enough to experience, is the meaning of annihilation. It is like this that a pattern

developed in which the continuity of being was interrupted by the patient's infantile reactions to impingement, these being environmental factors that were allowed to impinge by failures of the facilitating environment. (Winnicott, 1974, p. 93)

Likewise he considers that this theory can be generalised to encompass emptiness, belonging to the past, when a lack of psychological maturity meant that it could not be experienced "to understand that it is necessary to think not of trauma but of nothing happening when something might profitably have happened. It is easier for a patient to remember trauma than to remember nothing happening when it might have happened. At the time the patient did not know what might have happened, and so could not experience anything except to note that something might have been" (ibid., p. 94).

A research participant clearly makes this point as he describes the sense of emptiness he associates with being an infant:

> [...] on one occasion watching a mother who seems to be deliberately ignoring a child who was in this clearly very distressed, agitated state [...] and I just couldn't bear it, so I just know from the number of times I've had that kind of experience [...] this is something to do with me as a baby [...] and I'm [...] made acutely kind of aware, emotionally aware, not by observing it so much, but by just feeling.

Winnicott sees this fear as carried around in the unconscious of the client until it emerges within the therapy, for the client there remains this hidden aspect where ego integration is "too immature to gather all this phenomena into the area of personal omnipotence". Winnicott asks the question—why is the patient worried by something that belongs to the past? He answers that it "must be that the original experience of primitive agony cannot get into the past tense unless the ego can first gather it into its own present time experience and into omnipotent control now (assuming the auxiliary ego-supporting function of the mother [analyst])". Without the necessary support in infancy the client is unable to continue development in this area but must continue to search for "the past detail which is *not yet experienced*. This search takes the form of a looking for this detail in the future". To summarise, along with Winnicott (1974), the fear of breakdown is a fear of a past event that has not yet been experienced because it was psychologically unsafe to do so, and the therapeutic relationship means that it becomes safe to do so. When safety is thus provided "the past detail which is *not yet experienced*" becomes experienceable. This emerging trauma then becomes literally present. The patient's need, and an aim of this therapy then, is to enable the patient to experience it with a new significant other (the therapist) who is able to be dependable, soothing and affect regulating (Van Sweden, 1995, p. 91).

A research participant describes her experience and understanding of her early trauma. She describes revisiting a place which she thought of as total death:

> [...] in hindsight it took me right back to the death anxiety that I always maintain I was born with [...] she (mum) told me a story about holding me in her arms a few hours after I was born, looking down the road and seeing a hearse, and she told me, as a child, and, well, as a baby, that "poor Mr. so-and-so, he had to die to make room for you to be born", and this myth hung around for me in a very frightening form, that if, if, somebody has to die in order for a new baby to be born, so you can imagine, new life, for me, or knowledge of new life, was quite terrifying because I didn't know if it would be me that was chosen to be the one that was, sacrificed, if you like [...] having been a child with a very conscious fear of death, it had led me into all kinds of bizarre behaviour as a kid, like I'd be put to bed at seven o'clock and I would make about half a dozen trips downstairs to make sure that my mother was breathing, and to make sure that her [...] I knew how to take my mother's pulse as a little child—strange that I end up in the medical profession, but, or certainly in the nursing profession, but I was very aware that it was my job to keep her alive, so I thought, and I, it filled me with night terrors and lots of neurotic behaviour. [...]

Hurvich (1989) considers that pathological annihilation anxieties are a consequence and correlate of psychic trauma, ego weakness, object loss, and pathology of the self. He sees that annihilation experiences and anxieties are universal in early childhood, where psychic dangers are regularly experienced as traumatic. He makes the link between annihilation anxiety and the threat to psychic survival, experienced as a present menace or as an anticipation of an imminent catastrophe.

Hurvich describes the experience of overwhelmed helplessness as having much in common with Jones' "aphanisis", Klein's "psychotic anxiety", Schur's "primary anxiety", Winnicott's "unthinkable anxiety", Bion's "nameless dread", Stern's "biotrauma", Frosch's "basic anxiety", Little's "annihilation anxiety" and Kohut's "disintegration anxiety". Derivatives of underlying annihilation anxieties are fears of being overwhelmed, destroyed, abandoned, mortified, mutilated, suffocated or drowned, of intolerable feeling states, losing mental, physical or bodily control, of going insane, dissolving, being absorbed, invaded, or shattered, of exploding, melting, leaking out, evaporating or fading away. Neuroscience indicates that inadequate regulation brings feelings of overwhelm. Traumatic experiences block the ability to differentiate what was a past experience from present experiencing (Siegel, 2015).

The fear in such clients is seen as of catastrophe and fragmentation resulting in an extreme fear of annihilation. Little (1958, p. 84) writes: "There is only a state of being or of experiencing, and no sense of there being a person [...]. There is only an anger, fear, love [...] but no person feeling anger, fear or love [...]. It is a state of undifferentiation, both as regards psyche and soma, experienced as chaos." Gottlieb (1992, p. 254) continues "it is terrifying to reach this state since it implies losing the already fragile sense of identity. The patient teetering on the brink of fragmentation "becomes for the moment only a pain, rage, mess, scream and is wholly dependent on the therapist for containment". It is this area of infant development that is considered by some theorists to be the source of seemingly unpredictable terror states in adulthood.

This primitive process is described by two of my research participants:

> [...] it was like a life or death decision, and I turned round and went head first, tracking this pain in my shoulder, butting out of this confined space, and you know, eventually kind of, collapsed onto the floor, you know, not being really able to really make much sense of it [...] which was like a battle for my own life really, it was a life and death thing [...] quite a profound experience.
>
> I recognise that if I was in situations where there was a lot of anger around me I completely dissociated [...] in terror [...].
>
> [...] and I wouldn't be present, but I would look like I was, and that happened to me at work [...] I spent a lot of time dissociated in a way that I don't any more. [...]

Grotstein (1984, p. 211) recognises that primitive defences which developed to ensure survival in early infancy remain present in the individual, often causing great distress and relational failure. He sums it up as follows: "When innocence has been deprived of its entitlement it becomes a diabolical spirit." I know that many therapists and clients will recognise the truth in this statement. The feeling of being at the mercy of unconscious forces and the desperate need to try to control them in order to function in everyday life will be a familiar struggle. I will now look in more detail at the primitive defences that can develop originally as a survival mechanism but which now are part of the sequelae of that early infantile trauma.

## Primitive defences

Early infancy is a dangerous time for both humans and animals, when they are totally dependent on their caretakers for their survival. It is imperative that the infant stays with the caretaker, and primitive defences develop to "wall off unbearable anxiety" (Adams, 2006, p. 132) thus enabling the infant to defend against feared annihilation and enable psychic survival. Kalsched (1996) refers to the anxiety that results from cumulative traumas resulting from unmet dependency needs, using Winnicott's (1963, p. 90) phrase "primitive agonies" and Kohut's (1977, p. 104) term "disintegration anxiety" which he describes as "an unnameable dread associated with the threatened dissolution of the coherent self". He considers that this threat of annihilation must be avoided at all costs and that "because such trauma often occurs in early infancy before a coherent ego (and its defences) is formed, *a second line of defences* comes into play to prevent the 'unthinkable' from being *experienced*" (Kohut, 1977, p. 1). In psychoanalytic terms these defences are known as primitive defences, and "both *characterise* severe psychopathology and also (once in place) *cause* it" (ibid., p. 2), that is, those defences which once enabled survival now are the source of the client's problems.

Wilkinson (2010, p. 157) recognises dissociation as an effective defensive system designed to manage the traumatised aspect of life allowing the "apparently normal personality" to go on with the business of life.

Winnicott (1963) considers that the commonly used word "anxiety" insufficiently describes the "primitive agonies" experienced by the infant. The experience of these "primitive agonies" leads to the development of primitive defences against a repetition (1974, pp. 89–90). Because the levels of anxiety experienced by the child, who is not regulated by the parent, are beyond its tolerance, defence mechanisms are born. Moving into adulthood, these defences outlive their value and the defences which served to save the child now cause problems in the adult's life and often bring them into therapy. He describes his understanding of primitive defences using his own particular phrases. Other theorists have different ways of describing these defences; however, I will use Winnicott's descriptions to introduce each section, introducing other theorists' contributions as appropriate.

## Disintegration (a defence against the return to an unintegrated state)

According to Winnicott (1965), prior to the development of self the infant psyche can be considered to be unintegrated. This is not a problem if the environment supplies that which the infant needs without too much interference or overwhelming of the infant. Where the environment is unaccommodating of the infant's needs the infant may split off parts of experiences, which cannot be integrated. Bick (1968, p. 56) considers that the infant searches "for a container" which can "momentarily [...] [hold] the parts of the personality together". Ferenczi (1930) considered that the continuity of being is maintained by psychic fragmentation, which although resulting in unbearable pain allows survival. He recognises that repeated and early onset failures of the environment are more severe, resulting in splitting or separating off aspects of experiences which cannot be understood or integrated, but which can remain within the psyche, resulting in fragmentation. Adams (2009, p. 132) proposes that "repeated shock states within attachment relationships and unrepaired distress during the formative years contribute to an inherent vulnerability to psychic shattering and abrupt fragmentation". Therefore, no resilience is built up in the infant—each trauma adding to the weakness of the structure as a whole. Bollas (1987) would also recognise that experiencing the state of unintegration brings with it the passivity of disorientating confusion. Neuroscience offers us an understanding of this structure.

My research participant describes this experience in her own words:

> [...] once things became unlocked they tumbled out, I couldn't stop
> them, I couldn't put the lid back on, and part of me didn't want to,

> I didn't know where it was going, I didn't know sometimes if I'd
> ever get better, if I'd ever feel normal, or the sense of normality I
> thought I'd had before, which I realise wasn't really normality at
> all. [...]

Her words describe her experience of the lack of integration occurring in aspects of her personality. It is evident from the participant's words—"part of me didn't want to" that she holds this concept as a way of understanding herself. When she is experiencing the feelings described above she highlights the feelings of disintegration.

### Self-holding (a defence against falling for ever)

In early infancy the infant is completely dependent on its caregiver. When that dependency fails because the caregiver is unable or unwilling to respond the infant must look to itself to "hold together". Symington (1985, p. 486, in: Adams, 2006) identifies this self holding which results in a subsequent fear of dependency, (what has failed once cannot be trusted again), leaving only the self to be relied upon. He recognises that "the primitive fear of the state of disintegration underlies the fear of being dependant; that to experience infantile feelings of helplessness brings back echoes of that very early unheld precariousness, and this in turn motivates the patient to hold himself together." This is especially triggered in psychotherapy where the invitation is to be held by the other, and is described by my participant:

> [...] the terror is based in reality, that, and in the relationship with
> my Mom, and then obviously consequently in lots of other relation-
> ships since [...] I felt that "you need to pull yourself together, why
> would you need this, why would you want this? You need to grow
> up and get on with it." So that it was that sort of terror of being
> shamed in that, in that way is there in the reality for me.

In her words "you need to pull yourself together [...] you need to grow up and get on with it" she clearly identifies the defence that she adopted for herself as the best way to survive in her environment. This seems to correlate with Symington's (1985) thinking that where dependency cannot be relied upon, the self must supply the holding.

## Depersonalisation (a defence against failure to indwell)

This can be seen as the inability to feel alive and real, when aspects of the self are split off from experience, this can result in a "self" which feels alien to the main personality structure. Grotstein (1994, p. xviii) recognises: "The infant who feels critically unable to *attach* to a mother who may have difficulty in *bonding* may experience him/herself to be at risk for annihilation and may therefore seek to preserve him/herself by *withdrawal into alienation*—from the mother and from the self" seen by Winnicott as "failure to go on being".

Eigen (2001) describes the way that terror, whether from an external or internal source leaves an imprint on the personality of the individual. "The individual was born into a frightened and frightening world, a world in which being frightened plays a significant role" cited in Wilkinson (2010, pp. 24–25). When a person has split off aspects of themselves it is difficult for them to know what is missing. Some clients might describe feelings of emptiness and inadequacy. This mirrors the infant's parents' failure to recognise how they were failing to help their child to develop a sense of his/her self through misattunement to the child and its needs. Borgogno and Vigna-Taglianti (2008, p. 321) recognise that as adults these individuals feel an "intense uneasiness", but are unaware that they have been deprived. They consider that they can only discover this in analysis when they obtain, through "experiencing it" a psychic environment different from the one they grew up in, recovering at the same time within themselves those resources they had never imagined they could have.

## Exploitation of primary narcissism (a defence against loss of the sense of realness)

When aspects of self are split off to defend against experiences of repeated neglect or trauma this could result in a feeling of not being real, so to avoid this feeling, a further defence is required. Some theorists including Winnicott (1963) and Adams (2009) consider that such a defence system uses primary narcissism.

Kalsched (1996) writes that Winnicott considers that the failure of the environment/mother to provide "good enough" care can result in an effective relationship between inner and outer reality. If this care is impoverished or neglectful "a split opens up between the infant's psychosomatic "true" self, and a (primarily mental) "false self", which has emerged as a protection against further trauma. Winnicott sees this as a division to protect from "unthinkable agonies" from early trauma, emphasising the caretaking nature of this splitting. Kalsched (1996) highlights its persecutory dimension. It is undoubtedly a survival measure, but one which causes immense damage to the relationship with self and others.

## The development of autistic states relating to phenomena (a defence against loss of the capacity to relate to objects)

Autistic in this context is reflected by the roots of the word— "aut—self" and "ism—orientational state"; a tendency to be preoccupied by one-self, implying that the individual sees things in terms of fantasies and dreams instead of reality. It was a phrase originally coined by Bleuler (1911) for an aspect of schizophrenia and does not describe autism as a developmental disorder.

A number of authors have attempted to explain why our experiences of infancy are not usually available to everyday consciousness. Hopper (2003), in reviewing the aetiology within cumulative trauma and failed dependency in disavowal, dissociation and splitting, considers that "in order for life to continue and psychic paralysis [to be] avoided the entire experience [of annihilation anxiety] is encysted or encapsulated, producing autistic islands of experience" (2003, p. 59). Tustin (1990, p. 123) also recognises this "autistic encapsulation" seeing it as an inchoate defence against trauma which can be remembered either by events in the here and now, or result from therapeutic re-experiencing. These states enable the individual to compartmentalise painful, dis-tressing experiences which were unable to be processed at the time to be shut away so that the individual can continue with the other tasks of development.

Data from my research supported the concept of encapsulation of infancy experiences which are largely kept away from everyday experi-ence by powerful defences like inner walls behind which dwells these unintegrated experiences. These defences serve to cover over develop-mental wounds, submerging emotion and leaving the client "frozen, starving and unable to ask for help" (Adams, 2006, p. 130). She recog-nises that these clients are susceptible to emotional flooding and dis-ruptive functioning under stress.

This experience is described by a participant below:

> I was utterly exhausted, I wouldn't sleep all night because I'd be so triggered around stuff happening for me and my whole body was on hyper-alert, I just couldn't relax enough to sleep, and I would quite often have strong memories of things in those sleepless nights of first memories of things I had completely forgotten, shut away, sometimes had no idea where they came from, it's like they came from another life, I kind of knew things that I'd never known, but the problem with that was I was always on my own. [...]

She is describing experiences that she considers to be re-emergence of encapsulated or primitive states, these autistic islands of experience (Hopper, 2003, p. 59) which defend the person against the experience and allow them to continue with life. From a therapist's perspective the following participant describes experiences with a client which illustrate an autistic world:

> [...] there was never any love between her and her mother and she'd always refused to accept any dependency on her mother and as far as she knew even as a baby. And she'd created some form of thinking in language for herself which was to do with hand gestures so that she had a complete almost dictionary of hand gestures which had certain meanings and she could either form them on her hands and then there was this autistic world between her eyes and her hands. [...]

This description exemplifies how the pain and anxiety experienced by the infant must be encapsulated to enable psychological survival. Adams (2009) concurs with Berenstein (1995) regarding the enduring nature of these primitive defences "it is impossible to live with such anxiety. The mind springs into action to save the child; the defence mechanisms are born. Inevitably, however, the defence mechanisms outlive their value. The child grows older and more competent, is no longer realistically on the brink of destruction, yet the defences refuse to die. Not in touch really with the real world, the defences insist that if they are abandoned then death will follow. The terror of this possibility gives them continued life at a terrible price; little by little they get in the way of a child's development, isolating him from reality and the warmth of other human beings" (Adams, 2009, p. xvii). She quotes Hopper's (2003) comparison of these encapsulated selves to sets of Russian dolls. These selves develop in parallel to each other, and the encapsulation, or autistic state, defends the individual from the experience of the loss of relationship with others, and emphasise safety at any cost.

Van der Kolk and Fisler (1995, p. 9) discuss the critical differences in the ways that people process traumatic memories, seeing the nature of traumatic memory as dissociated and, therefore, stored without a coherent narrative. The authors highlight that their research subjects "remembered" the trauma "in the form of somatosensory flashback experiences" through a variety of sensory modalities. Their study supports Piaget's notion that memories remain unintegrated when they cannot be processed linguistically. They draw a distinction between those who have suffered adult onset trauma and those with childhood onset trauma, in the latter case abuse was remembered in olfactory and kinaesthetic sensations which they see as supporting the notion "that childhood trauma gives rise to more pervasive biological dysregulation, and that patients with childhood trauma have greater difficulty regulating internal states than patients first traumatised as adults" (Van der Kolk & Fisler, 1994).

Van der Hart et al. (1993) cite Janet (1904, 1919) in his observation that the lives of traumatised individuals appear to have had the evolution of their lives arrested by the trauma "they are 'attached' to, an obstacle which they cannot go beyond. The happening we describe as traumatic has brought about a situation to which the individual ought to react. Adaptation is required, and adaptation is achieved by modifying the outer world and by modifying one's self. Now, what characterises these 'attached' patients is that they have not succeeded in liquidating the difficult situation" (Janet, 1919, p. 660). They acknowledge, with Janet, that putting the event in words, establishing the narrative, reconciles the experience and restores continuity in personal history, that is, integration of the traumatic event has occurred. This has echoes of Winnicott's (1965) concepts of impingement upon the developing self, resulting in reaction by the infant and subsequent difficulty in moving beyond the phase when this occurred.

Having looked at the primitive defences which are responses to frequent misattunements which can be seen as traumatic and cumulative I will now look further at cumulative trauma.

## *Cumulative trauma*

Cumulative trauma describes the repeated instances of trauma frequently occurring, eventually resulting in damaging effects to the whole personality.

Eigen (2004, p. 590) gives this powerful description of the effects of cumulative trauma, "Injury unites injury, spreading through psychic time dimensions, wounds linking together from early to late, late to early, symphonies of injury, creating vast seas of suffering drawn together in one insistent pain point. Trickles of pain unite with other trickles, forming networks of suffering through the psychic body and often in the body itself. Trauma hits soul and body in one blow, in many blows."

The following participant describes how unaddressed infantile trauma is reconfigured to re-emerge when a trauma occurs in adulthood:

> A recent example in my life would be when there was a complaint about some of my work by a client which had to be investigated [...] and that occurred at a time [of] relationship breakdown with psychotherapy supervisors [...] and I think that triggered some quite intense regression so that [...] I could not rationally assess what had gone on in interactions between me and other people where I couldn't be sure that I wasn't reacting through some intense paranoid shame type feelings.

Another participant describes her experience:

> [...] crouching underneath the table in a corner, like foetal, just shaking from head to foot with no sense of how to ground myself, no kind of understanding of what was happening [...] completely freaking out like a frightened animal, er, so I know that I, you know, I had lost [...] I'd completely gone. [...]

She is describing her response to trauma and the loss of her "self" in this process. When Khan (1963) describes "cumulative trauma" he considers the impact of seemingly minor events which coalesce into significant accumulations of traumatic sequelae, which can have devastating effects upon the individual. Repetitive misattunements, non-availabilities, deprivations, in early and later childhood impact upon the individual, and have all the character of Post Traumatic Stress. Borgogno and Vigna-Taglianti (2008, p. 317) recognise that "[…] omissive and depriving parents […] have been at the very source of these patients' psychic grief". Kalsched (1996, p. 1) considers these experiences as overwhelming the usual defensive measures which Freud (1920g, p. 27) described as a "protective shield against stimuli". Kalsched (1996) shows how, as a result of cumulative or acute trauma in early childhood, defences which originally developed to protect the individual, can become malevolent and destructive resulting in a repeated inner traumatisation. He quotes from Jung (1928, paragraphs 266–267):

> Traumatic complex brings about the dissociation of the psyche. The complex is not under the control of the will and for this reason it possesses the quality of psychic autonomy. Its autonomy consists in its power to manifest itself independently of the will, and even in direct opposition to conscious tendencies: it forces itself tyrannically upon the conscious mind. The explosion of affect is a complete invasion of the individual, it pounces upon him like an enemy or a wild animal.

Experiences of trauma vary from acute experiences of child abuse, to the deprivations experienced when normal infancy needs are unmet, identified as "cumulative traumas" (Khan, 1963). When individuals describe trauma they are often describing a discrete event or events which are in isolation from an individual's everyday life. Cumulative childhood trauma, however, relates to any experience that causes the child unbearable psychic pain or anxiety, meaning that it overwhelms normal defences and ranges from experiences of child abuse to "cumulative traumas" of unmet dependency needs (Khan, 1963) including the deprivations described by Winnicott as "primitive agonies" which are "unthinkable" (1963, p. 90). Blum (2004, p. 20) comments on the definition of trauma and the wide spectrum of traumatic effects from a "transient loss of ego regulation to the regression, helplessness, disorganisation, and paralysing panic of massive trauma," considering that:

> Trauma may be so narrowly defined that the ego is considered totally overwhelmed with no possibility of adequate registration of the trauma or response to the trauma. At another extreme,

trauma may be loosely identified with any noxious experience or developmental interference.

Hurvich (2004) also acknowledges the overwhelming nature of the experience of trauma. He quotes from Greenacre (1967, p. 128) "any conditions which seem definitely unfavourable, noxious, dramatically injurious to the developing young individual". Trauma theorists clearly identify the loss of ego function which is associated with trauma and traumatic sequelae, however, theorists recognising cumulative and pre-verbal trauma as resulting from infantile deprivation see the trauma developing prior to the development of the ego. In both cases there is no ego present to mediate or integrate these traumatic events.

Having explored the experience of trauma resulting from a non-facilitating environment in early infancy and its subsequent effects, I will now look at how the therapist's role can begin to contain and heal such experiences.

## The therapist as transformational object

Responses to trauma and terror can be recognised as the earliest defences which are laid down in infancy. Therefore, a return to elements of the infancy state could enable new ways of responding to traumatic events to develop. Borgogno and Vigna-Taglianti (2008, p. 317) consider that "the intrapsychic can relive within the inter-psychic, becoming a masterly key for recognition and transformation of traumatic and traumatising past events." What hope there is in this! The intrapsychic world of the client can be reprised within the inter-psychic therapeutic relationship and so offer transformation.

Gottlieb (1992), in striving to understand Bollas's (1987) concept of "transformational object", formulates that patients seek within the transference such a transformational object which she calls "transformational transference" which is associated with early environmental deficit. She connects such patients with high levels of demand and dependence, and the need for maternal containment. This maternal presence is viewed by Hedges (1994a) as a "protective shield", protecting the infant against stress, strain and trauma. Where this protective shield has not developed the individual can in adult life break down in times of stress and trauma. The therapist's aim can be to help the client to develop, within a long term relationship, such a protective shield. In this section I will specifically consider how the therapist, because of the nature and depth of the relationship, can help to regulate and contain the client's experiences of trauma and terror in a way that should have been available to the child in infancy.

Little (1990) describes the type and depth of relationship in regression to dependence and views it as "a means by which areas where psychotic anxieties predominate can be explored, early experiences uncovered, and underlying delusional ideas recognised and resolved, via the transference/countertransference partnership of analyst and analysand" (Little, 1990, p. 83). She is referring to those areas which Winnicott would view as the state of being prior to the development of the self. Kalsched (1996) acknowledges Winnicott's and Kohut's assertions that "unthinkable anxiety" originates in the symbiotic stage of development when the infant is dependent on the mother for the mediation of experience including anxiety. He identifies that in a distressing situation for the baby then ideally the mother's presence will transform and regulate the baby's state. Cohen (1985, p. 180), cited in Steele et al. stated that "the traumatic state cannot be represented [...] therefore cannot be interpreted [...] [it] can only be modified by interactions with need-mediating objects". Kalsched (1996) acknowledges that both Winnicott and Kohut have placed a level of "unthinkable" anxiety within the symbiotic stage of development where the child is totally dependent on the mother. The mother's role is to regulate this anxiety. If for whatever reason the mother fails to regulate the baby becomes distressed and eventually traumatised.

The following participant describes an evocative experience in her personal therapy in which she re-experiences some aspects of her infancy. She has experienced a trauma in her early childhood which is re-experienced as a result of the therapeutic relationship:

> [...] when this regression began in my analysis I think it would probably be about six or seven years through treatment, and I was seeing him four times a week at that time, and I sensed a [...] I sensed a real "going-down" sensation, the nearest I can get to it is if I talk about what I experienced when I had to be resuscitated after my breast, my first breast cancer op, was a sense that all of life was draining away from me, I'm [...] sort of reliably told by the medics around that's exactly how I looked, as if life was draining away from me, and it didn't turn out to be a scary thing at all in

reality, but in my analysis feeling that all of life was draining away from me was a very terrifying place because I thought I would lose contact with my analyst [...] I was lying on the couch one day and I felt very little, and I kept saying to him, "you're like the weather men", now I don't know if you remember all those years ago, you used to get clocks and there used to be the lady came out on a fair day, and the man came out on a, on a miserable day, and I kept saying to him, "you keep coming in and out, you keep [...] one minute I think you're there, and the next minute I, you're gone again and I can't find you", and I couldn't find him visually, even though my eyes were open and he was sitting behind me, if I turned my head I could have seen him, but I wouldn't have seen him; I was eighteen months old when I had a second operation on one of my eyes, and in those days when they operated an eye, and had to cover it, they covered—crazy, crazy thinking—they covered both eyes because they thought you'd strain the good eye, so what came out of this, regression with (therapist's name) was I had suddenly become the blind child, the child with both eyes covered, and I couldn't find the people that I needed even though I'm told I was in a cot and there were cot-sides up in the hospital, the sense of people coming in and out, and that still for me today, I can sense when people are moving, well, I feel they're moving in and out of consciousness, unconsciousness, visibility, whatever, my eyes are really important, response mechanism to me is when a person is really here with me, or whether they've gone somewhere, so that was another illustration of what came out of the regression, but I can think of times [...] I just remember a descent into, it was a real going-down place where I no longer had any vision and I did still have sound though, I could hear if he, if he moved in his chair and then it was something very physical, and I remember saying, I think I said this at the time or maybe it was some sessions afterwards, but I had the physical experience of my heart breaking and the grief of a broken heart which was one hundred per cent, no "a little bit dead and a little bit alive", it was just a total, total place and the thing, I mean I've lost a lot of the information around that time, but what I remember him doing was, it was winter and he picked up my jacket that was on the chair and he just placed it very gently over my face, now I do remember my face as being [...] I was just awash with grief, and I think I'd got tears and snot and everything else, and I hadn't,

> couldn't, I couldn't clean myself up, I couldn't do anything [...] and so he put this coat over my face, and I thought he'd just dropped soil on my coffin, I thought, I, that's all I could think of what's happening to me, "oh, now I am really dead, now I'm really dead".

In this powerful story she links her infancy experience and the later experience with her therapist, making the connection with the life or death nature of these experiences and identifies the feelings of terror which are associated. Indeed, so profound are these experiences that some authors, such as Siegel (2003, p. 9) claim that they affect the individual at a neurological level:

> Overwhelmingly stressful experiences may have their greatest impact on the growth of the mind at the time when specific areas of the brain are in rapid periods of development and reorganisation [...]. Trauma during the early years may have lasting effects on deep brain structures [...] specific "states of mind" can also be deeply ingrained as a form of memory of trauma, a lasting effect of early traumatic experience. States of fear, anger, or shame can re-emerge as a characteristic trait of the individual's responses.

Fromm, (2004, p. 2) in his commentary on Winnicott's 1977 paper, recognises that during these times of infantile trauma, what is missing is an "other" who is able to help the infant through the difficult experiences. He writes:

> If only there had been someone at the point of crisis to encompass the child, to recognise that the child has feelings about what is going on, and to help him through the shattering effect of losing all that is familiar, then perhaps some of the shock and trauma could have been absorbed.

He goes on to describe how Winnicott links this early trauma with a reaction to trauma in the here and now, seeing that responses to trauma are laid down in early infancy and are then repeated in response to later trauma. He describes how an early trauma which has occurred in a relationship of dependence has resulted in a defence of self-sufficiency to contract the child against his/her own need, and he describes how, through the process of therapeutic regression and the re-experiencing in the here and now of such trauma in relationship could result in the patient referring to this part of her therapy as "the time when I began to want to live". He describes Winnicott's therapeutic stance as "about the developmental fact that moments of pain must be experienced—and can only be experienced if another person is present—in order for them to be transformed into moments of truth". Many clients present for therapy with self-sufficiency as a defensive position. When they have been let down in their first beginnings by those who should have cared for them, unconsciously they are guarded against being in that position with any other person again. They value their abilities to sort things for themselves and are extremely shocked and frustrated when these defences cease to enable them to overcome their current difficulties. They can be resistant to anything that looks like dependency, even though this is the very relationship which can bring healing through the reprise of a significant relationship of the same quality as their earliest relationship. My personal therapy was marked initially by high levels of shame and fear from which I could not allow myself, or any other, to know the depth of my need. I also experience this with my clients, who try to self-sufficiently use their habitual cognitive defences, to *intra*personally solve *inter*personal problems. They have learned this stance because historically there was no one willing or able to support them in times of difficulty or trauma.

Steele et al. (2001) have identified that strong social support is essential to prevent trauma related disorders because most chronically traumatised individuals have insecure attachment through basic security never having been achieved. This must first, then, be provided by the therapist before addressing the trauma. They also identify that *dependency need* emerges in the work with this client group.

Trying to address the trauma with the client prior to the establishment of a supportive alliance with the therapist could lead to re-traumatisation (Steele et al., 2001).

This participant is describing his understanding that early relational damage must be addressed through the therapeutic relationship prior to the addressing and resolution of trauma and distress:

> Her trauma was the sudden death of her father, and her mother going crazy, which we could not repair because there was already a lack of emotional security with that mother before that, although she kept going back to that scene. I needed to go back and be that good

> mother before we could come back and deal with that (traumatic
> memory) [...] Khan coined the term "cumulative trauma" when
> you're dealing with that accumulation and that lack of reliability
> on someone, then you've got to go in and establish that first, before
> you deal with [...] those painful traumatic incidences ... With
> depressed mothers, you can't really do a great deal of work with
> the traumatic incidences that come along in life, until you repair
> the lack of vitality from the depressed mother [...] beyond the basic
> fault, actually, but *to* it for the sake of repairing and finding the
> security. [...]

If we accept the theory that clients, having had early stage developmental deficit where ego boundaries have not yet developed, are still
searching for a transformational object in order to develop a coherent
inner world and so repair the "basic fault" then it is clear to see the
possibilities for the therapeutic relationship to be a source of emotional
repair. When the "injury" is seen to have occurred prior to the development of the self, then clients will re-experience these archaic feelings.
The therapeutic relationship taking on some of the aspects of the early
infant caretaker relationship then becomes a vehicle to contain the
client's dependency. Steele et al. (2001) making the link between the
experience of dependency and its relationship to survival needs, concur
with Mitchell (1991) and his understanding that dependency desires
expressed in therapy can represent ego needs, not symbolic wishes or
fantasies and that these needs must be met before anything else can
occur in therapy. They recognise that in failed dependency situations,
where the environmental provision has been insufficient for the infant,
there is a risk to the client of "severe deterioration in functioning, self-
destructive acts and disintegration." Adams (2006, p. 257) also recognises consequences of failed dependency in an impoverished psychic
organisation forming a "black hole" and so connecting it to Balint's
(1968) "basic fault" and Grotstein's (1990) "implosive centripetal pull
into the void".

These participants describe their experiences:

> [...] it wasn't until I got deeper into therapy that I was realising
> that I was dependent [...] and like if my therapist had to move to a
> different room it was like I'd get in there and say, "I just can't work

in here" it was just like every little thing was almost impossible
[...].

I was utterly exhausted I wouldn't sleep all night because I'd be
so triggered around stuff happening for me and my whole body
was on hyper-alert, I just couldn't relax enough to sleep and I
would quite often have strong memories in those sleepless nights
of first memories of things I had completely forgotten, shut away,
sometimes had no idea where they came from, it's like they came
from another life. [...]

## Negative therapeutic reaction and juxtaposition

Some clients, as the therapeutic relationship develops and starts to
become more intimate and meaningful, experience what is known as
negative therapeutic reaction. This is a phrase used to describe the aversive and resistant reaction as traumatic material first begins to emerge
from the unconscious. When this happens, clients are frequently thrown
back on primitive defence structures and it is at this point that clients
can sabotage their lives, their relationships or their therapy. An attempt
to give her client an object for security is described by this participant:

> This is the client group that I have often felt the desire to give, pro-
> vide some kind of transitional object, and the difficulty in introduc-
> ing that into the work, sometimes, the feeling of them wanting to
> have, and yet, not allowing themselves to take, has been difficult,
> and therefore sometimes meant that that's not happened, or that
> it's somehow destructed the intention of the transitional object [...]
> for example, Christmas I bought a client a scarf and put some per-
> fume on it that he particularly likes, that he's smelt on me when
> he's been close to me, and met with his absolute rage when I gave
> it to him, that he couldn't have that, that that couldn't be tolerated
> [...] I feel like I hit that ecstasy and pain place a lot with this client
> group.

The client rejected her offer because the threat of the re-emergence of
these previously destructive experiences and defensively felt they must
be avoided at all costs as there is a threat to the very organisation of the
self and fragmentation.

Kalsched (1996) accounts for negative therapeutic reaction by identifying that the process of integration is not experienced as desirable for these patients.

> These patients do not experience an increase of power or enhanced functioning when the repressed affect or traumatogenic experience first emerges into consciousness. They go numb, or split, or act out, somatise or abuse substances. Their very survival as cohesive "selves" depended upon primitive dissociative operations which *resist* integration of the trauma and its associated affects—even to the point of dividing up the ego's "selves" into part-personalities.

Hedges accounts for these experiences thus, "Reviving memories of failed attempts at connection entails reliving primitive organising experiences which are bound to emerge as the early developmental period comes into focus" (Hedges, 1994b, p. 5). Kalsched (1996) accepts Guntrip's understanding that the child originally,

> […] must feel that it is too frightening to be weak in an unfriendly and menacing world. […] and if you cannot change your world, you can try to change yourself. Thus he comes to fear and hate his own weakness and neediness; and now he faces the task of growing up with an intolerance of his immaturity. (Guntrip, 1969)

Van Sweden (1995, p. 174) recognises the difficulty in negotiating this stage of the therapy "Initially, the analyst's efforts to establish an emotional connection may be looked upon by the analysand with suspicion and distrust. What basis does the analysand have for believing that this connection with the analyst will be reliable if the original connection with the mother was not?" Etherington (2003, p. 16) asks the question,—"How do we learn to relate to others intimately when our early and most important relationships have caused fear, shame and distress?" Clients who have been shamed for their vulnerability and need in infancy and childhood are ashamed of their dependency needs emerging in the therapeutic relationship. This shame persists even when the client has insight into their story, because to re-enter a dependency relationship re-awakens the fear and "unbearable anxiety" associated with re-entering the trauma, such anxieties can make a client resistant to change and the therapist must work persistently and consistently to develop and maintain the client's trust.

The dependency which results from the regression (Steele et al., 2001) is described by the participant below:

> [...] and she'd say things like, "why would I tell you?" because she'd gone back to that place where there was no point in, you know [...] "You don't tell adults anything, you don't communicate" she had her own [...] so there'd be moments in therapy sessions when she'd be doing all this sort of thing, so there was definitely a real regression there and it included a lot of dependency [...] the demand on me as therapist was very intense [...] We had sessions twice a week and the sessions were an hour and a half because it seemed that for her to do any work, to really get into it and then just [...] in whatever way possible to come out of it again [...] [took] an hour and a half or longer.

In the regression to dependence process the client can re-experience the early mother/infant relationship. Within this re-experiencing is then the emergence of terror, pain, and rage that resulted from the original maternal failure which is frightening to experience, but the client can be helped and supported to understand causality and reparation (Van Sweden, 1995).

Little (1990) concurs with Winnicott's assertion that the mother's inability or unavailability to transform the baby's distressed state results in trauma, implying that the baby has experienced a break in the continuity of life and that primitive defences would be rallied to defend against "unthinkable anxiety" or "a return to the acute confusional state that belongs to disintegration of nascent ego structure". The unconscious threat of a potential return to a dependent relationship refigures the previous failed dependency and so can involve "a frightening return to the earliest unintegrated state". She describes her first therapy session with Winnicott as bringing a repeat of an experience of terror and how Winnicott held her and managed her during her regressive experiences. She identifies how the healthy part of her and this traumatised part of her existed together within and how during her therapy there was a challenge: "which would prove the stronger, the sickness or the health, which were both there" (Little, 1990, p. 70).

My personal experience resonates with Wilkinson's comments (2010), seeing that in early psychoanalytic understanding regression was viewed as a primitive state of mind and that abstinence on the part of the therapist could replay original traumatic experiences. My therapist was very comfortable with silence, yet his silence often triggered for me a traumatic re-experiencing of being with my depressed mother and her unavailability. This misattunement was very painful for me and hard to tell my therapist about because I was protecting him, as I used to protect my mother. Wilkinson (2010) advocates for the therapist's attention to affect, to enable regulation of the amount of arousal experienced by the client. She considers that the therapeutic relationship has at its heart the creation of a sustaining, containing relationship in which unintegrated affect can be integrated and fear and terror attenuated. She cites Krowski (1997, p. 171) "it is only when a containing maternal object has been internalised [in therapy] that rage and hatred [...] can be faced". She concludes that "it is the internalising of the containing maternal object that is at the heart of a regression process in treatment that emerges as truly therapeutic" (Wilkinson, 2010, p. 160). The therapeutic relationship will then be a dependent one, where the needed regulation, containment and support will be provided by the therapist in a way that recognises the needs of the client but still acknowledges the adult aspects of the client in the here and now.

The following participants identify how their therapists were available to them and able to offer reparative relationships, transforming their distressed states:

> That I might be able to ask for reassurance from her, that I might be able to ask for some affirming of me, that I might be able to ask for her to hold me, I might be able to ask for her to tell me how I appear, or to tell me how I come across, or just to tell me how I'm perceived [...].
> It was how she leant forward about two thirds of the way into the work, and how she just very, very gently just touched me just there on the hand, it was just that kind of a touch and with it pulled me and her into a closer space. [...]

The importance of the therapist's presence and touch as a form of nonverbal contact is highlighted here. Wallin (2007) makes a clear link between the development of a secure therapeutic relationship and the

TERROR   89

client's ability to confront trauma helpfully. He considers that the goal
of therapy is to resolve the patient's trauma, whether that be an acute
traumatic event or of the chronic nature of cumulative trauma. He
understands cumulative trauma as the child's repeated experiences of
fear, helplessness, shame and abandonment requiring the development
of primitive defences which may remain into adulthood. He advocates
for the development of a new secure attachment relationship with the
psychotherapist. This empathic, attuned relationship attenuates the
impact of original trauma and provides a barrier between the old, traumatic attachment patterns that enrage and terrify and the here and now
of relationships that are supportive and empathic. He views working
with the body as a key aspect of therapy with such patients because of
the propensity of traumatised infants to use dissociation—the "escape
where there is no escape" (Putnam, 1997) which he describes as having
two aspects; a failure of integration of the trauma together with a hyp-
noid state, or separate state of mind, where the relation of self to reality
is altered. The presence of dissociation, he says, makes it very difficult
or impossible to confront and address the traumatic experiences. The
loss of contact with the body which dissociation brings means that the
somatic markers of clients' stories can be inaccessible.

Wosket (1999) identifies ethical and appropriate use of touch as a
therapeutic intervention for some clients. Hedges (1994a, 1994b) recognises that specifically where there is early development damage some
form of physical touch is required to transform states and establish connection. The importance of touch in establishing connection is identified by the following participant:

> Largely not in words, largely in action her knowingness of me, but
> letting me know in, in an often very non-verbal way, a touch or a
> gesture, or a look, more than a word […] something about being
> loved, I think, and having a sense of being loved.

Both personally and professionally, I consider touch and sometimes
physical holding to be necessary and advisable to provide that sense of
physicality and regulation which has been missing for these clients. In
identifying that clients are in touch with more inchoate states then those
means of contact which are appropriate to early infancy are useful to
establish contact. Communication with infants is largely non-verbal so
interventions of touch and holding are key. Van Sweden (1995, p. 165)

identifies the value of remaining "with" the client, and conversely, "withdrawal" through misattunement or emotional unavailability can "precipitate psychotic disorganisation". He notes that the therapist should initiate and maintain contact in ways that support the dependent relationship. This statement goes with the usual proviso that this must be fully considered in supervision and the appropriateness or otherwise be ascertained prior to a move into this area, however, I think that avoiding touch and holding where there is cumulative trauma means that the client is unable to benefit from that sense of physical containment and affect regulation which make for a sense of security both within the therapeutic relationship and outside of it. I agree with Lazarus (1994, p. 256) who says: "One of the worst professional and ethical violations is that of permitting current risk management principles to take precedence over humane intentions."

## Countertransference as means of repair

The therapist's response to the client's transference, their countertransference, is a vehicle for understanding the client and their story. We have seen in an earlier chapter how these responses can be used to inform and guide the therapeutic process. Gottlieb (1992) identifies that the medium of transference/countertransference recreates within the therapy the previous early deficit relationship. She describes this situation as the area of the "basic fault" (Balint, 1968) where during the developmental stage of dependency damage has occurred to the infant's nascent being. She recognises that "so much damage has occurred that a well-defined ego cannot be said to exist and the predominantly psychotic anxieties about fragmentation, disintegration, and loss of identity are paramount" (Gottlieb, 1992, p. 1). Because of this damage ego boundaries are not well established, there is no "me" and "not me" and no internalised good object. This results in the search for the good object in the external object. Van Sweden (1995, p. 156) acknowledges the opportunity for the therapist to become a "maternal constant within the transference" so providing the opportunity for integration and developmental progression. Erskine (2007, p. 137) understands this process thus:

> Through the psychotherapist's awareness of his or her own emotional reactions and associations to the client, together with an

understanding of child development and self-protective reactions, that the therapist can sense the client's unconscious communication of relational conflicts or traumatic experiences of early childhood and that through affective and rhythmic attunement and an awareness of the importance of relational needs, they can create a sensitive phenomenological and historical inquiry that allows such pre-symbolic emotional memory to be symbolically communicated through a shared language with an attuned and involved listener.

Kalsched (1996) describes how, in the intimacy of the transferential relationship, it is possible to observe moment-by-moment changes, to re-experience aspects of the original trauma within the therapeutic relationship and undo the primitive defences. Ferenczi (1932) also considered that revisiting traumatic early events was necessary in order to integrate the experience, and that the therapeutic setting was the place to do this. Bollas (1987, p. 33) recognises that in the early developmental phase the mother is not "identified as an *object* so much as a *process* transforming the infant's experiences". Through the "resolution of discomfort" by the mother providing milk "the pain of hunger, a moment of emptiness, is transformed by mother's milk into an experience of fullness. This is a primary transformation: emptiness, agony, and rage *become* fullness and content". Gottlieb (1992) then identifies that the mother is not known as an object, but rather as a process with the capacity to transform the infant's world. Thus cumulative transformations, because of their constancy, result in the differentiation of ego and object which, together with the emergence of the infant's ego development "may further transform the object world" (Gottlieb, 1992, p. 256). What is recreated in the therapeutic relationship, if all goes well, is a process which has the capacity to transform the world of the infant within the adult, having the possibility to result in the development of a sense of self and of security. Killingmo (1989) sees the therapeutic relationship as agent for change, recognising that recent literature and research sees that insight and relationship work hand in hand, and that the therapist's role as a "new object" is the catalyst for change. This participant describes the relationship with her therapist and its effects:

It's like my therapist was my whole world, I just lived for the sessions [...].

> I have much more of a sense of liking me [...] I've had much more of an "ok"-ness of who I am [...] And more of the physical sense of myself, I feel a lot less fragmented physically.

Fromm (2004) in describing the work of C. Winnicott (1980) comments that her client "having achieved the ability to truly depend on Ms. Winnicott, [...] could then re-connect with her very early depending on a teddy bear and on her mother as well". He notes that Volkan (2006, p. 3) calls this "the re-libidinisation of the patient's inner world—meaning the coming to life of early experiences with people who really mattered to the person, experiences that reassure the person about the foundations of their place in the world". This is exemplified by the following participant:

> [...] it was a life and death thing, and it was quite a profound experience [...] this was a real developmental stuff about separation, identity, about coming into the world, about that survival, so that is, that is the memory that most comes to mind in that, and although there weren't transitional objects that were given to me, from that experience, actually making sense of it was really important [...] it was actually within the therapy room. [...]

In describing such patients and the difficulty in working with them Borgogno and Vigna-Taglianti (2008, p. 316) recognise the inability of the patient to speak or think about their pervasive difficulties until such time as there is a therapeutic container for them and how this "occurs when we are facing histories marked by pre-verbal traumatic events that have created such damage to the structuring of the ego that the patient's dramatic nature can no longer be 'dramatized' and, instead of anxieties, catastrophic terror has settled in". They go on to describe the analyst's role: "these are precisely the situations in which the analyst, along with his hard work of decoding and 'interpreting' the dissociated feelings and roles, will have to provide and to give existence to those parental functions and those aspects of the infantile self that have been omitted and are lacking in the patient's history" (p. 317). Erskine (1999) would describe this as playing a part in an archaic story having the same elements, and yet having a different ending and outcome.

This participant has experienced her client's terror in the session:

But I stood, and I could hear voices in the room [...] and all of them agitated and worried, it was quite crazy-making, you know, if I, you know, hadn't got a handle on it and not understanding what was going on, so you'd think, "I'm going barking here", but I kind of had a sense of what that meant, you know, it was the levels of terror that were in her really. [...]

When trauma originates in the pre-verbal period this can be felt by the therapist in the countertransference. Borgogno and Vigna-Taglianti (2008, p. 314) describe this as the "domain of non-occurred or non-completed symbolisation, that with the passing of time can be slowly reintroduced into the analysis by the functions that the analyst performs, so that the patient will eventually be able to find the symbolisation within himself" thus enabling "the transmission of the emotional alphabet that is needed to master the lived experiences." They highlight the significance of neglect as traumatic because something that should have happened has not happened (Ferenczi, 1932; Winnicott, 1963; Bokanowski, 2004; Borgogno, 2005, 2006).

Siegel (2003, p. 48) identifies how individuals with unresolved trauma use the attachment relationship to enable them to re-enter terrifying states within the therapeutic relationship to permanently alter the primitive defences. This safety is not through words but through the nature of the relationship "traumatic states can be re-experienced, communicated if possible, and altered into more adaptive patterns in the future".

One view of development is that it involves the organisation, disorganisation, and re-organisation of patterns in the flow of states of mind. In this manner, development requires periods of disequilibrium in order to move forward in its ever-changing trajectory. In unresolved trauma, such forward movement has stopped. Restrictive or chaotic states preclude adaptive development from occurring.

Schore (2003, p. 108), recognised that "the loss of the ability to regulate the intensity of affects is the most far-reaching effect of early traumatic abuse and neglect". He highlights the fact that contemporary studies focus on the connection between early traumatic attachment experiences and the inability of some personality developments to regulate fear and terror states. He considers that there is evidence to connect neurobiology with attachment theory, hypothesising that the infant's "capacity to cope with stress" is correlated with certain maternal behaviours. He views the attachment relationship between mother and infant as crucial in developing the capacity to regulate emotion. He argues that a secure attachment relationship can facilitate the ability to self-regulate in later life. Schore's conclusion in this process is that "the dyadic regulation of emotion", psychobiologically, modulates positive states, such as excitement and joy, and also negative states, such as fear and aggression.

Goleman (1996) believes that it is the element of perceived helplessness which makes the experience of trauma overwhelming for the individual. The impact of trauma upon an individual is subjectively experienced and the closer the relationship, the more significant the impact upon the individual. This also means though that as the relationship with the therapist becomes close then that relationship is significant in helping the client to change and develop.

This participant describes traumatic feelings of helplessness and powerlessness:

> [...] that sort of intense feeling of pain and sort of wrongness and powerlessness about something terrible going on, to me that something [...] to a small child that's [...] terrible, that's the word for it.
> [...]

It should be noted that the fear of breakdown and psychological collapse is heightened in some individuals, but it may not be evident at the outset of therapy. Kalsched (1996) considers that "fear of breakdown" can come to the fore as a "dominating factor" when therapy is progressing well. He considers that in high functioning clients who are well compensated against their need for dependency it may not emerge early in the relationship. When the relationship moves to this level the therapist's failures and misattunements result in fear and anxiety culminating in "fear of breakdown". He describes the meaning as "a failure of a defence organization" (Kalsched, 1996, p. 88). This breakdown that is so feared is the breakdown of the self, because the organisation of the ego is threatened. Indeed, this could be seen as a reprise of the breakdown that occurred when the "false self" was created in order to protect the "true self". The therapeutic task is to help the client to begin to develop a narrative to express the experience, and to find words to express the primitive emotions. This dual conception of the self, involving a highly developed, socially adroit "false self" and a more primitive, emotional, "true self" can help us understand the therapeutic value of regressive experiences. One way of seeing the client's regression in therapy is as a way for them to tell the story of their developmental experience and so identify their developmental needs. This pre-verbal communication is not available to consciousness, it arises as a result of the development of attachment in the relationship, emerging in pre-verbal memories made manifest in behaviour patterns, emotional responses and relationships. In regression to dependency, experience is not available in the form of a narrative memory, but recollections of abandonment, neglect and cumulative trauma can be stored on a physiological level (Erskine, 2007).

## Conclusion

> Living with terror changes you. It burrows into your soul. It pulls
> you apart thought by thought. It inhabits your sleep. It visits when
> you least expect it, even when you are miles or years from its home.
> It recreates you, unbidden and unwelcomed [...] it is impossible to
> speak directly of terror. The experience of terror falls beyond the
> capacities of our normal language. (Hudnall Stamm et al., 2004,
> p. 370)

In this chapter I have described the emergence of terror in the life of the adult client, and particularly within the effective therapeutic relationship. I have described how trauma resulting from maternal deprivation which has occurred prior to the development of language, re-emerges and is revisited in a therapeutic relationship which recognises, allows and facilitates regression to dependence. When trauma relating to nascent relationships emerges, it can provoke a re-experiencing of the terror of disintegration and breakdown. I have described how terror originates in the infantile experience, leads to the development of primitive defences in relation to cumulative trauma, highlighting the power of the relationship, and the therapist's response and capacity to transform.

The experience of terror and trauma can disrupt functionality, and some orientations and medical professionals seek to avoid such disruption by using cognitive interventions and strategies which assist the client to manage their symptoms rather than resolve them. This treatment of symptoms is not appropriate for the clients who are the subjects of this work. Such experiences haunt and oppress the lives of these clients, and should therefore be addressed rather than avoided. The therapeutic relationship can offer the means for such resolution. Data from my study has identified how the terror, panic and anxiety symptoms which some of them have experienced prior to and during therapy have been alleviated or transformed as a result of the therapeutic relationship.

The development of a secure and attached therapeutic relationship is necessary to enable the client to feel sufficient safety to begin to regress, bringing with it the emergence of disowned feelings of rage and fear. When the relationship is strong enough to survive the expression of rage and fear, and the client is able to relate to the therapist from the "true self", and this is accepted by the therapist, then defences are not rebuilt and eventually the client can integrate the needs and emotions of the "true self" and become whole. Successful negotiation of the regression to dependence can resolve such primitive anxiety by providing reassurance and continuity of being, allowing the prematurely stopped forward movement of development to resume its trajectory. The therapists who have participated in my research have identified feeling moments of risk from clients whose rage was expressed. My own rage and terror scared me and it did get acted out. My therapist contained me, physically and emotionally, and accepted my rage and its manifestation as one would an infant's, with tolerance, love and acceptance—through management not interpretation (Winnicott, 1963).

It seems appropriate at this point to apprise the reader of my experience of writing this chapter. I have written it during a particularly difficult time in my own life when I have been experiencing terror as a result of current serious health concerns, and life or death has been ever on my mind. To be immersed in the data on terror has been very difficult and I could not have done it without the support and love of those who are important to me. It has been very difficult to put into words that which I know, both personally and professionally. The lack of control and the sense of helplessness has put me into existential fears. The support of those who care for me has enabled me to continue to grow and develop. This is a similar situation to that which my clients and participants have also found themselves in, and why they have struggled so much to live in an adult world whilst at times feeling very small and vulnerable and unable to rely upon themselves.

Having highlighted the presence of terror in the regression to dependence process I will now focus on the repair that the therapeutic relationship can offer.

CHAPTER FIVE

# A relational response

## Introduction

In one of Helen Keller's letters, there is recognition that: "The best and most beautiful things in the world cannot be seen or even touched; they must be felt in the heart" (Helen Keller, 1904, p. 203).

In identifying the intangibility of "the best and most beautiful things" she highlights the importance of things being felt in the heart. The process of psychotherapy is at its most powerful in the intangible, the intuitive, and the tacit knowings. These things are truly facilitative, yet this intangibility is hard to articulate and in describing a helpful therapeutic stance I do not want to present a formulaic set of rules, which would constrain the very spontaneity, which I view as essential to true healing. Clients who have been wounded by relationship must be healed in relationship, and the source of this healing is the development of a new attachment relationship of love. One of my participants expresses her experiences of her therapist's love:

> [...] it was utterly unconditional and she didn't want anything back,
> it wasn't a possessive love, it was a non-possessive love. [...]

Many clients entering therapy have never experienced unconditional love, having only experienced the absence of such love in their early development. Early experiences of neglect or abuse lead to the development of defences and ways of being, essential to survival, but which, in later years, negatively affect relationships. Hedges (1994b, p. 8) describes how these defensive patterns result in resistance to relationship, "Where love once was, or might have been, is now blocked." When a new and significant dyadic relationship is formed with the therapist these resistances come into the relationship and can be re-experienced, understood and finally given up. It then becomes possible to experience a new, formative relationship with the therapist.

The importance of the therapeutic relationship to the client's successful development is not a new idea, having been acknowledged at various times over the history of psychotherapy. Ferenczi believed that it was the love of the therapist that actually heals the patient, enabling them to develop a meaningful and anxiety-free relationship with the therapist, which then can lead to a capacity for other anxiety-free relationships to be possible. Thus the therapist has taken the role that the mother originally would have taken in being a starting point for relationship. Stern (1985) ascribes to the caregiver the role of a "soothing vitality affective mother". He argues that it is the live response of the mother that brings a vitality affect to the infant, so defining and helping them to know a sense of self and emotional relatedness. He relates this to therapy and describes "now moments" as being akin to the vitality affect in the early relationship. It could be argued that these "now moments", which Stern describes as occurring in therapy, provide healing during the process of regression, so enabling the aspect of the sense of self, which was damaged or arrested, to repair and grow. The purpose of psychotherapy then is to restore the client to full membership of society. Suttie (1935) considered that the whole of the development of psychoanalysis seems to have been dominated by the unconscious purpose of utilising love in practice, while repudiating any such activity in theory. I would go further, recognising that the presence of love can be an explicit theoretical construct, where such love is known and acknowledged between therapist and client.

Data from my research highlights the therapist's perception of this on-going process:

I think learning to love this client, 'cos she's very lovable, I think that's a hell of an important dynamic and we don't talk about love enough, I think, in the therapeutic relationship. She's lovely and she's become very dependent on the therapy and that's very obvious [...] if I'm away she ricochets, she feels the loss again, it's like a mini death to her, like the loss of her mum and her dad [...] and she's aware of that, but still it happens so she's [...] depending upon me, not in a kind of, unhealthy way, but in a way that helps repair [...] some of those lost, or never developed self-functions [...] she's finding a secure base that's located in me and my therapy room.

As therapy continues the client is subsequently able to use this secure base and reach out into the world. This need for security is recognised by Giovacchini (1990) as being essential to effective healing, seeing that a client must feel secure in order to comfortably regress to the more infantile aspect of their psyches. The therapeutic relationship provides the secure base to enable the client to tolerate regression to early traumatic experiences.

The United Kingdom Council for Psychotherapy (2013) identifies the purpose of psychotherapy thus:

> Psychotherapy aims to help clients gain insight into their difficulties or distress, establish a greater understanding of their motivation, and enable them to find more appropriate ways of coping or bring about changes in their thinking and behaviour.

Those who have experienced abuse and neglect in their early lives cannot be helped by insight alone "any more than a baby who has had a bad fall can be helped by being made to understand itself. From the point of view of the person giving help, there is no point in aiming at the capacity to understand intellectually (because it is not there)" (Klein, 1987, p. 7). More is required than this. Whilst understanding and insight are important, the ultimate objective of relational/developmental psychotherapy is reparative. Kohut (1977, p. 178) recognised that some clients enter therapy searching for the developmentally needed reparative relationship and its reactivation in therapy naming that search as the "original developmental tendency", and so it is the therapeutic task to offer such a reparative relationship.

In this chapter I identify how psychotherapy can facilitate regression to dependence, highlighting both specific interventions and the therapeutic attitudes, which address the relational needs of regressed clients. I will use theoretical literature informed by my research to show the therapeutic relationship as a potentially secure attachment relationship, having similarity to the original relationship with the caregiver of infancy. I will also identify the possibility of malignant regression and how this occurs.

## Remembering and re-experiencing

It is the therapeutic setting itself which is considered to induce the remembering and re-experiencing of the past, allowing the client to experience the therapist based on early experiences which may or may not be part of linear memory. Because this re-experiencing then occurs in the presence of the therapist, a new opportunity is offered to re-work relational patterns, thus making a new beginning, with new ways of relating being learned and experienced over time. This is illustrated in the following excerpt from my data where the participant recognises that her intrapsychic process has changed, and that re-experiencing in the relationship with her therapist has enabled her to learn new ways of being:

> I know and trust generally that what my therapist is saying, that if that isn't how she's feeling, then that's not how it is for her [...] so I'm less likely to have that transference, but actually even if I see it now, I give it less weight, that actually even if that is there, and even if that were truly there and somebody was irritated with me, I'd be more likely to say, 'well, I'm still gonna ask [...] something changed on that level. [...]

In order to facilitate the regression to dependence process an adjustment in the therapist's behaviour and the management of the client is required. This involves a move away from interpretation and the developing of insight towards the management of the client's transference and dependency. Developmental needs that are unaddressed in the appropriate developmental stage remain searched for in adulthood, and these needs and needed relationships can re-emerge in the psychotherapeutic relationship, where it is possible to attempt to offer resolution and repair. The therapeutic task is to attune to the client's ego state, matching the client's needs to the provision of care, support, understanding and acknowledgement. Gill (1991) recognises that such provision can allow a therapeutic re-experiencing, as described in the excerpt below by one of my participants:

> [...] it was something about that constancy, and also just the hold-
> ing was a very relaxed holding. That made me remember, when I
> was little my mother would come and say goodnight to me, but
> she would have to dash off, she wouldn't stay, she'd just come and
> tuck me up, and there was something about the level of holding I
> was getting, the person wasn't dashing off, it was a sort of relaxed,
> physically to be with, that was a calm, not an anxious person.

Such presence, engagement, involvement, and non-defensiveness by the therapist are necessary to effect relational repair.

### The therapeutic setting and the holding environment

Bion (1962) helps us to understand the nature of the mother's function. He considered the mother as container for the infant's projected over-whelm. He identified the mother's role in transforming that which the infant could not digest into more palatable elements, to be re-introduced to the infant in a transformed state. This understanding enables us to link Bion's description of the mother as container and Bollas's (1987, p. 259) description of the therapeutic setting, which he describes as "like being held by the mother". This sense of being held offers an invitation to regress, providing proximity, the attentiveness of the therapist, and security. Bollas (1987) highlights that the therapist should understand the need (not wish) to regress, be attuned to the process and understand the phenomenon. Winnicott (1965b/1984) identifies that anxiety in the infant has its roots in being insecurely held, this is an important point for therapists in terms of establishment of the holding environment. So that, just as in the maternal setting, the therapeutic setting can provide an attitude of acceptance, encouragement and responsiveness along with the dyadic regulators of physical comfort, warmth, quiet and the absence of interruption. Such regulation has not been provided by the caregiver in infancy, resulting in a response to trauma which negatively affects the development of self, and a failure to develop self-regulation.

Winnicott (1958b/1984) described how the mother's immersion into her infant's world, her primary maternal preoccupation, enables her to know the infant's expectations and needs, and the infant's self therefore, to begin to exist, not just react. He theorises that the mother through spontaneous sources within herself brings about this source of creative activity and that some analogous attitude needs to be present in the analyst in regard to their patient. In this particular matter, Bion and Winnicott are very close in their thinking. Just as a mother cannot learn how to mother from books or advice, when her baby spontaneously reaches out towards her in gesture or in action, neither can the therapist rely upon a mentor or a book in some difficult moments. However, a mother can be taught a lot: she can be shown how to hold a baby, how to feed the baby, how to wind the baby, how to bathe the baby and so on, but only she can know how to respond to the infant's look, noise, etc. This is also true for the therapist; theory and supervision offer teaching and support, but at some point the client will make demands for something that comes spontaneously and uniquely from the therapist. Fisher (2015) identifies the flexibility and spontaneity needed when working with complex clients. "These survivors have given me a window into the inner experience of the legacy of trauma, taught me what always to say and what never to say, helped to validate or disprove what the experts and theorists were claiming".

One of my participants described to me how she demanded such spontaneity from her own therapist, who seemed to be placing the techniques of her therapeutic modality before the real relationship with her client:

> I think that I pushed through her model of therapy and demanded that she be real with me [...] I demanded it, and when she did it she realised she had failed her own discipline, her own model.

The client's demand for spontaneity may come verbally, or be generated by the emotional intensity of the situation, placing a responsibility on the therapist to act. This action may be to move or not move, to touch or not touch, to remain silent or to speak, but whatever it may be, the client needs an attuned gestural response coming from the therapist's "true self", which by definition has no antecedent.

Bollas (1987, pp. 271–272) highlights the importance of suspending interpretation, dismissing residual guilt and using silence appropriately while the deeper parts of the self begin to emerge. This can result in the client experiencing an altered state of mind, going to a place of musing to sensory awareness, olfactory sensations and perceptions, intense feelings and discoveries. When I asked one of my participants about her memories of her experience of therapy, she illustrated this point:

> The first thing I think about is the room, and that's quite surprising, because my picture now is of the room actually without her in it, and the view outside the room, because I used to stare outside the room a lot, so the trees outside the window [...] and the sort of silence, the wordlessness. [...]

When clients are regressed in this way they are in a less integrated state, and experience elements of merger with the therapist, as in the original mother/infant relationship. In therapeutic contexts, the creation of a situation akin to the holding environment offers a sense of safety and protection, allowing the client to access hitherto split-off primitive agony and rage resulting from the original maternal failure, and accounting for the sometimes extreme and troubling emotions experienced in therapy or when any interruption in the therapist client relationship is threatened. Because of the profound and overwhelming emotions it will often have to contain, the development of the holding environment must be firmly established through a series of therapeutic successes in order to gain maximum benefit. The therapeutic alliance is an aspect of the therapeutic relationship, which holds both parties together even when the relationship at times becomes difficult. Depth psychotherapy involves working with negative aspects of the relationship and the client sometimes experiencing painful feelings. In order to sustain the client through this period client and therapist need to have established sufficient relationship to avoid the work being disrupted by negative experiences. Greenson (1967) described it as "the relatively non-neurotic, rational, and realistic attitudes of the patient towards the analyst".

The importance of the therapeutic alliance is identified below by one of my participants:

> They've got to have a knowledge of the way back, so that, that alliance elsewhere needs to be in a place, needs to be very clearly in place [...].

>so I need to have a way of assessing that I can get them into that other place, say I've got it wrong, or it's going to take them into distress, or memory, or whatever, I've got to have a knowledge of the way back. [...]

Ellman (2007) identifies that as love develops in the therapeutic relationship the ruptures occurring as a result of transference are more easily recovered from, and the survival of these ruptures enhances the trust between the therapeutic couple. Such an experience of love begins to fill the empty spaces in the client's psyche, helping them to know that they are no longer alone at their core of their being.

## Affective attunement

Van Sweden (1995) and Erskine (1993, 1994) specified that the therapist must attune to the client's presenting developmental stage and respond appropriately to provide a reparative and emotionally nurturing relationship, recognising that in an atmosphere of affective attunement the needs and feelings of the client can be expressed and appropriately responded to. This attunement will be based on verbal and non-verbal cues and is similar to that of mother/infant in the infant's pre-verbal phase. Affective attunement requires intuition, understanding and empathy which are developed through shared knowledge of the experiences of the client, the use of the unconscious material in the countertransference and the processing by the therapist of unconscious confused material; in short it means being totally in tune with the internal experiences of the client (Van Sweden, 1995). Affective attunement using the countertransference allows communication of the therapist's experiencing and understanding of the client's pre-verbal experiences. Erskine and Criswell (2012, p. 2) identify developmental attunement which is described as "thinking developmentally, sensing the developmental age at which the client may need therapeutic attentiveness, and responding to what would be normal in a child of that developmental age", in particular, touch and tenderness are important here. Kohut (1971, 1977) identified empathy as one of the main requirements of the therapist in relationship, together with engagement, involvement and non-defensiveness, and upholding the importance of working with the relationship between therapist and client, so uncovering unconscious processes developing.

I have stated earlier, that in formulating inchoate feelings as needs, a narrative is established which helps both therapist and client to have a sense of the direction of the work, a kind of map of shared understanding. However, just as in the mother/infant relationship, until the child achieves the ability to verbalise their needs, wants and desires, there is a necessity to tolerate ambiguity and live with not knowing which is echoed in the therapeutic dyad. Stewart (2003) considered that work on this area of analysis has not received the recognition it deserves because of the adaptation of technique that it requires, and the necessity of the therapist living in the difficult position of not knowing for long periods. But this is the nature of this work, and, in order to have an effective outcome, offering the possibility of a 'new beginning' to the client, the therapist's adaptation is required. This adjusted stance is described beautifully by my research participant:

> [...] the key times, the critical moments were definitely those points of regression, it wasn't the regression itself, it was the moving through the regression, there was something about being met, and feeling safe enough in my own therapy [...] once things became unlocked they tumbled out, I couldn't stop them, I couldn't put the lid back on, and part of me didn't want to, I didn't know where it was going, I didn't know sometimes if I'd ever get better, if I'd ever feel normal, or the sense of normality I thought I'd had before, which I realise wasn't really normality at all, but I kind of knew I needed it out, so I think I trusted that process somewhere, even though I was often scared [...] She held me, she stroked me, she sang to me, she covered me up with a duvet, she stroked my hair, she read me stories, we played in the sand, we drew and painted, you know, finger painting, foot painting, we did all kinds of things that were beyond my life experience that needed to happen for me to be able to inhabit another (name) who'd never had a voice, never had a place, never had any form of expression, and all that was really moving work, the painting, really moving work, and very beautiful, and she handled the time boundaries brilliantly.

She has described how her therapist nurtured her and attuned to her relational needs, some of which could be met. Therapist and client have worked together to construct and make actionable their situation in these terms. She has described an experience which is significant developmentally both in her internal world—intrapsychically, and in her external relationships—inter-psychically.

Another of my participants describes how he attunes to his clients:

> [...] the real thing is my capacity to be attuned to them and meet them where they're at which includes really respecting all of their reluctance and resistance to regressing. The other thing is identifying the regression when it's embedded and hidden amidst all of the adult stuff [...] so what I have learned is that when people are in that quiet regression to make comments like, I'm still here, I'm watching over you, I'm still listening even though you're silent, you don't have to, you don't have talk, so I make statements about my presence [...] But I don't turn it into an enquiry [...] if I know some people well I might say it's so important to be silent, or if you're quiet there's a safety [...] I watch the little body movements that signal agreement or disagreement [...] And if I see an agreement then maybe five minutes later I'll say it again so as not to abandon them.
>
> I might get hold of their face and turn it, and say, "look at me, look at me, what are you seeing", I might, I might move quite clearly into body work with somebody, there is a specific move, and I think the way in which I would conceptualise it is that when I see a child who's distressed, or distraught [...] a little one, obviously there needs to be an appropriate attunement to what's happening, I don't expect them to deal with themselves, I see it as—that's the other, the other's responsibility, so I will specifically work there, it depends on what I'm getting though, age-wise. [...]

When working with such clients it is important to equip oneself with useful items to facilitate the therapy; this might include sand trays, books and paints, all of which can bypass cognitive defences, helping to access and meet the clients' archaic needs.

I will now explore further the theoretical understanding of relational needs.

## Relational needs

This participant shows us the individuality of relational needs:

[…] she looked after me […] and I don't really know what that
means […] I do actually think a lot of it is in the word "look" […]
'cos it isn't about providing drink or tissues […] 'cos it's more than
seeing, it's watched […] watching me, just watching and waiting
[…] you know, a bit like watching a child sleep.

As theoretical understanding has moved away from the internal world
of drives as in Freud's understanding, into a world of relationship—the
influence of the other—then theorists and therapists become part of the
therapeutic encounter in a different way. They are viewed as relational
partners rather than experts who provide knowledge and insight into
their patient's inner world. They are partners in a setting whereby their
client is experiencing deep and painful feelings and they may be sitting
with the discomfort of being with their client who is without words.
Therapists and theorists have formulated the therapeutic process as one
of "meeting needs" perceiving that these needs existed independently
of and prior to the therapeutic process. This happens as a result of the
theoretical stance whereby these inchoate feelings are located by developmental theories in early infancy and so a narrative starts to develop
in turning these feelings into needs. When these feelings are named as
needs, the therapeutic partner can start to do something about them,
i.e., either name them and/or attempt to act upon them. This narrative
then forms part of the client's story and gives words and meaning to
their inner experiencing. It also means that the therapist and the client
can start to know rather than living with the discomfort of not knowing. For me this then has echoes of the early infancy dyad, where initially the infant experiences and protests, the caretaker is prompted to
respond and because the source of discomfort may be unknown, then
alternatives are tried in an attempt to offer resolution. Over time the
needs of the infant become more recognisable based on the trial and
success or failure of the previous experience—experimentation. The
feeling for the parent in these early days is very uncomfortable. Their
empathy can be aroused, but it is difficult because of not knowing what
the infant requires.

In establishing such an infancy narrative and re-enactment there is
not only a narrative, but also a way forward and an agreed and understood treatment plan for the therapeutic work. That is, what the individual requires can then be supplied, initially by the other, as in the early
infant relationship. Erskine et al. (1999) argue that needs that can be

met through relationship grow out of, and nurture, human interaction. As needs are present in all relationships, both client and therapist will have them, but in the therapeutic relationship it is the client's needs that are at the core of the interaction. Needs are often out of awareness, only coming into awareness when they are unmet. The needs which arise in the therapeutic relationship must be met with the therapist's genuine affective response of spontaneity, warmth and care (Erskine et al., 1999). They identify eight relational needs, although, in reality, there are as many relational needs as there are individuals, which should be acknowledged and addressed appropriately by the therapist. A contactful supportive relationship in infancy can result in the emergence and satisfaction of relational needs and the same is true of a psychotherapeutic relationship.

Contact in relationship involves the sensitive meeting of the other, and results in the ability to authentically acknowledge oneself. Where such contact is disrupted by insensitive attunement or neglect, then the relational needs which are appropriate at this time become problematic and cause pain. This can result in the infant putting them out of awareness, splitting them off to avoid the pain of dissatisfaction. These needs can then re-emerge in the therapeutic relationship, along with the other relational needs that would be expected of any adult to adult relationship. The client who experiences regression to prior developmental stages will also experience relational needs for security, valuing, acceptance, mutuality, self-definition, making an impact, having the other initiate, and the need to express love. Clients often recognise that their parenting has been inadequate, and that they have been inappropriately responded to in their infancy. They therefore have both present and past relational needs. The necessary attunement and response appropriate to both should then be available (Erskine et al., 1999).

My metaphor for attunement is a memory of an old TV set in which the required channel can be found by turning a knob, left or right, until some sort of picture is seen. As I remember it, in this tuning in process one would make large movements first to locate a picture, and then increasingly fine movements to obtain the best picture available. My understanding of attunement has its origins in being a mother. With a new-born a mother has to "guess" what her infant may need at any given time. This "guess" is based on both her innate knowledge of what infants need, and on her own experience of being an infant, held in her unconscious. Over a fairly short period of time the mother learns to "tune in" to the signals given by her infant, and is more and more accurately able to interpret and subsequently meet the need of her infant until such time that they are able to identify their needs. As a psychotherapist the process of getting to know the nuances of any individual client is a similar process.

Clients are individuals with individual needs and the recognition of their individuality is important. Because of the level of damage they have sustained, many clients do not recognise their own needs and so cannot identify them to the therapist. In regression to dependence the moment-by-moment attunement and acknowledgement of the therapist will identify nuances of behaviour which can help clients to begin to recognise and acknowledge their own needs (Erskine, 1998). The following participant identifies his awareness of how unmet relational needs took him into therapy:

> [...] but I'm also aware of becoming increasingly aware that there were needs in me that weren't met, that weren't met in my relationship, there were gaps, I was constantly hungry for those needs to be met through my relationship, and they couldn't be, and a constant level of frustration around that, so I guess that was my sort of primary driver [...] for what I needed to do in therapy was to find out how to meet those needs, relationally [...] with someone other than my partner [...] Now I could see that (I was) sort of forever being on the edge of relationship, forever getting a bit of relationship, seeing the possibility of that opening up slightly more, and then feeling short-changed, feeling like I couldn't quite have enough [...].
>
> I suppose I make sense of it as taking me back to a neediness that hadn't been met, it was about unmet needs, so it took me back to a place of unmet needs. [...]

This excerpt highlights that search for the developmentally needed repair (Kohut, 1977, p. 178).

Another participant shows her understanding of her therapeutic position in the dyad:

> Consistency is really important [...] and respecting of the level of needs, and trusting that they'll grow through that, consistency even to the point of sometimes, if they're really traumatised, of wearing

> the same clothes as when they last saw you, same jewellery [...]
> Sometimes it feels like a real straight jacket and it's important,
> I think, for me, to trust that it won't be forever [...] So they're
> allowed dependency [...] and I said, "Well, that's what children do,
> you know". So normalising as well is important I think, yes very
> important. It's so important just to be the same I think, to be the
> same person. [...]

From my own experiences as a client, tenderness, kindness, and gentleness are the instruments of healing.

When a client is regressed to a former developmental stage, the appropriate intervention by the therapist can itself lead to a re-experiencing of a past interaction, but with a different outcome. Bringing insight and remembering is important to help the client to understand their difficulties and to cognitively apply themselves to change, but, both Gill (1991) and Erskine (1998) see the relational repair as being "transformed experientially"—a re-experiencing with "a therapeutic twist". Stewart (1992) describes his conviction that where an experience has been psychically traumatic, in order for change and psychic growth to occur, both intellectual knowledge and understanding of emotional states involved need to be brought into consciousness. This knowledge and understanding is brought to fruition by experiencing. This participant describes how she works with clients to address the client's developmental needs and begin to establish a narrative for the experience:

> [...] what are the developmental issues here, what's not being met
> historically, what are the issues with, I mean I've got a newish cli-
> ent now always experiences that kind of nameless dread of things
> emerging [...] in regulatory terms, a terrible, real difficulty with,
> with regulating, or affect and her anxieties [...] She, she gets very
> panicky at night, very panicky [...] once it's set up it gets repeated,
> so yeah, for her I think there's early stuff [...] we haven't got to the
> earliest, but I know it's early something, but we're getting some of
> the narrative.
>     [...] this is pre-verbal, because if you haven't got a sense
> of life-affirming given to you in those first few months of life
> it's going to be phenomenal to get it, so I go back to there with
> clients.

"But if we sensitise ourselves to think developmentally we begin to sense what a traumatised or neglected child of that particular age may require from a caring and contactful adult" (Erskine & Criswell, 2012, p. 2).

This participant clearly shows her considerations regarding working with regression:

> [… ] looking at it from the "now", and thinking with any client what is it that's preventing them, living as wholesomely and as holistically as possible in the "now". So that would be my kind of starting point with anybody, and from that then I'll have choices, from those choices, regression i.e., for me actively inducing a decent, or a change into child ego is one of the choices, and I guess the question's like anything in life is, what's going to be the most effective and ethically most appropriate i.e. have I got the competency to achieve, and with regression it would be very specifically to extend and more likely into the process of gratification, so it would mean becoming an active component, or the continuance on of something that I felt was needed developmentally that hadn't occurred. […]

When infantile experiences re-emerge in therapy and become re-enacted with the therapist they can be reparative when the experience is *almost* re-lived; if it is fully re-lived, it will be re-lived in the original way, using the same self-protective pattern and resulting in trauma. Clearly it must not have the same ending as the original event, but be similar enough to trigger the emotional processes belonging to the event. Re-experiencing can bring about the re-emergence of archaic pain and catharsis and this should be met with support, acceptance and containment to ensure a feeling of safety around such processes for the client.

One of the interpersonal needs originating in childhood is for touch. I will now discuss therapeutic responses to the need for touch.

## Touch as therapeutic intervention

Hedges (1994a, 1994b) considers that human contact, often manifested in some form of physical touch, even if token, is necessary to transform reflexive mental states into symbiotic bonding patterns. He, in fact, questions whether this transformation is possible without touch. The foundation of human relatedness is now understood to be related to actual human contact.

Grotstein (1994) acknowledges that psychosomatic theorists such as Hofer (1978, 1981, 1982, 1983a, 1983b, 1984) and Krystal (1988, p. xxi) recognise the importance of skin and of "the touch modality that contacts it". "The infant's senses in general and perhaps that of touch in particular, seem to be the conduit of earliest contact with the object."

When the client is regressed and in contact with the early infant ego, the only form of contact with the infant is through sensory contact, and this includes touch. Little (1981, p. 144) recognises that, when dealing with the primitive layers of a patient, modification of boundaries may be necessary using non-verbal means "to carry interpretative effects [...] linking them with words to make the interpretation complete and to join up the primitive with the advanced layers". I would highlight that this joining up may come much later. Little (1981) describes work with a patient in emotional despair reaching out for her "I put my hand on his. He took a deep breath and burst into a storm of weeping, and great relief followed." She argues that emotional material at the primitive core of her patient "would not have been reached but for the body happening of his hand movement, accepted both verbally and non-verbally by me. It was the body injury that showed me the need for the body response". She has been able to identify the developmental need, and respond to it.

Hedges (1994a, 1994b) considers that in order to reach the somatised psyche touch may be a necessary part of the therapy at this time. He holds the belief that some physical contact is necessary to help the clients remain in contact at the time of re-experiencing "memories" of previous relational trauma.

Infant research concludes that touch is necessary for infants' well-being (Spitz, 1957). Psychotherapeutic research which focuses on the infant within the adult client also suggests the necessity for touch when addressing early infantile need. Erskine (1994) identifies the sense of unworthiness that can be experienced in the adult client resulting from a lack of physical touch in childhood.

A participant in my research, speaking of therapeutic work, describes working with touch:

> I've worked, focusing a lot on physical holding, with this client group and allowing them to determine what they need from me

physically, so a lot of experimenting with getting physical contact to feel right for them, and allowing them some freedom in being able to do that, using touch, to experiment what feels good, what doesn't feel good, allowing them to make some physical contact with me, to feel a sense of my physicality in the sense of my, my boundary, my solidness has felt important.

Erskine and Moursund (2004) recognise the link between the use of touch and the increase in dependency in the client, and is therefore facilitative. Polster and Polster (1974), Durana (1998), and Toronto (2001) have all viewed touch as therapeutically advantageous, both as a means of establishing contact and of completing unfinished business.
My participant illustrates this point:

> There was a terrific amount of risk taking and pro-activity on her behalf. She was unashamed about using herself physically as a mother would [...] physically so comfortable, and so comfortable in her own body, so I never had to go through that excruciating thing of thinking, "I need someone to hold me", it was just so seam-lessly done. [...]

She realises the difference between what is available in this relation-ship, and the nature of her parental relationship. The fact that the thera-pist initiated physical contact seems to offer some repair:

> [...] it was good that she initiated it because it was something I'd not had with any physical contact as a child, I really thought that it was really strange when she suggested it, but the being held was really, was important because somehow it meant that my body which I hadn't felt before, and there was something about somebody actu-ally saying "I would like to hold you" [...] to feel connected, I think, as much as anything, this person's given me something because they understand. [...]

Another participant describes how the use of touch enables her to feel connected and soothed:

> So the therapeutic touch was like [...] I remember it now, it was just so [...] it wasn't invasive, it was just like warm electricity going

through me … it brought tears to my eyes because it was soothing, you know […].

[…] she obviously recognised that need and at the point of very, very deep need went into the session I would need a hug before we started […] It was something about that constancy, and also just the holding was a very relaxed holding […] Well, she was constantly reaching out to me. […]

Sometimes clients dream, or daydream, about their therapy session. Rennie (1992, p. 227), in his research on client reflexivity and change, identifies the "reflexive moment" as a "safety zone" where a "course of action can be contemplated" seeing that reflexivity is "the form of consciousness in which a decision may be reached about a contemplated action and in which the decision may be converted to action". This is where the individual has a choice and I would view dreams and daydreams about the therapeutic encounter as means of reflexivity whereby the client incubates desires, wishes, and needs, making choices about action. My experience is that clients often picture themselves and their therapist and their needs in a therapy session, but shame can be experienced which blocks identification of this need to self and to the therapist. Sometimes I ask clients if they picture how our session might be, and often needs can be associated with this. One of my own pictures, a sort of waking dream, was of being held in a way I saw a colleague at a workshop being held by the facilitator. It was months before I was able to stutter out this need to my therapist, because of my experience of shame.

Winterson (2011, p. 9) writes of the power of stories:

I believe in fiction and the power of stories because that way we speak in tongues. We are not silenced. All of us, when in deep trauma, find we hesitate, we stammer; there are long pauses in our speech. The thing is stuck. We get our language back through the language of others. We can turn to the poem. We can open the book. Somebody has been there for us and deep-dived the words.

Wosket (1999) describes a client using reflective writing to experiment with the possibility of disclosure of issues considered shameful as a means of experimentation with the possibilities. Such reflective writing can have the same defensive distancing possibilities as the use of metaphor. She also advocates for the negotiation with clients around the use of touch, sharing dilemmas and exploring possibilities. I think of this as bypassing the defences against shame in the way that some clients use metaphor to create the "as if" experience which reduces their level of shame. Erskine (2001b, p. 2) considers metaphors to be "an expressive communication that emphasises our emotional and developmental perspectives". Tomkins et al. (2005, p. 2) consider that metaphor helps the client to create new internal experiences based on the evolution of a chosen metaphor. The use of metaphors enables the client to gain some distance, to see from a perspective which uses all of the client rather than them being engulfed in only the shamed ego state. They also identify that working with metaphor has verbal and non-verbal components, highlighting that clients will use metaphor to express "something abstract in more concrete terms, capture the whole, or the essence of an experience, or talk about something obliquely". Talking about issues that are perceived as shameful, in an oblique and metaphorical way can help to titrate shame, so that the client is able to tolerate exploring such issues.

Leijssen (2006) considers the use of the body in conjunction with verbal psychotherapy, seeing it as providing additional information and in order to improve awareness, to deepen experience, to release body memory and to explore new possibilities. She highlights the importance of the therapist's validation of the body and the use of touch. She notes that the therapist can also make use of the spontaneous bodily expressions of the client to understand their story.

These participants describe their ways of working with touch and holding:

> I think I learnt quite early on in my career how often physical holding was appropriate and good and learnt by the seat of my pants really just learnt not a very good metaphor but in this context but learnt just learnt how it worked basically by following what your clients needed.
>
> [...] the symbolic holding is, you know, really, really important 'cos if you're not doing that the whole thing [...] now whether or not you go for holding in terms of physical holding, I have used physical holding only if it felt useful for the client, and certainly with a number, well, the one I've just spoken about was another client, who was very, very badly abused with a kind of cultic context,

not just holding, but actually smelling, primary scents sense, trying to differentiate good smells from bad smells, it was really an important part of our, of our work, so that she could hold in her sense memory that the scents sense of me in the world, still existing, and quite literally I would rip off an old shirt of mine and stuff it up my jumper, refuel it with my smell, and give it back to, you know, to her for the next week so that she'd got, she could smell me in the world, so holding in that sense was enormous [...] certainly with this, this client there was sight, sensory memories of bad smells, bad smells, smelling bad smells in the room and then inviting her to smell me, acute startle responses to the slightest noises, you know, out there or out there, and holding [...] working at those sensory levels I think it's really important, but it's meticulous and careful work really, and often working with gut feelings. [...]

This participant describes how she experiences her responses to the client and her understanding of how she titrates her responses to meet the needs of the client in the moment having regard for their defences and her previously assessed understanding of their ability to tolerate such interventions:

> [...] it would depend [...] upon how robust they were at what stages [...] different levels of their development [...] what they were capable of [...] if I were to [...] move across and put my arm around somebody, I know I'm pushing them into something else, therefore they've got to have a level of allegiance with me elsewhere, cos I'm taking them into the bit that they might not have. [...]

Touch is a controversial issue in the world of psychotherapy, yet I believe it to be an important intervention to be considered when working with regressed clients. Using touch and holding requires a concept for both therapist and client to understand the experience, and a narrative is developed to enable a shared understanding.

## Establishing a narrative

Etherington (2000, p. 9) recognises that "making a coherent narrative out of experiences of childhood trauma is perhaps one of the most difficult tasks we can set ourselves". Establishing a shared narrative with an other (the therapist) can give people a voice and words on which to hang their experience which has previously been wordless. Narrative is the client's story, their understanding of how they came to develop as they are. For the therapist, narrative can help to develop a shared language for the client's experience, which then can become actionable, providing a shared treatment plan.

This participant describes his way of working therapeutically with narrative:

> [...] I think what you're doing here is half reliving, or trying to tell the story of a little baby, but I wouldn't label it as birth trauma or I wouldn't label it as mother abandoned you. That's much more the old psychoanalytic way. I have done things that have looked like and felt like re-birthing and I don't say anything but it's some kind of emotional experience but they might say, yes it was like I was being born again. I say, well tell me about it, how was it for you, well I had to push, or struggle, I thought I was going to suffocate, what do you know about your birth. [...]

Stern (1985) highlights how narratives are constructed in therapy and he sees the clinical infant, that is, the perception of the client's infancy narrative reconstructed in the course of clinical practice, as a construct which is discovered and altered by both teller and listener in the telling. He identifies the competing theories around early life: "the early life narratives as created by Freud, Erikson, Klein, Mahler, and Kohut would all be somewhat different even for the same case material. Each theorist selected different features of experience as the most central, so each would produce a different felt-life-history for the patient". In this way Stern demonstrates how therapeutic narratives are not used simply to discover what actually happened, but also to create "the real experience of living by specifying what is to be attended to and what is most salient. In other words, real-life-as-experienced becomes a product of the narrative, rather than the other way around" (Stern, 1985, p. 15). He recognises that the establishment of a narrative is an important clinical necessity.

The following participant offered a word of caution:

> I do think that's really important [developing a narrative], but I think it's got to be co-created, not over-defined by the therapist,

I think it can rob a client of their real internal experience [...] I love those moments when the client comes and says, "Do you know I've been really thinking about this [...] and it seems as though I've been in this place, you know, and does this make any sense to you?", and I say, "Well yeah, where are you with it?" So you know it's come out of something organically, but I'm not imposing it in an interpretive. [way]

## Transference within the therapeutic relationship

This participant is describing an experience in her own therapy, which illustrates the importance and nature of the therapeutic relationship to her. She has arrived for her therapy whilst the previous client is still leaving:

[...] as I walked in the hallway the door opened and my therapist hugged the client and was really tender towards her, and, and the client left, and I was devastated by her, absolutely devastated that, they'd become like my parents that didn't notice that I'd really needed her to be there and be waiting for me and notice, and she really wasn't there and she really didn't notice me, and, and she said that she'd even forgot that I was coming, and that, that part of the therapy has been really difficult for me, being forgotten, not being noticed, makes me rage as to why it's still happening, how I can be so forgotten and so unimportant. [...]

She identifies feelings that may echo sibling rivalry, where there is competition for parental love, and indeed, how this can be carried into adult romantic attachments where there is a demand for exclusivity.

Cozolino (2006, p. 50) states that the brain should be understood as "not a fully formed structure, but as a dynamic process undergoing constant development and reconstruction across the lifespan". There is then hope for the "re-formation" of brain processes into more helpful patterning as a result of therapeutic intervention. Wilkinson (2010) calls early relational trauma "the old present" where she identifies how early relationships bring with them the patterns and emotions from past relationships. Hurvich (2000, p. 19) describes the experience in regression whereby the "distinction between past and present is lost, so that the past is experienced as if it is happening now (Schur, 1953). There is a decreased ability to integrate experiences and a restriction or temporary loss of the sense of self" (Pao, 1979).

This participant describes the emergence of a different experience of herself:

> [...] I think that constantly working with that transference [...] allowed me then to free up around what I might need, that actually if I wasn't gonna get annihilated there for being vulnerable that actually I might be able to ask for stuff from her [...].
>
> That I might be able to ask for reassurance from her, that I might be able to ask for ... some affirming of me, that I might be able to ask for her to hold me, I might be able to ask for her to tell me how I appear, or to tell me how I come across, or just to tell me how I'm perceived.
>
> The thing that touched me when I went to see her was she just felt like a warm, tender person and I think that was just the thing that caught me, and brought out that little boy who just needed that [...] and yet I guess it was stirring up a lot of intense emotion because I think it, it was mainly my relationship with my mother.

During regression to dependence the nature of the transference can lose its "as if" quality, because the client perceives the therapist in an authentic way where he/she really is the parent in that experience. This aspect of regression to dependence is psychotic, in the sense that the "as if" aspect of the transference is lost, (Federn, 1952, p. 26) and the transferential relationship is seen as reality. The therapist does not have to become the mother to the dependent infant, only to accept the developmental needs and to offer appropriate response. When working with the regressed ego therapeutic misattunements can cause the client to experience deep shame and pain, the effect of which should not be minimised (Clark, 1993; Simon & Geib, 1996), but as in all therapy these misattunements can be successfully used to deepen the relationship, and, with successful reparation can allow the client to feel loved. The therapist's occasional and unintentional failure for the client can actually help the client to recognise the normal failures which are a part of life, and to become robust and resilient. In the dependency stage of early infant development the caregiver does not know what the infant's needs are, but makes an educated guess of what might be needed. When this is wrong then the infant protests and the caregiver learns more about the infant's needs. Similarly, the verbal and non-verbal protests of the client assist the therapist to correctly attune to their needs. When the therapist fails the client, the transgression may seem minor, yet to the client it can be experienced as an impingement which can engender pain or rage, getting the balance right is a tightrope to be walked by the therapist during these phases. Too many impingements can result in a return to the despair of childhood and if this is not recognised by the therapist, the client can terminate therapy. When my therapist failed me, usually by misattunements, I raged and felt let down once again, the pain I experienced was overwhelming and immense, and my response was to return to my normal defensive patterns and to lose hope. Because I had learned that I had a right to protest about this to my therapist without adverse consequences I began to be able to address these feelings with him. I learned over time that these powerful feelings do not have to cause an end to relationship, or abandonment, but instead can develop the relational depth. There was also a sense of relief from my almost permanent feeling of being wrong when I was able to feel that he was wrong instead, for once my critical internal voice, normally directing feelings of wrongness and rage towards myself, was directed outwards towards a relational other that could contain them. Even these apparent failures, however, serve a valuable function in that, provided that the relationship is strong enough to contain any overwhelm, they are part of the process of developing healthy inter-dependence. As Winnicott (1971, p. 10) says of good-enough mothers: "As time proceeds she adapts less and less completely, gradually, according to the infant's growing ability to deal with her failure." The failure then is what prompts independence.

## Countertransference

"The therapist is forced into shapes determined by the client's earliest relationships and is further influenced by the human tendency to repeat certain old patterns" (Kahn, 2001, p. 115).

The therapist's response to the client's transference is known as countertransference. Currently and historically there are significant contributions to the body of knowledge on countertransference from varying perspectives. The scale of this research does not permit for a full exploration of this concept therefore I have only selected such literature as is relevant to the issue of countertransference in regression.

Countertransference is usually considered to be the therapist's feeling towards the client. It can be divided into pro-active, that which the therapist brings of their own history or process into the relationship, and re-active, the therapist's response to the client's transference (Clarkson, 2003). Pro-active countertransference is largely problematic resulting from the therapist's unsolved conflicts. Here I am considering re-active countertransference as a response to the client's story, spoken or unspoken.

This participant describes his countertransference which engenders parental feelings, and he explains how he uses these responses to inform him of the client's needs and ego state or history:

> [...] what I remember most of all, is holding them one series of memories, and it's often right, it's analogous with the feeling engendered in me, the nights I had to stay up with my own sick children when they had been young and they have a fever and I hold them all night long and I you know I never really get to sleep myself, I'll doze for five minutes but they'll move or they'll cough or something like that and yet you know if you put them down the baby will wake up they don't sleep then you can't lay down with them and you have to sit up and hold them all night and that's often the feeling engendered in me when I'm holding a regressed child.

Racker (1968, p. 2) describes it "as a technical instrument, that is, an essential means to the understanding of the psychological processes (and especially the transference processes) of the patient". He (1968, p. 15) sees it as the patient's transfer of "infantile and internal conflicts to current situations and objects which are out of place and inappropriate." That is, the client sees the therapist through the lenses of previous relationships. For many therapists the process of transference and countertransference is an effective tool to understand the client's early relational history which becomes manifest within the current relationship. Young (2005) considers that transference and the therapeutic process itself are based on a mistake, that is, that the client experiences the therapist as someone else. He notes that many psychoanalyst colleagues of Winnicott and Little considered that the relationship between them went beyond the appropriate boundaries. Working at the pre-verbal regressive level does involve an awareness of boundary and the potential for the movement of boundaries. In responding from the countertransference Winnicott met with the infantile aspects of Margaret Little and his countertransference response was to step outside the normal boundaries of the analytic frame. So countertransference then can be seen as a catalyst for movement of the analytic frame (Little, 1990).

Young (2005) considers that "the frame must provide a bounded space in which it is bearable to do the work. Space—space for the patient to be safe enough to explore what is unsafe." He also discusses those theorists who have used the countertransference and subsequently stepped outside of the analytic frame with the aim of meeting the patient's needs and effecting a repair. My belief is that countertransference is an important key to understanding the client and a guide to the relational stance needed to offer repair. When clients have experienced infantile, pre-verbal trauma their ways of being including transference and defences will operate on a more primitive level. Borgogno and Vigna-Taglianti (2008) consider that not only the patient but also the analyst is involved in primitive experiences. They consider that the unconscious relationship of transference and countertransference occurs to "create the affective inter-psychic conditions that will enable the transmission of the emotional alphabet that is needed to master the lived experiences" and that this will be long-term therapy to allow such transference to be established "since such a patient is lacking a piece of experience connected to subjectivation (Botella & Botella, 2001) and consequently trauma for them would consist of the very fact that something that should have happened has actually not occurred". I would then assert that countertransference and the consequent meeting of relational needs is the means to effect relational repair. An instance of such countertransference is described by a participant:

> A client that I was holding [...] there was nothing, no words going on, but I had a sense that his head was really tender, like a new-born, like how you would protect a new-born baby's head, and I put my hand on the top of his head, on the crown of his head, and something really changed in his body, his body *went* in that, and there was something really met in that, and he did, he was able to tell me a few sessions after that that had been really powerful.

If countertransference is viewed as an inescapable part of the imaginative work of being able to think one's way into the client's concerns then it can be viewed as a major vehicle for empathy; but it is more than empathy—Maroda (2004, pp. 67–70) sees countertransference "as the sleeping giant". She believes that the countertransference can be as important as the transference and that the therapist can be almost as important as the patient. She quotes from Benedek (1953, p. 208) "[...] the unfolding of an interpersonal relationship in which transference and countertransference are utilised to achieve the therapeutic aim. This definition places the therapeutic relationship as the most important agent of the therapeutic process", a concept identified by Norcross & Prochaska (1986).

Countertransferential feelings are identified by this participant as a means of contact with a regressed client:

> [...] it feels like a felt sense, just a hunch and not being too over-defining of it, but to be curious, just to hold in my doubts and uncertainties really, and tracking, observing eye contact if there is any, very often there isn't, observing my own counter-transference responses, observing body posture, and even doing just gentle feedback, even to say that "it's me [...] I'm still here" so that they can be more grounded in present reality [...] but very delicately you know. [...]

She illustrates her use of countertransference to understand her client's story:

> It was almost as though I was being induced into sleep, and I was struggling to a) stay awake, and b) understand what was going on, suddenly had this image, and they were holding so many different ways, and we would communicate in different [...] this, but this image of this mother with a small child, with the mother unavailable, fast asleep, and I just said to her, "did you, did your mum fall asleep with you and you were desperate to try to wake her up?" and, "stop" [...] up came the memory, yes, she was a, she was a sherry drinker, you know, she recalled the clock falling on her knee and trying to wake her up [...] she was out of contact. [...]

Reflecting upon the feelings I have as a therapist working with clients undergoing these kinds of regressive experiences has been a source of increasing insight and knowledge. My countertransference when working at these developmental levels often involves maternal feelings and a desire to meet the infant ego in whatever way is necessary. This can be through eye contact, the expression of understanding, touch, physical holding or through silence. When clients are dealing with such a high degree of psychological damage that they need to revisit these pre-verbal times, then their needs become appropriate to their developmental age of the time. Clients who are regressed struggle to cope with cognition, thus, as Winnicott (1965b/1984) advised, interpretation during these times is not useful and may be experienced as an impingement. My own experience has underscored the way that countertransference also involves an experience of one's own infancy needs. One of my participants illustrates how his personal work as a client now influences his therapeutic work:

> [...] she obviously regressed in the therapy to the point where we could only do the work as long as I was actually physically holding her and that gave a kind of security which enabled some very intense feelings of lostness. I can also remember occasions where I tried physical containment and it didn't work at all it wasn't the right thing for that client [...] Because I think holding and not being held are very much part of my stuff from very early in my life which means I am very acutely sensitive to it and probably quite good at you know at picking up the vibes and reacting to the clients need or where things went wrong in their lives.

If the therapist has not worked with these needs they may rely on the client to fulfil them, hence the need for a personal experience of this depth of work. Therapists may also experience the threat of chaos and psychotic process. This can be frightening for the therapist who has not met this in themselves, or address their own vulnerabilities.

My participant identifies this experience in her own therapy:

> I stood for something that she'd not faced in her own life [...] I don't think she'd looked at it in herself. And I think I knew that, but I was still going to take the risk of showing, and watch what she did, and I think that frightened her [...] I think it opened up on her own need.

Powerful feelings can be engendered by in-depth psychotherapy, which can be psychological and physical. My participant describes a powerful physical response in countertransference with a particular client:

> [...] it's like holding a child rather than an adult. I've held some beautiful, attractive looking people in my arms, but once they get into regression it's just like a little kid. Now, where have I gotten sexually excited, 'cos that's an important part of the question. Intriguing to me the people I have sat in a session with and started to get an erection with. Talking about everything later I discover they are a sexual abuse victim and they've kept it a secret. I'll give you one example and it has nothing to do with attractiveness. I was sitting with a very ugly woman who does not smell good to me, who is obese and aggressive. Yet each time I see her somewhere in that session, I start to get an erection. Its two years before we get around to the sexual abuse with her father, which was a very seductive abuse, not a painful abuse, not a rape, but a slow, easy, seductive abuse which is why this woman has never been married. In her adult life she has sort of been a virgin, as a child she wasn't, that's her fending people off. And yet I could pick up that energy and my body is picking it up and responding, because while she's fending me off she's also seductive [...] And those are the wonderful countertransferential resonances. It's where we are resonating with them at a physiological level.

He is describing sexual arousal in response to his client's countertransferential story. He has identified his experience that this countertransference is often present where there has been sexual abuse. Maroda (2004) highlights that discussion of such sexual feelings towards a client is a controversial area. She cites Gorkin (1985, 1987) concerning different aspects of such countertransference, and Mann (1997) identifies the experience of either distaste for the client, which he describes as "transference resistance", or a desire to respond to the client's unconscious process. Of course, either of these positions is problematic for the therapist and is controversial for the profession, but the participant illustrates his therapeutic use of such feelings.

A high level of skill is needed in management and tolerance of these processes, and I feel particular insight was gained from having undergone these experiences in my own therapy. Nathanson (1992) considers that "It is axiomatic that therapists treat their own patients in a manner and style somewhat akin to the way they themselves were treated" (1992, p. 22). He considers that therapists minister to their clients as they were ministered to by their personal therapists. I would enlarge this to say that therapists who have not experienced repair of early infantile relationships may "parent" their clients as they have been parented.

Therapists can make use of the way that their own awareness may develop as a kind of response to the patient's immaturity and dependence as they regress. In Winnicott's account, the good-enough mother is willing to let go of her identification with her infant as soon as the infant is capable of become separate. Because of maternal attunement and empathy the mother knows how the infant feels and is able to meet its needs for holding and environmental provision. In the therapeutic relationship this attunement and empathy is present in the counter-transference and skilful use of this enables identification of and adaptation to the client's needs and recognition as the client develops and as needs change. As in the mother/infant relationship, when the therapist fails to attune to the needs of the infant/client they will experience this as an impingement or, as Khan (1963) would describe it, a psychological affront to their sense of self.

In order to meet the client's needs in regression the therapist must be reliable, non-defensive and aware of the risks involved. In this phase supporting and managing the client's experience is more necessary than verbal interpretation. This involves accepting the client's anger and rage without interpreting it as transference or identifying previous patterns, it is not the time to offer logic or teach self-support. The client needs their experience to be accepted, and for the therapist to offer necessary support within the session and sometimes outside of the session in the form of texts and phone calls or additional sessions. Winnicott (1974) believed that this process involved a frightening return to the earliest unintegrated state, which would involve a primordial fear of annihilation which can have a physical reaction in the startle reflex. The therapist must be able to stay grounded in reality, retaining their sense of identity whilst being able to experience the anxiety, fear of annihilation and loss of identity that the client faces. This requires the same qualities that a "good-enough mother" provides. The development and maintenance of such a relationship involves emotional effort for both parties. Clients can access powerful primitive emotions and catharsis of rage and fear during the regression to dependence process, as can be seen in the participant's descriptions in the chapter on terror, but my experience suggests that, with sufficient support, this is generally manageable. I consider that the question for the therapist in private practice is, "given my situation, the client's functionality, and practical facilities is this client containable and manageable by me?"

This participant illustrates his concerns:

> [...] certainly a fear that it would [...] that I would be unable to hold it with her, that it was so overwhelming, that "was this a good idea?", you know, "should I be doing this?", but I also knew it could happen to her even outside a therapy session, it wasn't necessarily the therapy that was triggering it, and it meant that the session would always go on longer than an hour, and it meant [...] and it was exhausting, physically and emotionally, mentally exhausting to stay with. [...]

Some clients' levels of distress and lack of internal and external emotional support mean that additional support in the form of Mental Health Services may be required. The client's history, functionality and psychological style should be considered at assessment, although sometimes it is not possible to anticipate the emergence of a high level of distress prior to beginning work. In a private practice setting the therapist's ability to work with high levels of distress must be considered, they must be supported by supervision, and elicit the support of other agencies if necessary. A research participant relates an experience with a client who was receiving support from Mental Health Services:

> [...] her consultant had formed the opinion that this was some kind of re-living of trauma, and was a dissociative episode, and not, not a normal psychotic breakdown, but she didn't enamour herself to the staff in those phases, but in sessions with me the whole room could get filled with this kind of sense of tension and terror.

Bollas (2013) addresses this issue with the recommendation that a team of supporters is assembled in order to deal with such crises. This may be possible for such a high profile practitioner, but would be much more difficult for most practitioners when they are unknown to local psychiatrists. The prevailing wind of CBT also has an impact here. Previously, when I have sought support from psychiatry for a client in crisis the response has been for the psychiatrist to refer the client for a course of CBT which would divert the client from the issues of their internal life by attending "to a time-limited cognitive project. Just as a parent resolves a toddler's crying by diversion" Bollas (2013, p. 2). He considers that this action would forestall a "necessary" crisis. I concur with this position, considering that to fail to address this emergence of what I consider to be the "true self", leaves the client forever in a place of fragility and compromise and a victim of the short fix, revolving door nature of cognitive therapies.

Piloting distressed and regressed clients makes it essential for therapists to access supervision from practitioners experienced in this type of work in order to gain support, advice and assistance in recognising if it is appropriate to work with a particular client, to obtain help in understanding transferential aspects of the relationship and to ensure that the relationship remains ethical. Once all this has been considered then it is the combined efforts of both participants that bring "the mother/infant emotional upheaval" to the foreground of the therapeutic relationship. When this is successful, integration of disconnected feeling states can occur. The provision of a containing environment, affective attunement and acceptance of dependence allow the regression to occur. Van Sweden (1995, p. 210) recognises that "these provisions support ego integration, encouraging developmental progression to take place." Winnicott (1958b/1984) also identifies that given the provision of a safe setting and the facilitation of regression to dependence then the hidden self can become integrated into the total ego, there can be an unfreezing of the environmental failure and the expression of anger related to this. Subsequently there can be a return from regression to dependence with instinctual needs and wishes becoming realisable.

Bollas (1987, p. 230) considers that:

> [...] patients convey their internal world through the establishment of an environment within the clinical situation, and they necessarily manipulate the analyst through object usage into assuming different functions and roles. This is so because the patient cannot express his conflict in words, so the full articulation of pre-verbal transference evolves in the analyst's countertransference.

Maroda (2004) also recognises the regressions of both therapist and client and their immersion in the symbiotic phase of treatment whereby the work centres on the pre-verbal and the patient requires more of the therapist's self.

My experience of working with regressed clients has involved being in touch with my pre-verbal experiencing, that is my connection with the infant part of me. As my need to be developmentally met has been addressed I am able to use such experiences as a diagnostic tool to guide the process of the relationship I am working in. In writing of Winnicott, Khan (1984, p. xi) described that he "listened with the whole of his body" and that his "psyche and soma" were in perpetual dialogue and debate. Van Sweden (1995) recognised that in this process much of the analysand's communication is pre-verbal and therefore increased emphasis is given to the countertransference of the therapist.

In his chapter on the meanings and uses of countertransference Racker (1968) refers to Freud's "third meaning" in the transference. "It is in the transference that the analysand may re-live the past under better conditions and in this way rectify pathological decisions and destinies." Racker continues to look at the three meanings of the countertransference, seeing the third meaning as affecting:

> [...] the analyst's behaviour; it interferes with his action as object
> of the patient's re-experience in the new fragment of life that is the
> analytic situation, in which the patient should meet with greater
> understanding and objectivity than he found in the reality or fan
> tasy of his childhood.

He also quotes from Heimann (1950) "the basic assumption is that the analyst's unconscious understands that of his patients". All of these theorists are seeing countertransference and the understanding which can arise from it as a means to interpretation which ultimately would result in the analysand obtaining insight, which is the main aim of psycho-analysis. My hypothesis would be rather that the countertransference can help us to understand the client's story, both subjectively and objectively, and this insight can then help us to respond to the client in ways which offer a relational repair. In "Interpreting the counter-transference" (1992) Hedges gives an account of his experience of countertransference and how his understanding and use of countertransference reactions has influenced his work. In Hedges (1994b)

"In search of the lost mother of infancy" he has further developed his understanding of countertransference as an indicator of the presence of pre-verbal material and as a guide to eventually engaging the relational components of the work, and on removing blocks to interpersonal relationship, therefore seeing the aim of such understanding as transformation through connections which may include physical contact.

## Secure attachment

Clients who need to re-visit early developmental epochs will need to develop a long period of secure attachment with their therapist in order to create a safe, secure base in which to explore these painful experiences. In this process the infantile relational needs are believed to re-emerge and the developmental relational stance will require some gratification of these needs (Van Sweden, 1995).

Siegel (2003) describes psychotherapy as a form of attachment relationship in which the client seeks proximity, is soothed, and develops an internal working model of security based on the experience and subsequent learning of the nature of the relationship between the therapist and client, seeing that an effective change in brain function and in the attachment process can help the client to self-regulate. Stewart (2011) describes the possibility of developing a secure attachment after a successful long-term therapeutic relationship. Some attachment theorists (Roisman et al., 2002; Phelps, Belskg, & Cmic, 1998) have called this "earned secure" which describes the attachment relationships of adults who have had early traumatic relationships, but have created a narrative for their experience and have entered into a reparative relationship. The development of attachment, the understanding of object relational needs, working within transference whereby early relationships are reprised within the therapeutic relationship where the client can experience a new relationship and risk regression and dependency with a dependable other. Ultimately it is possible for previously held disorganised, insecure attachments to move towards more secure attachment relationships as a result of the therapeutic relationship. My participants have identified that this attentive, loving care, when provided within the therapeutic relationship through adaptation of technique, allows clients to rediscover themselves as worthy and loveable, and to develop secure attachment patterns. This attachment is considered necessary by Steele et al. (2001) seeing that in the treatment of trauma the client has a need for emotional and physical safety, and the attainment of a secure attachment to a consistently responsive and caring therapist is necessary to enable the client to recover from traumatic injury.

## Ego boundaries

Winnicott (1965b/1984) frames the provision of ego-support by the therapist as a reprise of the mother/infant relationship whereby the mother lends some of her ego to the infant. I have experienced this in my personal relationship with my therapist. In a regressed state I have needed protection from impingement, whether that is impingement in the form of interruption of my reverie or silence by my therapist or by some outside agency or event. I have also received ego support in the recognition that I might need soothing when such an impingement occurs. Both of these forms of support have enabled me to remain in my regressed state without needing to react, my therapist has done the reacting for me. There have also been failures in this aspect of my therapy, where my therapist has misattuned to my need in the moment and in a lack of spontaneous gesture in response to my action. On one occasion I remember playing with my therapist's hand and my expectation was that I would be met in this. My therapist did not respond and I felt shame and reacted, resulted in a premature return from regression into an experience of shame for being regressed.

Winnicott considered that working with a regressed client may require the therapist to lend some of his own ego to the client. He views that a regressed and dependent client in some circumstances—such as where the client is unsafe to leave the therapeutic setting—unsafe to drive, etc.,—requires a change in the therapeutic stance whereby the therapist takes appropriate responsibility for the client's actions, feelings, behaviours. He considers that when the client is regressed the therapist will need to "take care" in the way that a caretaker would with an infant. Therapists may also, in the client's interest, need to allow their own boundary to move in order to accommodate the client's need. The client's need may penetrate the therapist in the same way that the infant's need penetrates the mother, though at times this may be uncomfortable for the therapist/mother. The therapist may also need, in the client's interest, to give the client more of themselves than they normally would—this too may be uncomfortable.

Giovacchini (1972, p. 301) comments on the propensity of even healthy patients to regress given certain circumstances. He considers that evidence can be found of:

> [...] fusion during the transference regression. This should not be surprising because if one accepts the existence of a symbiotic fusion as a beginning developmental phase, one should expect its persistence in the context of more integrated superstructures. During regression it can become activated again.

Within this there can be an experience of the loss of self and of the client's inner world. Bollas (1987, p. 254) describes this process of mutual regression "only by making a good object (the analyst) go somewhat mad, can such a patient believe in his analysis and know that the analyst has been where he has been and has survived and emerged intact with his own sense of self". Little (1981) describes her work with "borderline" patients, commenting that "the work shifts and changes continually and calls for a high degree of sensitivity, stability, and flexibility in the analyst". She recognises that this is a difficult task in which the analyst must face his own anxiety and inner processes, having freedom of imagination, the ability "to allow a free flow of emotions in oneself, flexibility of ego boundaries", may all be necessary in the treatment of the patient. This participant describes her feelings towards her clients and her response:

> With love, actually, with feeling love for these clients [...] but also letting myself feel all the other things, too, letting myself feel all the countertransference stuff that's horrible [...] how do I meet it and how do I envisage meeting it [...] through touch, through look, through sensory experiencing more than the verbal word.

She describes her immersion into the client's world, by giving an example of how her inner boundary, her sense of separateness becomes subsumed into the client's world:

> [...] the ecstasy and pain, it felt like, that [...] and I feel like I hit that ecstasy and pain place a lot with this client group.

Balint, in recognising that in a "benign" regression there is a potential benefit for the client in resolving experiences of the past which have caused damage, he also recognises that the therapist "must accept and carry the patient for a while, must prove more or less indestructible, must not insist on maintaining harsh boundaries, but must allow the development of a kind of mix-up between the patient and himself" (1968, p. 145).

In this formulation the aim of addressing these early developmental needs is to help the client to "catch up" with other aspects of the self, which have not been fixated by failed dependency and the primitive defences which have surrounded the experience. Transitional objects are indicators of the developmental stage that the client is in and can also evidence the development of the beginning of internalisation of a more secure relationship.

Dosamantes (1992, p. 361) in linking the pre-verbal dyadic couple with the therapeutic dyadic couple writes:

> [...] while in a state of symbiosis, the dyadic couple blurs the boundaries between them and together they create the illusion of at-oneness with one another. In this merged state, words have little meaning for them, and communication transpires primarily through touch, sensation, and mental images.

## The use of transitional objects

Winnicott wrote of transitional objects originally in his 1953 paper. He describes the movement between what could be called "subject" and "object", or "me" and "not me". Initially, the infant experiences every-thing as himself, such as his thumb. Eventually the infant recognises an object such as a teddy bear or blanket. Winnicott describes an "interme-diate area of experiencing". In this intermediate area the infant uses an object to represent the relationship that reduces anxiety.

A transitional object is any object (although usually a soft toy, com-forting blanket, or some other item) which is in the infant's/client's possession and can be used symbolically to soothe in moments when the mother/therapist is not available because it is believed to represent the soothing power of that relationship. Winnicott (1953/1984) consid-ers that the infant uses an object to describe the intermediate area of experiencing, the between. This object comes to represent the holding relationship between mother and infant in the time before the infant is fully able to have a sense of self and other. Litt (1986) identifies that Winnicott considered that such attachments represented an important aspect of ego development which ultimately led to the development of the sense of self. He introduced the terms "transitional object" and "transitional phenomena" to identify the area of experience between "oral eroticism and true object relationship". He described an intermediate area of experiencing in-between the infant who has not yet developed a sense of self, and the infant who has grasped the sense of self and other, a transitional area to which inner reality and external life impact, again a transitional area (Winnicott, 1958b/1984, p. 230). The term "transitional phenomena" describes the use of soothing acts in order to reduce anxiety. This transitional tendency develops at the point when the infant is moving out of oral eroticism towards recognition of "me" and "not me". The point at which the infant begins to incorporate "not me" into its soothing technique is described as "transitional phenomena", when this consistently becomes one such object this is known as a "transitional object". Winnicott made clear that it is not the object itself that is referred to, but rather the possession, and the intermediate position between the subjective and the objective (p. 231). In using a transitional object the infant possesses it. The infant can then use the object in times of anxiety as a means of soothing. Winnicott considers that the root of symbolism in time is highlighted by the transitional object and shows progress towards experiencing.

Within the therapeutic relationship a therapist can also use this formulation of infant development in the period before the client has fully developed the sense of self and other. It is seen to support the client between sessions, enabling them to hold externally a sense of the relationship with the other.

This is described by a participant:

> [...] if she was on holiday for a month it was like I'd got something of her [...] the scarf I used to keep under my pillow, the cardigan I'd put on at night and [...] To feel [...] to feel connected, I think, as much as anything, this person's given me something because they understand, therefore, even if I'm feeling unloved, I know [...] so it's somehow it affirmed [...] At the beginning of therapy I had a stone I used to keep in my pocket, later on I had a scarf (and a cardigan).

> Yeah, it was just so, it was just like I needed this contact and to
> know this person wouldn't disappear. [...]

Little (1981) describes how the attention to a client's physical needs made it possible to reach psychological material which may not have been possible otherwise.

When infants have experienced being shamed by caretakers for their needs or vulnerability, they can reject and disown those aspects of themselves. When these aspects of themselves are brought back to awareness through the process of therapy, they are often thought of with disdain and there is a process which needs to occur in which clients start to reclaim and integrate those previously unintegrated self-aspects.

The symbolic nature of the transitional object is described by the participant:

> I still have a cushion from my therapist's room which I, which is my, you know, the baby, for me to, you know, talk to, love up, soothe, stroke or blah, and that was really important for me to be able to take that home after, when I actually made contact with her I was able to see her and recognise and acknowledge the deficit, and feel a kind of, you know to integrate her, I needed to have her in-between sessions [...] and I've still got it, and I think I'll always have it.

Winnicott (1960), Tustin (1990), Bick (1968), and Hedges (1994a) in different ways consider the infant's skin as both a container of the internal world and a connector to the external world. Infants (and regressed clients) seem to find comfort in soft, warm items such as fabrics. The items that infants seem to choose have such characteristics, and the participants of this study have also largely described the finding and acquisition of such items to symbolise the soothing that they experience within the therapeutic relationship. These items seem to have their place for both infants and clients for a time in their development and are relinquished when they are no longer needed, as acknowledged by these participants:

> I would say [...] "when I've left here I can't hang on" [...] this was when I got things like phone calls [...] and transitional objects [...] to take home [...] I can't remember exactly [when I stopped needing

them] but I think there were things that I didn't need so much, I'd still got them, but I didn't cling on to them.

[…] she'd taken a photograph of herself […] she'd clearly kind of thought and felt herself back into it […] she kept the tape recorder running for three or four weeks […] then she'd cut and edited snippets and threaded them all together […] she did that, and that was lovely, and eventually I lost the tape […] it was actually right to lose it in the end […] the work was moving on and actually I didn't need it.

Having looked at how therapy can effectively be considered to facilitate regression to progression it is important to mention an aspect of regression which is neither helpful nor healing.

## Malignant regression

Balint (1968) recognised that there could be negative aspects to regression. He considered that these negative aspects involved patients who, rather than needing regression to allow progression in their development, regress in order to avoid change and maintain their defensive structure, that is, those patients who demand caretaking from the therapist, not with a view to repair and then progression, but in order to maintain their fragile self-structure. In this construction the therapeutic task would be to challenge the regression rather than to facilitate it. Regression in the service of progression has a clinically different feel from regression in the service of gratification. Where there is a *need* for therapeutic intervention in the service of growth what is offered by the therapist can simply be what is needed, whether that is touch, or time or some other need. Where there is a *wish* for therapeutic intervention for the purposes of gratification the therapeutic response is different, involving recognition of the client's wishes together with appropriate challenge of habitual ways of relating.

The following participants are referring to this possibility, that is that the client may come to rely upon regression as a means to get their needs met rather than as a means of progression to maturity. This participant seems to echo Balint's position:

I feel the risk could be that it could just be staying there, so that I'm very careful, I don't just offer it. […]

She recognises that there was a potential for this within herself:

> [...] I believe with myself that could have been a risk, but actually it didn't become a risk.

She also identifies how clients may fear that regression and dependence may become permanent:

> I've experienced their fear of that [...] they won't get stuck like that for ever, but I can understand their fear.

This participant illustrates the complications that can occur when working with regressive processes:

> [...] this woman has been regressed now [...] this is her fourteenth year [...] the only thing that would meet her originally when she was in the three/four year old stage was for me to put my arms around her and hold her tightly, until she could feel her edges again [...] I don't think I can really heal something, there's been too much destruction, and she's not sure she wants to live either, so I do sometimes think, and I did question her very gently over it, that maybe she's afraid of getting better [...] because she's also afraid that our relationship would come to an end.

Maroda (2004) notes that "the more disturbed the patient, the more difficult and traumatic" the therapeutic re-enactment (the out-playing of the story) will be. Van Sweden (1995) recognises where there is a high level of disturbance within the therapy it can be difficult to differentiate between benign regression and malignancy at this time. This is because at the heart of the regression it is difficult to see progress or identify the direction of the work.

I have reservations regarding the concept of malignant regression. Whilst there can be regression in the service of gratification, which would not be towards progression, the reasons for this search for gratification rather than progression can be found in the client's early history, and, with the appropriate therapeutic relationship, can be addressed by the acceptance of this need and the appropriate holding of boundary, resulting in a regression towards progression. A previous client of mine (I shall call him Fred) has progressed by being given minor gratification from me. Sometimes, when wants are not met there were hot protests. Overall his needs were such that without these minor gratifications to ease his anxiety he would not have been able to stay in therapy. Eventually, he was sufficiently supported to conceive of the idea of change and progression, at which point there was no further unhelpful regression.

## My experience of the facilitating therapy as a client

Throughout this work I have reflected upon my personal experiences as a client and as a therapist, but in this section I want to describe my experience of the facilitation of my therapist. I have been hesitant to give detail because the relationship is intimate and therefore private. I consider that my gift as a therapist, supervisor and trainer is in sharing myself with the other, yet on the negative side of this, I can easily give myself away and open myself to those who do not value my offerings. Yet I believe that being open to share our experiences is essential. Winnicott describes the process of the psychological development of the self, and it is this description which has so closely matched my own experience as a client. My therapist, although highly trained, did not fully understand the regression to dependence process, yet he was able to stay with me through it because of his ability to live without knowing, to accept my experiences and to love me through them. The most important times for me were when he allowed his own spontaneity into the regressive process. Where he seemed to know how little I was feeling and would reach out to me. On one occasion I was experiencing a high level of distress and he needed to go to the toilet. He took off his jumper and gave it to me to hold until he returned. Not only was my panic contained by this gesture, but also I was able to see his understanding of where I was and his acceptance of that. There were many other instances like this where he facilitated my development. I was very dependent for a long period and he managed to tolerate this, attending to his own needs and yet continuing to support me. He made many misattunements and mistakes, but the relationship we had developed enabled quick recoveries and he was always ready to own his own errors and failings. Coming from a family where no one ever said sorry this was really important for me. I consider that he gave me the gift of himself. He taught me how to have an intimate relationship and how to be non-defensive and accepting of myself and my clients.

Throughout this time I was functioning and practicing as a therapist. His support enabled me to work and function sufficiently and I saved my falling apart until my therapy sessions. I was a therapeutic infant.

## Real infants, therapeutic infants

Stern (1985, pp. 14–15) highlights the difference between the infant observed by developmental psychology, and the infant reconstructed using theories about developmental psychology in the course of clinical practice with adults. He describes this infant as a joint creation between therapist and client; the client an adult who became a client, and the therapist who has a theory about infant development. He considers that "this recreated infant is made up of memories, present re-enactments in the transference, and theoretically guided interpretations". Like Winnicott he considers that both clinical and observed infants are necessary to think about the development of the sense of self. He highlights how "the story is discovered, as well as altered, by both teller and listener in the course of the telling. Historical truth is established by what gets told, not by what actually happened".

This participant recognises her expectation of her therapist's response:

> I trusted I would be responded to in a way that I hadn't experienced being responded to—as an actual child. [...]

Bromberg (1991, p. 417) recognised that:

> [...] the child in the patient is a complex creature; he is never simply the original child come to life again, but always an aspect of an aware and knowing adult. In this respect it is fair to portray the relationship between analyst and child as simultaneously real and metaphorical. Regression in one respect is a metaphor, but not only a metaphor. It is also a real state of mind.

The powerful and overwhelming experiences of shame, rage, anxiety or loss of contact with reality experienced in therapy could usefully be formulated as a kind of reprise of much earlier traumatic incidents which have been experienced in the early parenting of the client.

## Conclusion

In this chapter I have demonstrated how therapy in regression to dependence can facilitate repair by looking at the relationship itself and the particular setting and interventions which are facilitative. I have identified how the therapist's use of self within the transference relationship can both tell the story and change the story. I have written of the importance of the relationship between therapist and client, the development of a love relationship, and data from my research participants has been used which demonstrates aspects of this relationship. I have described the importance of re-experiencing, not just remembering, and have identified by what means the therapy is facilitated. I have identified the importance of touch in regression and why this is important when working with nascent relational needs.

Clients who need regression to dependence have within them elements of chaos, the chaos which emerges prior to the development of self, and often the chaos present within their early environment. Order proceeds from love, and the therapist, in facilitating this therapy, offers love in the midst of relational damage and disturbance. Winterson (2011, p. 211) describes how her chaotic upbringing has led to hurt and damage, "And the people I have hurt, the mistakes I have made, the damage to myself and others, wasn't poor judgement; it was the place where love had hardened into loss." She recognises that she "would need to find the place where my own life could be reconciled with itself. And I knew that had something to do with love" (2011, p. 146). The therapeutic aim then would be to acknowledge this loss, and the effects of loss, but to repair with love. In clients with such early relational damage the theory helps to identify how this love can be offered in ways that address relational needs which originate in early infancy.

Bryce Boyer (1993) recognises that there has been a change in attitudes regarding the treatment of more complex patients because of increased knowledge of character structure, psychopathology, and deeper understanding of early object relations and development. He notes that treatment of patients with primitive disorders, that is, relational disorders believed to have originated in infancy, demands heightened understanding of the interactions intrapsychically within both therapist and client. My aim has been to demonstrate how theory can heighten understanding, so making therapy effective with this client group. Stewart (2003), though, considers that this area of psychotherapy has not received the recognition it deserves because of the adaptation of technique that it requires, and the fact that the therapist goes with the client into unknown aspects of themselves, for however long it takes, and without the benefit of technique or interpretation to lead the way. Stewart sees this as the necessity of living without knowing. I would add to this the degree of difficulties for the client, the length of time and commitment needed by both therapist and client, and the costs involved. However, many clients who have reached this point in therapy recognise that it is their only hope. I know for myself that it has been well worth it.

I chose the quotation at the beginning of this chapter because it speaks to me of love. I have found this love in my personal therapeutic relationship and I offer it to my clients. Whilst the ways of being, and techniques of therapy, are referred to in this chapter, ultimately it is love that heals. In a loving parental relationship, the parent is keen to do what is in the best interests of their child, and in a therapeutic relationship the therapist's aim is to do good for their client. Ultimately, whilst I have talked about various theories I do believe that the relationship itself is the main agent for change. Wachtel (2008) identifies the importance of relationship to the practice of psychotherapy. He considers that psychological change is effected by relationship; this is also evidenced in contemporary research regarding important factors in therapy, one of which is the relationship between therapist and client (Norcross, 2011).

Such a relationship is based upon the therapist's attunement to the states and needs of the client which can change moment by moment. Winnicott (1965), Balint (1959), and Van Sweden (1995) all discuss the importance of silence in regression; however, my participants did not mention the importance of silence in particular, they did however, describe the importance of their therapists' attunement to the client's moment by moment experiencing and that it was this attunement that was significantly different from their original infancy experiences.

Revisiting experiences which are believed to have occurred prior to the development of self can result in the re-emergence of terror and of shame, which is a reprise of the original nascent experience. Erskine and Trautmann (2002) describe the process of integrative psychotherapy whereby the client's childhood needs, their experience process, and interventions, including touch and holding, as dictated by the client's developmental age in regression are appropriately addressed within the therapeutic relationship.

144 BETTER LATE THAN NEVER

In Erskine's (1993, 1994) works, he identifies the necessity for the therapist's attunement to the client's presenting developmental stage, and to respond appropriately to provide a reparative and emotionally nurturing relationship. Erskine recognised that in an atmosphere of affective attunement the needs and feelings of the client can be expressed and responded to, these needs may be emerging from archaic stages or from the current relationship. Erskine (2011) describes the therapeutic response when working with clients for whom contactful, sensitive, and attuned parenting has not been consistently or dependably available. He considers that such clients, whilst requiring the usual needs present in a here-and-now relationship, also present with the unmet relational needs of past insecure attachment. Erskine considers that therapeutic presence, attunement and involvement should be engaged with the archaic needs, this does not mean that they must be satisfied, but they must be acknowledged, explained and validated.

# CHAPTER SIX

# A question of boundary

> [...] I usually made her a drink when she came, and if I wasn't very
> careful at the beginning she would sit holding her cup, she would start
> drinking and then she would just start staring, and she would just
> stare, and I'd suddenly realise she was going, if I was able to contact
> her at that point I would do, get the cup out the way and things, but
> she would gradually just go deeper and deeper and deeper, and she
> might start crying, she might start coughing and heaving 'cos she'd
> been orally abused, sometimes she would shut herself away into the
> corner, and occasionally I would have to just go out of the room,
> get a duvet, give her the duvet and leave her, and she used to go to
> sleep after the session, and that was often the only way she would
> come round, so she [...] I used to assign four hours, so that she'd got
> time to have the session, time to get her back from her [...] wherever
> she'd gone, and then I'd let her go to sleep, and then wake her up
> with a cup of tea, and then she'd go home.

## Introduction

In the above extract one of my research participants is describing her
work with a regressed client. It is evident that she has acted in ways

that some psychotherapists might have concern about. I have already identified in earlier chapters why I consider that boundaries might need to be adapted for work with certain clients. I will explore this now in more detail.

The boundary around therapeutic work is fundamental to its process. Braudel (1995, p. 18) defines boundary; "The question of boundaries is the first to be encountered; from it all others flow. To draw a boundary around anything is to define, analyse, and reconstruct it." From the birth of psychoanalysis attention has been given to how the therapist should behave in relation to their client, and in current day, the professional bodies that govern counselling and psychotherapy describe the ethical and professional responsibilities of the therapist and seek to describe a setting that is accountable and safe.

The two main professional organisations governing counselling and psychotherapy are the British Association for Counselling and Psychotherapy, and the United Kingdom Council for Psychotherapy. Both organisations have codes of conduct for their members to adhere to. These are The Ethical Framework for Good Practice in Counselling and Psychotherapy—BACP (2010), and UKCP Ethical Principles and Code of Professional Conduct (2009). The BACP information sheet for prospective clients identifies both implicit and explicit rules, which are embedded in all therapy. It also recognises that specific boundaries may be negotiated at the start of therapy. This document identifies the difference between therapeutic orientations and the effect of such orientations upon the boundaries that the therapist holds, more humanistic therapists may use touch and self-disclosure, while more psychodynamic therapists may not.

Both of the above documents have at their heart the interests of the client. They do not offer a comprehensive list of dos and don'ts; rather they form a guide in which the therapist is able to identify the spirit of good practice, which is contained within. There is nothing regarding the boundary changes that I have discussed that is contradicted specifically in either document, however, within the profession itself there are accepted ways of behaving. Beginner training courses in both counselling and psychotherapy tend to have clear indicators that students stay within clearly defined parameters for the conduct of their therapeutic role, and this is absolutely appropriate. This will also be defined by the orientation of the training that they are undertaking. The NHS and other employer and placement agencies also have strict guidelines regarding the ways of conducting therapy that would include the timing of sessions, payment, use of touch, length of sessions and the importance of adherence to the therapeutic frame.

Wosket (1999) considers though, that rules can limit the effectiveness of therapy. She is not describing boundary violations, rather the boundary crossings that are in the interest of clients, much as I am describing within this work. These are the adaptations to the therapist's usual way of being in order to address the regressive needs of their client. The complex nature of boundary is recognised by Gutheil and Gabbard (1993, pp. 1–4) who acknowledge that "like many concepts in psychotherapy, such as 'therapy', 'transference,' and 'alliance'", defining boundaries "proves slippery on closer observation", noting that "clinicians tend to feel that they understand the concept of boundaries instinctively, but using it in practice or explaining it to others is often challenging". They identify that "the historical tradition that current therapists have inherited has resulted in some of the difficulty in defining appropriate boundaries, for instance the way that Freud described therapeutic technique is different from the way he practiced therapy". They recognise that "technique changes with treatments" and that therefore "there may be a built-in confusion between the notion of therapeutic boundaries and adjusting the technique to the ego organisation of the patient".

In this chapter I will explore such boundary adaptations, using some data from participants and comments from other theorists and practitioners. I will also describe my own experiences regarding this issue.

## The therapeutic frame

In order to identify the nature of these boundary adaptations it is important to understand the meaning of "the therapeutic frame". Milner (1952) coined the phrase "analytic frame" in writing an analogy between boundaries in therapy and a picture frame. The frame identifies the difference in reality both within itself and outside itself. Winnicott (1958b/1984) identifies the "setting" as the summation of all aspects of management. He has described it as the facilitating environment. Young (2005) identifies the frame as consisting of the physical setting, the contract and a state of mind. He considers maintenance of the boundary to provide containment whereby "the patient is being helped to hold himself together". Overall these theorists are trying to describe the analytic space, which contains the work of therapy.

One of my research participants relates the importance of boundary and consistency when working with clients who have experienced early relational trauma:

> I'd be thinking about boundary setting very clearly from the outset with this type of client, not with rigidity, but with clarity.
>
> [...] these are the type of clients that I would be wanting to see on the same session every week, and not making changes, so that we'd have, we'd develop some consistency in my contact with them over time. I'd also be wanting to focus a lot on containment and safety [...] I think with [...] this type of client that I tend to focus more on safety than I do possibly with other clients that have more of a capacity to contain themselves.

## Crossing boundaries

"Psychotherapists do seem to be able to help people; perhaps because they often manage to outgrow the handicaps imposed by their training. Wherever two or three psychotherapists are gathered together, confessions gradually emerge about their deviations from orthodoxy" (Mair, 1992, p. 152). Smith and Fitzpatrick (1995, p. 500) seem to concur, acknowledging that "boundaries are regularly transgressed by even the most competent of therapists, and such transgressions are not always to the detriment of the client". It is essential to highlight the difference between boundary crossing and boundary violation, where the former is a departure from accepted practice that may or may not benefit the client, and the latter is a departure from accepted practice that places the client or process at risk—the task for the therapist is to distinguish between the two. From their research Johnston and Farber (1996, pp. 391, 397) cited in Wosket (1999) concluded that clients infrequently challenged their therapist's boundaries, but when they did so "psychotherapists accommodated their requests in most cases". recognising that this "stands in opposition to the generally accepted image of the psychotherapist standing firm in the face of persistent attempts by the patient to challenge existing boundaries, and suggests a spirit of cooperation and good faith underemphasised in theoretical writings".

Pope and Keith-Spiegel (2007, p. 638) consider that decisions about boundary must be grounded in an ethical approach. They explain that non-sexual boundary crossing can "enrich psychotherapy, serve the treatment plan, and strengthen the therapist/client working relationship". They also accept that boundary crossings can "undermine the therapy, disrupt the therapist–patient alliance, and cause harm to clients." They highlight the importance of the therapist and the client sharing the understanding of the adaptation of a boundary. The therapist's motivation to adapt a boundary should be thoroughly explored in supervision and the therapist must ascertain the client's understanding of such an adaptation. Any boundary adaptation must be viewed in the light of the client's needs and their personal relational history. Totton (2012) concurs with this position, yet observes the widely held belief that all clients at all times should be treated within the same set of boundaries. He notes that Sandler (1983) considers that therapists rely upon "educated instincts" to form their response rather than consulting with the rule book. Totton considers that therapy culture "militate[s] against these adaptations and adjustments". Whilst recognising that some well-known therapeutic celebrities have revealed their boundary crossings, others, like Winnicott, never revealed to his peers that he worked with touch. He voices the concern that the codification of the concept of appropriate boundaries for psychotherapy "increasingly forces all therapists and counsellors into defensive practice", considering that such defensive practice results in the avoidance of the possibility of litigation at the expense of therapeutic treatment.

As I have reflected on these issues I have remembered supervision sessions where I was reluctant to tell my clinical supervisor that I had stepped outside an accepted boundary for a therapeutic advantage, such as allowing a client to go a little over time or allowing contact outside of a session. In each circumstance I had a clear rationale and a treatment plan for such boundary changes, yet I was afraid of the judgement of my supervisor, who I believed held tightly to all boundaries. If the rules about boundary are not made specifically, they are there implicitly to the point that many therapists are afraid to talk about touching their clients or other boundary adaptations or describe the use of self with their peers and supervisors. Wosket (1999, p. 13) recognises that the professionalisation of counselling and psychotherapy, and the professional assessment of competence can lead to the repression of those therapists who take an individualistic or unorthodox stance. She identifies the dichotomy between that which is shared by therapists privately, and that which is shared in the public domain, maintaining that "healthy unorthodoxy has been driven underground" and that therapists "are becoming squeamish about admitting publicly to aspects of their work that may be misconstrued, for example touching clients or engaging in regressive work". She fears that we are in danger of succumbing to "therapeutic correctness". On page 133 she states her belief "that rules can limit therapeutic effectiveness even as they also importantly define the boundaries of safe practice". Sandler (1983, pp. 36–37) recognised the "conviction of many analysts [is] that they do not do 'proper' analysis [...] that what is actually done in the analytic consulting room is not 'kosher', that colleagues would criticise it if they knew about it". But he explains that "any analyst worth his salt will adapt to specific patients on the basis of his interaction with those patients. He will modify his approach so that he can get as good as possible a working analytic situation developing".

In his 2013 contribution, Bollas is describing his work with clients in breakdown phases of their analysis, and how it may be necessary to change the therapeutic frame in order to manage the phase of therapy that they are in. He identifies the difficulty he has faced in sharing his ways of treating these patients with some practitioners and professional bodies. He clearly demonstrates the caution that many practitioners feel when discussing their client. I have also become aware of some of my own implicit rules which would have been influencing me to stay within the therapeutically accepted "safe" boundaries, and how my failure to comply would result in my feelings of shame, yet to fail to meet the client's therapeutic needs would transgress my value of beneficence. I feel this so strongly because my therapeutic home is largely within the theory (but not the clinical stance) of psychoanalysis. Gutheil and Gabbard (1993) highlight that boundaries are different for different therapeutic ideologies, the bottom line is—is there a body of professional literature, a clinical rationale in existence. Other orientations may not have the same difficulties with letting go of these accepted boundaries (Wosket, 1999), however, orientations which accept some alteration of the frame, such as CBT and other short term cognitive interventions, may not work within the unconscious relationship, and may not have an understanding of the impact and meaning of boundary upon the client.

The UKCP acknowledges that considerable personal variation exists within the field, that relationships between patient and therapist vary from therapist to therapist and, of course, there are variations between patients with any one therapist.

## Regression and boundaries

As far back as the 1930s Ferenczi (1931, 1932, 1933) was successful in working with patients that were found to be unsuitable for analytic treatment by other analysts because he believed that in order to heal, some patients needed to regress to a former developmental state, and to do this required changes to the analytic stance, a movement of the therapeutic frame and a potential relaxing of boundary. Balint (1959, 1968) also worked with clients who had insufficient ego strength to work within the traditional methodology. His understanding of the importance of the dyadic relationship in psychotherapy meant that the role of the therapist was as an involved and responsive participant. Little (1981), although valuing psychoanalytic technique for most patients, also recognised that for clients having problems of existence, survival and identity, adaptations in technique were necessary. From an integrative and relational perspective the intent is to provide a corrective emotional experience, and where the therapeutic need is to work in areas of the mind prior to the development of language the reliance upon verbal connectedness is insufficient.

As we have already seen, working with regression in psychotherapy can have a significant impact on the therapeutic boundaries. This is considered to be particularly important when the client is regressed and, for the moment, is relating to the therapist from an infantile ego state. Winnicott (1958a/1984, p. 288) sees it thus, "In so far as the patient is regressed (for a moment or for an hour, or over a long period of time) the couch is the analyst, the pillows are breasts, the analyst is the mother at a certain past era." Winnicott is identifying the loss of the "as if" component in the transference and views the client's way of relating to the therapist at that time as originating in an earlier phase of development. Because the client is mainly relating from this regressed phase then for that period the therapist must be aware that the client's normal functioning capacity may be absent for minutes, hours or days.

This research participant describes her state of mind after such an experience in therapy:

> [...] I was in such an altered state of consciousness, I think if I'd been the therapist I'd have been very worried about me leaving and driving [...] in fact, I did nearly kill myself on that occasion.

Some theorists identify that clients who present for therapy therefore may initially appear to be high-functioning whilst concealing a heavily defended, vulnerable self-state. Adams (2009) quotes Siegel (1999) regarding the co-existence of these two aspects of the self, seeing that the client can be triggered into "low-road" functioning. Many clients can present with distress and confusion regarding the dichotomy between these very different self-states. I recognise from being a regressed client myself that these experiences can be very frightening, and it is important that therapists allow for the neediness that may develop, rather than expecting the adult part of self to manage. Where there is this level of need and vulnerability a change to the usual boundaries may be necessary. This potential change has been recognised by many theorists, Balint (1968), Winnicott (1958b/1984), and Van Sweden (1995) have all written about the need to step outside of the boundaries in order to work with patients who experience early relational trauma. One of my research participants described some of the changes in boundary that she accommodated when working with a client:

> [...] some days she'd stay all day (at the facility) and then late afternoon ask to see me again and often, quite appropriately, she'd finally worked something out or come out of something and could see me again and tell me that she had worked something out or come through something but it had taken four or five hours, and needed to see me again to finish off.

The therapist's ability and willingness to recognise and respond appropriately to the immediate need of their client in the moment can begin to repair the client's capacity to see themselves as valid human beings.

## Movement of ego boundaries

In Winnicott's (1958b/1984) explanation of the requirement for a change in the therapeutic stance with regressed patients he again makes the link between mother/infant and therapist/client. He considers that, in the client's interest, the client's need may mean that the therapist is required to give the client more of themselves than they normally would, and that this may be uncomfortable for them.

Bromberg (2012) considers that the analyst's professional role "is subsumed within a shared personal field" and identifies the joint creation "of a relational unconscious that is mediated by state-sharing— a process in which analyst and patient gradually are able to invite increased permeability between their respective self-state boundaries". This has a flavour of Winnicott's understanding of the ego-support provided by maternal care and therefore also ideally provided by the therapist. Bollas (1987, p. 41) comments that "Winnicott knew that he was immersed in the patient's unconscious reconstruction of a child's environment, and I understand that it was a feature of his technique to adapt himself to the patient's ego defects and characterological biases in order to allow for the transference to evolve without the impingement of a premature use of analytic interpretation. From this experiencing of the early infant environment, the analyst could then interpret the past as it was re-created through the transference". He considers that the mother, in serving as a supplementary ego, (Heimann, 1956), transmits to the infant the language of their relationship through idiom of gesture, gaze, and intersubjective utterance. Therefore, he considers this first subjective experience of the object as transformational. He goes on to develop the theme that means that the adult patient seeks for this transformation of self which is a memory of this first relationship, "to remember not cognitively but existentially—through intense affective experience—a relationship which was identified with cumulative transformational experiences of the self" (Bollas, 1987, p. 17).

Little (1981, p. 57) describes the analyst's total response to the client's needs. She specifies that:

> [...] the analyst goes with the patient as far into the patient's illness as it is possible for him to go. There may have to be times— moments, or split seconds even—when, psychically, for the analyst nothing exists but the patient, and nothing exists of himself apart

from the patient. He allows the patient to enter his own inner world
and become part of it.

Modell (1969) considers that it is only when the analyst is willing to
fully experience the patient's pain that hope begins to be instilled.
Lipton (1977), in recognising the intersubjective nature of the therapeutic
relationship, noted that it is ultimately impossible to be precise about
the nature of the personal relationship between therapist and patient.
Weiss (2002, p. 12) identifies the difficulty for the therapist when the
client's dependency needs push into the therapist's personal boundaries. He identifies how the therapist's countertransference, which
initially may be nurturing and responsive to the needs, can become
withholding because of the therapist's feelings of invasion, and he
sees such difficulties as resulting from the therapist's unresolved issue
around dependency. Personal issues such as this are key reasons why
a therapist should consider their position regarding working with this
client group, making an informed and deliberate choice about it before
finding themselves with such a client. This work is not for all therapists
and knowing what types of presentations are effectively worked with
and the therapist's personal limitations are important professional and
ethical considerations.

## Adaptation of techniques

In his 1994b contribution Hedges formulates the re-experiencing within
the therapeutic relationship of the very earliest infantile organising
experience that results in a dread of contact and relational withdrawal.
He identifies the therapist's task to find ways of maintaining contact in
ways that are relevant and age appropriate to communicate with these
early aspects of infant personality. Balint (1968) considers that there can
be a gulf between the therapist and the regressed client that the client
cannot bridge alone. Balint clearly states his conviction that "in certain
cases, in particular with a regressed patient, [the therapist] may go further towards satisfying some demands in order to secure the existence
of a therapeutic relationship". Van Sweden (1995) agrees that the emergence of infantile relational needs requires adjustment in the therapeutic stance to allow for some gratification of these needs.

The participant quoted at the beginning of this chapter has identified ways in which she has adjusted the boundaries in the work with

her client in order to manage the process of psychotherapy. She has provided her client with a drink, has relaxed the time boundary, and has provided nurturing in the form of a duvet. In varying the boundary in these ways she would consider that such boundary adjustments were necessary to enable the client to stay in therapy and still function in her "outside" life. Her aim would also be to give the client an experience of receiving care and nurturing in a relational way. When this participant was describing her work with regressed clients I was aware of a trust being placed in me, because as I have highlighted, there is a degree of "we don't talk about this", which would have come from her training and from her experience within the profession.

Two of my participants have identified interventions used in regressive therapy:

> I might get hold of their face and turn it, and say, "look at me, look at me, what are you seeing [...]".
>
> I put my hand on the top of his head, on the crown of his head, and something really changed in his body. [...]

Little (1981, p. 143) formulates the development of ego defects as resulting from deficient mothering in infancy. When these phases re-emerge in their therapy (in regression) she considers that they are unable to use dialogue and interpretation and therefore need "a new set of experiences of good-enough mothering" before being able to develop sufficient ego use language. She recognises that this may be more difficult for the analyst, but is necessary for some people who otherwise would not tolerate the therapeutic process to remain in therapy. In her description of her therapy with Ella Sharpe, Little (1981, p. 290) describes Sharpe as lending her books and making her comfortable in her seat. She makes a comparison between Sharpe's "mothering", and Winnicott's, saying that "I learnt from Winnicott about the patient showing the analyst how to do his analysis, as a baby shows the mother how to handle it", and this was such a contrast with Sharpe's authoritarian way of "mother (or analyst) knows best". Giovacchini (1990) quotes from Winnicott regarding the conflict between the client's needs and the therapist's needs. He considers that a regressed client, from their point of view, is being reasonable in protesting about a gap in therapy because of the therapist's holiday. Management of this would involve recognising the need, but still addressing one's own need to go on holiday.

Erskine (1998) considers that the expression of love is a relational need which is to be seen, honoured and accepted by the therapist. When the therapist accepts the client's expression of love it is validating and respectful. This is demonstrated in my participant's hopes for the results of therapy, that is, that her clients are able to give and receive love in a healthy and appropriate way:

> [...] that they're able to express love and feel love (for the therapist) without pushing it away, or hungering to the point of starvation.

Little (1981, p. 151) also reflects upon the inter-relationship between the therapist and the client; she sees that although the therapist makes adaptations according to the needs of the client these are dependent upon his experience of himself, and how he experiences the client at that time "I do this, here, now, with this patient. I do not do that with him, now or ever. I do not do this with him at another time, I do not do this at all with another patient", making the point that the individual therapist must determine his own limits, but that someone who is unwilling to make adaptations may then be limited in either the range of clients, or in his results. Fromm (2007, pp. 5–6) in his writing about C. Winnicott's work identifies that she was able "to hold the analytic role within herself so fully that it was not threatened by stepping out of that framework to some degree". This is the process of developing expertise, when experience, theories and personal knowledge come together in an integration within the therapist, and the ethical position of acting therapeutically will be maintained even when stepping outside of normally held boundaries.

Research participants identified various ways in which they have relaxed the normal therapeutic boundaries such as contact outside of sessions, the giving of transitional objects, provision of physical touch and holding and other ways of attempting to meet the client's needs relationally, two of which are detailed below:

> I can remember him coming [...] or phoning me up, or texting me in the middle of the night, and [...] me phoning him back the next morning which was a Saturday morning, and I saw him on Saturday morning [...].
>
> I have often felt the desire to give, provide some kind of transitional object, and the difficulty in introducing that into the work,

> sometimes [...] the feeling of them wanting to have, and yet, not
> allowing themselves to take, has been difficult.

In these examples not only is the actual therapeutic boundary altered, but also the therapist's own personal boundary is affected. The relationship when viewed from a relational/developmental perspective is not as clear cut as the professional relationship originally advocated (if not practised) by Freud and traditional psychoanalysts. Van Sweden (1995) specifies that working within the two person relationship involves the use of the therapist's self, and therefore, their entire person. Winnicott (1958b/1984) establishes that this use of the therapist's self in the therapeutic dyad is comparable with the mother's response to the infant. Totton (2012) identifies the mutuality in the therapeutic relationship as "a place where two subjectives meet". He uses the word "boundlessness" to denote non-defensive practice where the therapist offers from their abundance.

The participants in this study have identified that the adaptations to boundary made by their therapists have been highly significant in terms of their development and repair, and that these moments have had great significance in terms of their growth and repair. I would echo this from my own experience. The times when my therapist has adjusted the boundary for me have felt caring and have given me a sense of his involvement in the relationship. These moments have indicated a depth of relationship which goes way beyond what might be seen in a basic counselling relationship.

## The real relationship

In her writing on the therapeutic relationship Clarkson (2003, p. 152) has identified a key aspect of the relationship as "real relationship" existing between therapist and client. This is also identified by Duquette (2011, p. 55), citing Greenson (1978) as "the realistic and genuine relationship" between therapist and client. Duquette (2011, p. 59) considers that the therapist's humanness is essential to the development of a real relationship, and that if the therapist allows their real self to enter the relationship then this relationship "can be used as a consistent referent" for the client. This view of the relationship concurs with Buber's (1958) stance that as therapist we should drop superiority and drop into the abyss, where the self of the therapist is exposed to the self of the client.

One of my participants describes working with in-depth relationships where there is a real relationship of love; where even after the therapeutic relationship has ended the love remains:

> [...] there've been clients that have lived on in my life for ever, they've never, ever gone out of it, I have no problem whatsoever at immediately recalling them, and seeing them in all different states and stages, they're there now in my mind [...] they will be a part of my, my inner life and on the times when I have seen them, coincidently or as part of other things, I know I am in theirs, so there is something about working at this level that isn't just about the therapeutic time, it's for ever.

Another participant describes her involvement with her client and the importance of the relationship:

> [...] every minute of those two years was hell, her rage was absolutely colossal with, and I understand it technically, but it was a lifeline for her and that lifeline was being cut, but I always promised her that she would never lose contact with me as long as I stayed alive, and so I do her cocktail of medicines every month, visit her at her home and do that. Now, I don't know if that's me acting out, or just being human, because I don't want to do it, and sometimes it feels like a humbug on my day off, but I know it's so vital to her, that I keep doing it, and I think some things, you know, they go on beyond treatment, really. [...]

### Boundaries and touch

Two of my participants below describe their experiences of touch and nurturing as clients:

> The therapeutic touch was like [...] warm electricity going through me [...].
> [...] she held me, she stroked me, she sang to me, she covered me up with a duvet. [...]

In any writing on the subject of boundaries the issue of touch will inevitably arise. There is a large body of literature concerning touch, largely focussed on boundaries around sexual contact. Freud considered that touch in the therapeutic relationship could lead to sexual entanglement. In the move towards two-person psychology starting with Ferenczi (1953) the idea that touch within the therapeutic relationship could offer some sort of repair was mooted. The relational turn in psychotherapy has resulted in the inter-subjective nature of the relationship being explored and some therapists consider therapeutic touch useful within the relationship (Toronto, 2001). The use of therapeutic touch in psychotherapy is still a contentious issue, raising fears in the therapeutic community of abuse and exploitation (Holub & Lee, 1990). A full exploration of the impact of touch upon the therapeutic relationship is beyond the scope of this work, therefore I am considering it from the perspective of its relationship to boundary rather than as a subject for discussion in its own right.

Chu (1998) warns of the dangers associated with touch with abused clients which can result in dissociation causing a sense of disconnection from themselves and from the therapist. For any intervention, and touch is just one of them, the impact, meaning and effect upon the client should be thoroughly considered, explored in supervision and discussed with the client on an on-going basis. Gabbard (1989) considers that any changes in boundary must be openly discussed in order to ensure the safety of the therapeutic relationship.

Some of my participants highlight their ethical considerations around the use of touch as an intervention:

> How can you do a serious early childhood or traumatic therapy without touch? Now how much touch, when is that touch initiated, what is the quality of the contract for the touch, what is safe touch versus none safe touch, those are all the issues that have to be decided on, on an individual basis.
>
> I might talk about touch rather than do the touch [...] to actually say you know, "I wish you were about this big because then I could just pick you up and give you a hug" [...] And there's a lot of ethical stuff about whether you do or not, and boundaries [...] I wouldn't avoid touch because of that, you know, I'd just make sure it was ethical and it was checked out etc.
>
> [...] the one thing I would do was to say, "My hand's here if you want to hold it", and she would sometimes hold it, but that was all within her control so that the minute she wanted to let go again, she

could, but rather than me doing the touching because at that point she couldn't handle it [...] it was like an invasion.

Gutheil and Gabbard (1993, p. 191) make an important distinction between the developmental needs of the client and libidinal demands:

> In attempting to delineate the appropriate role for the therapist vis-à-vis the patient's wishes and longings to be loved and held, it is useful to differentiate between "libidinal demands", which cannot be gratified without entering into ethical transgressions and damaging enactments, and "growth needs", which prevent growth if not gratified to some extent.

These participants identify the relevance of touch to clinical work:

> I want to be free to touch a client if I feel that's right, there are some clients I would never touch from the start to finish of therapy, but if somebody said to me, "if you work here you can't touch", I think I would say, "well, I'm sorry, I can't work here. [...]"

And how this might be contracted for:

> [...] it's also got to be negotiated. Somehow it's got to be contracted for. That contract doesn't always have to be in so many words, it can be simply be like [...] can I touch you and they just nod yes [...] the moment they stiffen up, when you reach out to touch them and they stiffen up, that's a no [...] how do I know? Agreement, contract the process of being together they're mostly non-verbally asking for it. But it's also thinking developmentally certain ages and certain activities of a child you would never hold them, because to hold them would stop their rambunctiousness [...] so it's thinking developmentally, really thinking about "what does a normal kid need in this kind of a crisis?"

In my contracts for psychotherapy I identify that I may work with touch as appropriate and with mutual agreement. The difference between a boundary crossing which is benign or harmful depends upon whether clinical judgement has been used to make the decision, whether adequate discussion and exploration have taken place, and whether documentation has adequately recorded details.

## Fear of litigation

Wosket (1999) expresses concern that touch, as an important therapeutic intervention, will be jettisoned for fear of accusations of abuse or litigation. She cites Hunter and Struve (1998, p. 67) "within the prevailing climate, most clinicians have resolved the cultural and professional tensions surrounding the use of touch by adopting a one word guideline: *Don't!*". Current society is highly litigious and professionals from all disciplines are increasingly concerned about legal action. The use of touch and holding is a sensitive area and one open to abuse. However, I do not consider this as reason to withhold it from the therapeutic relationship. Two of my participants after their interview told me that although they strongly believed that touch was essential when working with regression, and they believed that it had been essential within their own therapy, they felt unable to offer it to their own clients because of the fear of complaint, which in their working life was grounded in experience. Touch is a developmental need and many clients have been starved of it. I refer to Lazarus (1994, p. 25) once again, "One of the worst professional and ethical violations is that of permitting current risk management principles to take precedence over humane intentions."

## The importance of supervision

Steele et al. (2001) advocate for collaboration between therapist and patient and consultation with another professional. They quote Dalenberg (2000, p. 229) referring to "boundary crossings" for therapeutic advantage as opposed to "boundary violations", which are harmful to the patient. Pope and Keith-Spiegel (2008) discuss the use of self-disclosure as a therapeutic tool. They establish the importance of discussion in supervision regarding self-disclosures. Gutheil and Gabbard (1993) make the point that if there is physical contact and the patient expects it and grants consent; no actual violation occurs. They identify that risk management requires careful consideration of departure from usual practice together with recording of such together with consultation with another professional.

The type of therapy that I'm describing in this book is complex and involves the consciousness and the unconsciousness of both the client and the therapist. If issues are truly unconscious then of course we cannot know them, but they can emerge and remain powerful within the therapeutic relationship. What is needed is another who is able to look into the relationship from an experienced, supportive place. This is the place of supervision. It is essential that the therapist obtains supervision from a practitioner who understands their way of working and the client group that they work with in order to be able to offer support and appropriate challenge. The supervisor should know enough about the therapist's own processes to be able to ascertain their part of the therapeutic relationship, and finding the right supervisor is of key importance.

## Conclusion

In this chapter I have considered why therapists would choose to relax boundaries within psychotherapy. I have explored the client's need for this and the intrapsychic and inter-psychic processes which develop in a relational/developmental therapy. I have identified how boundaries may be appropriately relaxed, according to the needs of the client, as part of the regressive process. In the psychotherapy world currently there is a marked division between those who recognise powerful unconscious processes at play within the therapeutic relationship, but who see insight alone as the therapeutic goal, those who recognise the therapeutic relationship but consider that the work should be done in the here-and-now, and those therapists who understand and work with the unconscious processes and developmental needs but who see the here and now as an arena to offer the client a repair of archaic wounding. Wosket (1999, p. 164) asks, "What therapeutic opportunities might be afforded when a counsellor extends or moves beyond the boundaries normally governing their practice?" The participant's stories have given to me clear indications of the importance of a therapist's willingness to move outside of their own accepted boundaries within the relationship with them. In fact it has been as important as the actual intervention itself. It has provided evidence of the relational and mutual nature of their relationship.

Those who work with regression are not advocating for an abandonment of the therapeutic frame, far from it. A therapeutic need is being identified in some psychotherapy clients, which must be recognised and addressed if these clients are to be successfully worked with. As we have seen in earlier chapters, the movement away from the traditional tenets of psychoanalysis towards the dyadic relationship and the idea that the therapeutic relationship, through the process of transference and countertransference, could refigure and help to repair the deprivations of early childhood, meant that the therapeutic stance would change from one of professional distance (Gutheil & Gabbard, 1993) to a relationship whereby the needs of the client would be attended to within the relationship.

I will now move towards my conclusions of this work, reflecting upon the contents and process of my research itself and the themes which emerged from the participant data, making recommendations for clients, therapists, supervisors and trainers involved in the practice of psychotherapy when working with this client group.

CHAPTER SEVEN

# Reflections and conclusions

## Introduction

Winterson (2011, p. 144) quotes Hartley's (1953, p. 5) beliefs about the past.

"The past is a foreign country: they do things differently there." But she considers that revisiting the past has benefits too, "Yes, the past is another country, but one that we can visit, and once there we can bring back the things we need." In therapeutically revisiting the past (in regression to dependence) we are given a second chance to develop and take back the things we need as part of developing emotional maturity.

In writing this book I have sometimes used my personal stories, seeing them as an intrinsic part of my work. Reflexivity in psychotherapy is important, even more so when working with the type of client addressed in this book, and the use of myself is a significant aspect of my way of being, requiring self examination and self analysis throughout the therapeutic process. Reflexivity has also been an integral part of my process throughout this book and my research.

In my research I was looking for ways to understand this process in myself and in my clients, and I found a gap between psychological theories and clinical applications. For me, Winnicott and others offered a bridge for this gap, and a framework within which I was able to understand my own process, and the processes of my clients. Bornstein (2013) also acknowledges Winnicott as bridging theory and technique. He acknowledges that psychoanalytic theories of the mind are "rich and exciting" but that the technique associated with it has left him feeling anxious and frustrated. Bornstein (2013) identifies the gap between the description of what is occurring in the psychotherapeutic relationship, and what is actually taking place experientially. For me, this is one of the attractions of Winnicott's work. It moves away from dry, bald theorising into a more numinous, experiential arena. That said, it is still very difficult to articulate that which is experienced, in this work I have tried to do that as much as is possible for me.

My aim has been to develop understanding of the process and experience of regression to dependence. I have identified how holding a narrative for the client's early years can describe and account for the experiences of clients, how this narrative helps clients to make sense of their experience and enables an effective clinical formulation to be used within the therapeutic context. When practitioners have knowledge of relevant theoretical concepts and an understanding of the necessity to address the pre-verbal stages in an appropriate manner, they can offer a therapeutic "second chance" for their clients to have "a new beginning" which both mourns the loss of what should have been, and celebrates the emergence of their "true self" as the ultimate outcome (Balint, 1968). The education and training of psychotherapists is incomplete without an understanding of this process and the particular needs of these clients. Practitioners must be able to recognise such a process, and the potential for it, to enable recognition of the most effective ways of working.

## Regression to dependence

The subject of this book is regression to dependence, the concept that given the right environment, a person can return to their early developmental history and, through the unconscious process of the transference and countertransference, re-experience their early inchoate relationship within the therapeutic relationship. Working with this concept requires the therapist to have an understanding of infant development, because aspects of the client's presenting behaviour are viewed as pertaining to stages of infant development. Throughout this work I have described my personal and professional engagement that has allowed me to hold a unique insight into the process itself, and a belief in its usefulness and effectiveness. This then leads me to stress the importance of the therapist having a thorough understanding of infant psychological development and its relevance to client work in order to work with clients experiencing this process. Therapists should be able to recognise a regressive process occurring in the relationship with their client, and know how to facilitate this appropriately. To do this therapists need an understanding of what the need to regress represents developmentally, that is, a return to a needed relationship which holds the potential to revisit and repair aspects of self in a facilitating environment, and have sufficient understanding to identify and address the unmet need. As this is a relational engagement the therapist must be willing to be a participant in the needed relationship, taking on some aspects of the original needed relationship. To achieve this the therapist must be a safe, containing, holding, attentive and loving other.

The facilitation of such a process relies upon the development of a relationship that has enough similarity to the early infant relationship to facilitate the client's regression, yet which has significant differences in that it is safe, accepting, unconditional and non-judgemental. The aim of the relationship is both to identify the place of damage and trauma and to offer repair addressing any emerging infantile needs appropriately. These needs can be thought of as remaining in the psyche of the individual on an unconscious level, whilst being acted out or felt at a conscious level, as the search for the lost or insufficient relationship of infancy. The development of this new relationship requires the therapist to be aware of this process and be able to adapt to their client's needs on this developmentally needed level as well as at other relational levels.

It is essential that the therapist has experienced a successful dependency relationship, either in infancy or in therapy, so as to be able to have an understanding of the developmental needs of the client from an experiential perspective. If the therapist has experienced a therapeutic repair then they will also hold a sense of what this feels like as an adult, and how a repair can be offered. The therapist must be prepared to "be with" the very experience of the unfolding transference process, recognising and meeting the emerging, previously unmet needs, whilst keeping hold of an awareness of "what's me and what's not me"—their own boundary. The therapist must be able to engage with the regressive process in whatever way the client is available, be it emotionally, physically or psychologically, and either symbolically or literally. The therapist should be an object of transformation for the client, and offer a reparative experience.

The formulation of a client's distress as a return to the early developmental arena gives a narrative, which identifies a plan of action for both therapist and client. If both parties accept the narrative for the experience then there is the possibility that it can be worked with, the client can re-experience their early infantile unmet needs and the therapist, who takes on some aspects of the caretaking relationship, can acknowledge, validate, and sometimes meet them, and in this way offer a repair. Therapists should be able to find a voice and give narrative to the experience of being in the moment in the therapy, and begin to describe the process in which the client is immersed. Working with the likely narrative of both mother and child can help to identify that which was missing so that it can be understood, and disowned aspects of self can be integrated. The therapeutic importance of the development of a narrative between mother and child builds upon the concepts formulated by Winnicott, Little, Balint, and others.

The quotations from some of my participants, which I have included in this work, make it apparent that for many of them integration is a process which follows experiences of chaos and disintegration. Van Sweden (1995) acknowledges that the journey of regression to dependence is difficult. Once the dependent relationship is established the additional ego support supplied by the therapist is often sufficient to keep any psychological or emotional disruption within the therapeutic setting (Winnicott, 1958b/1984). A relational therapy minimises such disruption because of the potential for flexibility of boundaries, and the therapist's availability can sufficiently support the client. As I have described previously, when I was experiencing a high level of emotional disruption as my infantile needs began to emerge and I felt shame for them, the provision of increased and extended sessions, and contact in-between sessions allowed my functioning in the outside world to continue. It is the therapist's role to hold an awareness of boundaries, safety, touch, and the possibility of malignant (unhelpful) regression.

It has been said to me a number of times during my practice as a therapist, supervisor and trainer that I should not advocate for the use of touch in today's litigious climate, particularly when training new psychotherapists. I can understand why this is an area of concern. The use of any boundary adjustment and particularly touch, must have a rationale which is in the interest of the client. However, if touch is accepted as a necessary component of therapy in some cases, then it no longer becomes a boundary violation, any more than an osteopath is violating a boundary in touching a patient. As a practitioner I am always cautious and I ensure that touch is contracted for, in a formal way in my initial contract with clients, and verbally, moment by moment as necessary within clinical work. I have grave concern when fear of litigation prevents therapeutic interventions and repair.

It was my intention, in the publication of this work, to both inform and encourage practitioners to recognise this process, to develop an understanding of relevant theory in order to work with it or to refer on if that is more appropriate.

## Anxiety and panic attacks

Clients who present with chronic anxiety may find that their anxiety has its roots in the failure of their early relational environments. My research and my own experiences have led me to formulate this issue as existential and a potential pre-curser of an emerging regression to dependence. This may indicate to the therapist the possibility that the anxiety and panic attacks as experienced by the client may actually be spontaneous regressions. These existential feelings of life and death may be considered as remaining powerfully active at an unconscious level in those people who have not had their anxieties contained by a powerful and protective other in their early infancy. This containment takes the form of the parent not being fearful in themselves, able to handle and soothe the emerging emotion of the infant so that the infant learns that their powerful feelings are containable first by the parent and subsequently by themselves in adulthood. When this has not occurred, the infant, and eventually the adult, becomes afraid of their inner chaos, finding it difficult to tolerate any dysregulation.

This resonates with Winnicott's (1965b/1984) understanding of the development of the capacity to be alone, where the experience of the infant of being alone in the presence of mother implies a special type of relationship, one which Winnicott called "ego-relatedness" (p. 30). He has identified that at a very early stage ego-support from the mother is necessary in order to balance the immature ego. Winnicott considered that the development of this capacity to be alone is vital for the infant, and consequently the adult, to be able to truly relax. This is because the infant ego had been protected from impingement by ego-relatedness in the form of ego-support from the mother, which then in adulthood becomes internalised and introjected. This capacity to be alone is relational in that it involves being alone in the presence of another. Some clients avoid experiencing aloneness by distracting themselves by "doing". They thus remain in perpetual motion, of which anxious thoughts are a form and a defensive measure, in order to avoid the re-experiencing the immature aloneness that has not been supported in infancy. Recognising such anxiety as related to infant deprivation can enable the client to revisit this arena of primitive anxiety and, whilst it may take a long period of therapy, can resolve the terrifying levels of anxiety which bring many clients to therapy.

## The presence of infantile terror in the adult client

I have named the experiencing of childhood terror "a sickness of spirit", and living with terror does change you, partly because of the feelings of madness it engenders when strange phenomena are experienced. One only has to look at those suffering from post-traumatic stress disorder to see how their lives can be decimated by repeatedly reliving the experience. This experience though, is at least known and a cause is identified. To live with strange experiences and surfacing terror is very frightening and limits the lives of those who are affected. To help an individual to address these issues and to emerge from them with a sense of story, and the understanding and compassion for themselves that this brings, is a great privilege. During regression to dependence, the re-emergence of infantile feelings related to the environment present at the time, that is, the infant/caretaker relationship, can re-emerge in the therapeutic setting and the client can re-experience terror and fear.

This research participant demonstrates how the client's experience of terror can be communicated to the therapist through the countertransference:

> a fear that it would [...] that I would be unable to hold it with her, that it was so overwhelming, that "Was this a good idea" you know, "Should I be doing this" but I also knew it could happen to her

even outside a therapy session, it wasn't necessarily the therapy that was triggering it, it meant that the session would always go on longer than an hour, and it meant [...] and it was exhausting, physically and emotionally, mentally exhausting to stay with. [...]

Bollas (2013, p. 1) describes working with patients in the process of breakdown and the difficulties for the therapist when clients tip into psychosis. He makes an interesting statement though, about regression to dependence:

> If the analysand regresses to dependence in a rather ordinary way—lessening defences, opening up the self to interpretive trans-formation, abandoning disturbed character patterns—the self will usually break down in a slow and cumulative way.

The therapist must also have resilience and the capacity and ability to tolerate profound distress and emotional pain in self and other as it arises within the regressive process. Such emotive and powerful work often requires changes to the therapist's usual working practices and relaxation of certain boundaries. In such circumstances, understanding and safeguarding the therapy with appropriate boundaries is even more crucial.

## Integration and growth

One of the aims of integrative psychotherapy using an overarching relational/developmental framework is that aspects of the client's self, which may be constructed as "split off", disowned, disavowed or projected from the sense of self, can be integrated into a cohesive whole, disparate parts can be held together in a contained and cohesive way (SPTI, 2003). In regression to dependence, the aim for the client at the end of therapy is to have integrated split off infancy experiences, to have a narrative for the whole of the self, to be accepted by the self, and allow non-existence to become existence.

This participant describes her experience of the outcome of her regressive therapy:

> Physically I feel more joined up [...] my body feels like it belongs together [...] it felt much more fragmented than it does now [...] acting from a place of anxiety rather than acting from a place of the

> real me [...] I'm actually saying things that come right from the core of me and that aren't channelled through the anxious part of me [...] I have a sense of her [the therapist] feeling tenderly towards me, and that feels precious [...] I can be all that I am and still be held in a tender way.

This exemplifies such integration which regression to dependence can facilitate. Understanding this concept can then enable the client to be willing to allow the relationship and the transference to develop whereby the "primitive agony" may be re-experienced in a titrated form and then gradually be able to gather the "original failure of the facilitating environment into the area of his or her omnipotence and the experience of omnipotence which belongs to the state of dependence" (Kalsched, 1996, p. 91).

The aim in regression is to enable the client to progress and engage with their potential for growth and change, as illustrated by the participant below:

> [...] it felt much more fragmented than it does now, a lot of stuff about worrying about what other people think, sort of acting from a place of my anxiety rather than acting from a place of the real me, it feels like that's a big place that I'm finding now that, I'm actually saying things that come right from the core of me and that aren't channelled through the anxious part of me that worries what people think.

Working with this process has implications not just for the client, but for the therapist too.

### Regression to dependence—implications for therapist

#### The therapist's use of self

The therapist's use of self is an important aspect of integrative psychotherapy. This is much more than countertransferentially. It involves the therapist being willing to be appropriately seen and known as themselves by their clients. The data from my research has demonstrated how, when therapists are willing to be spontaneous and real with their client, and are willing to allow love to develop, then this can bring healing. This research participant acknowledges the importance of her therapist's love for her:

> It was a therapy of being [...] not a therapy of doing [...] and the last thing I think, she loved me. I thought she did and actually, later on, I knew she did, but it was utterly unconditional and she didn't want anything back, it wasn't a possessive love.

Suttie (1935, p. 215) also recognises that such love is the "effective agent in therapy". When practitioners reach the depth of relationship in psychotherapy, and experience the countertransferences which enable us to identify and address maternal need, an attitude of love has developed. These relationships are not easy options and require high levels of commitment from both client and therapist. When therapists talk about love, relaxing boundaries, and touch, other psychotherapists can make this uncomfortable for them. It is my experience that some therapists feel safer when in-depth personal relationships are not seen as aspects of therapeutic relationships, and may attempt to silence and shame practitioners who speak about this. I have seen this in workshops and conferences where rather than an attitude of shared learning and curiosity about difference there is instead a self-righteous posturing, which may result from personal fears of chaos, or of litigation and shame. Where practitioners focus on theory this may feel safer than focusing on what goes on between two people.

## The support of personal therapy

One of the key means of support for the therapist is personal therapy. Many psychotherapy graduates finish therapy at the end of their training, but in working with clients in the regression to dependence process, where the therapist's countertransference can be an evocation of their own infancy experience, the therapeutic aim is to establish primary maternal preoccupation, and to achieve this there must be a memory of maternal nurture in the therapist's experience of infancy, whether actual or therapeutic which also accords with Polanyi's (1969, 1983) valuing of personal and tacit knowledge.

This participant identifies how her experience in the countertransference may connect with her own infancy experience, and how she would be able to manage this therapeutically by, in effect, parenting her own child ego:

> It might mean, countertransferentially, that what I'm experiencing of them might trigger a reaction in child ego in me, but I would be expecting myself to manage that [expecting] the parent in me to be available to myself. […]

This is the main reason why I consider that therapists should have resolved their own issues around the maternal relationship in order to effectively work with clients. In my own experience, the nurture I received from my therapist is now modelled by me with my own clients, in the same way that we can learn how to care for others by being cared for ourselves.

## Therapy for the therapist

Most reputable training organisations, whose psychotherapy approach involves long-term work with complex and distressed clients, make personal therapy compulsory for those wishing to train as therapists. The professional body (UKCP) which oversees such psychotherapy training also requires long-term engagement in personal psychotherapy for students. There are two aspects to this, one is that the student is psychologically supported whilst in training, the other is to enable the student to gain insight into themselves, their motivations and their unconscious processes, so that they are able to successfully separate their processes from those brought into the room by their clients. Many therapists who work developmentally at depth with clients continue to engage in personal therapy over extended periods and re-engage as appropriate as an ethical stance. The participants in my research study were all practicing psychotherapists, and have commented on the importance of the psychotherapists' psychological ability to work with their clients:

> It does feel important to me that I have an understanding of this work, like a personal understanding of it; I'm not sure that mine will be the same as theirs [clients'] always […] it feels like I can only have so much of an understanding. If I'm not prepared to go there, if I'm not available to open up and work at depth in relationship

and be vulnerable myself, it doesn't feel like I can support the vulnerability of a client working in that way.

I don't think you can go into the client's inner world, object world, whatever you want to call it, without to some extent going into your own.

I think a big part of what I've learned from my own therapy and working with clients is that very often it isn't anything that I say, which I'd always thought it would be, I thought that it was gonna be that golden phrase that actually gets somewhere, but actually I'm far more free now at going with observing and just imagining what they might need at that moment, and going with that.

Some practitioners and theorists recognise that the therapist's own history and personal experiences can negatively impact upon the therapy offered. This is known as pro-active countertransference (Clarkson, 2003). Weiss (2002) identifies that the therapist's unresolved dependency issues can result in initial welcome of the client's dependence with the aim of meeting their own dependency needs, but subsequently withdrawing when the client's needs become too great. This participant identifies his experience of this issue:

> It's the people who push for regressive therapy out of their own unfinished business. The bigger problem is the therapists who are against regressive therapy because of their own unfinished business, and that's the bigger group. Now some of it is simply by theory and not knowing the psychotherapy field well enough, some of it was by group prejudice, "In our theory, in our association we don't do regressive work" [...] "Or we never touch because it's always going to become sexualised" or "you'll always be infantilising someone".

I consider my personal therapy to have been invaluable in enhancing my ability to work with regressed clients. Understanding, empathy, and intuition have helped me to recognise regression and respond to early relational need in an appropriate way. While not all therapists would have the need for personal regression to dependence, I consider that they must have addressed at depth their core experiencing in order to work at such depth with others. From my perspective this would mean that trainee therapists would have long term psychotherapy at a minimum of weekly sessions throughout and beyond training.

## The place of supportive supervision

Supervision is an important aspect of support for all therapists. In regression to dependence the supervisor should have an understanding of this process and be able to help their supervisee to recognise the potential for regression to dependence, and to be able to assess suitability of the supervisee to work with this process. Knowledge of regression to dependence enables the supervisor to support their supervisee through issues of safety, boundary, and holding. As I write this, I am reminded of a supervisor of mine who had a vast amount of theoretical knowledge and therapeutic experience. In one supervision session she told me not to touch the client (I had laid my hand on his arm) as I might confuse him, presumably she considered that he may interpret this movement of boundary as having a sexual motive. Caution with the use of touch is always appropriate, but my personal experience and theoretical understanding had led me to believe that with this client in particular, and in other similar circumstances, touch was an essential part of the therapy. At the time I experienced shame and professional doubt as a result, fearing that my supervisor knew more than me and that my tacit knowing of this client was misguided, yet believing that this client needed contact with me in a way that words alone could not achieve. It was after this incident that I began to search for a new supervisor. Working with regression to dependence is difficult, and the role of the supervisor and their understanding of this process are crucial for successful outcomes. If a therapist and client are embroiled in a transferential enactment then the supervisor may be able to keep an overview of the process as a whole. In my own practice a sympathetic and knowledgeable supervisor, with an understanding of the nature of this work and able to hold the whole picture has enabled me to tolerate not knowing and still maintain my equilibrium. This participant describes using therapeutic touch with his client to a supervisor:

> I later was talking to a supervisor who was extremely experienced
> in trauma work, and who I think initially listened to what I was
> doing and was willing to trust it, and then later decided that I must
> be in the [...] I must be wrong [...] [she said] "don't, you must never

use touch with, with such traumatised clients" that it could trigger off an episode of dissociation or whatever, just the touch itself, and I was trying to say, "well, this isn't the case for this particular client" but she didn't believe me, she thought I was wrong.

Therapists can experience such shame with supervisors and peers, but also experience shame within the therapeutic relationship.

## Shame in regression to dependence

Several of my participants have identified the toxic nature of shame, for example, describing multiple layers of shame, viewing shame as trauma, shame for being, and shame for existing. Bradshaw (1988) concurs, seeing that living with shame is life limiting, a person with toxic shame lives in fear; fear of discovery, fear of exposure, fear that their flawed self will be seen by others and rejected. When working with failed dependency in the pre-verbal arena shame is existentially present, and the therapist must expect to find it in both client and themselves. This participant relates her experience of shame as a practitioner within a therapeutic relationship:

> [I feel] constantly shoved away, constantly rejected, often feel that I'm going to be rubbished or attacked, I get very hurt by these clients [...] it feels very costly to engage in real relationships with these clients.

This excerpt demonstrates how a therapist can be effected by a shame process and so must have an understanding, not only of shame itself, but of their own vulnerability to shame and they should have sufficiently worked through their own shame issues in order to be able to get beyond being blocked by shame in the therapeutic relationship. Once again we return to the importance of personal therapy for practitioners. The nature of the shame process is such that it is largely ignored as identified by Nathanson (1992, p. 16) who describes humanity living "in an atmosphere of shame" seeing that "shame—our reaction to it and our avoidance of it—becomes the emotion of politics and conformity. It guides and creates fashion; its influence in civilisation is paramount". The avoidance of shame has also been significant in psychotherapy education and training. Psychotherapy training should include a focus on shame both for the client and for the therapist, helping the trainee therapists to explore their own vulnerability to shame, and the potential for it within regressive work. Therapists and supervisors of trainees should also have this awareness and capacity.

## Boundaries in regression to dependence

Boundaries are important in any psychotherapy, defining the relationship and making it known and safe. A client has expectations of boundary and so does the therapist. Research has shown that when boundaries are breached, the client usually suffers. However in regression to dependence, we are looking at changes in boundary to reflect the therapist's responsiveness to the needs of the client. These are boundary crossings which occur in the interests of the client's development. My research data highlighted the significance and meaning of therapists being willing to cross boundaries, experiencing such adaptations to the therapeutic frame to offer healing and repair. Therapists have choice about which boundaries are movable and which are not, and it is important to note that clients' needs do not always have to be gratified, only acknowledged as valid. However, working with regression to dependence does require more of the therapist, and therapists must be free to make a decision to work with this process or to refer on. I know for myself as a therapist that often I have felt discomfort when my personal boundaries have been challenged and it is at that point that I must acknowledge and consider my own needs as well as those of my client.

## Implications for training

Psychotherapists in training should be given sufficient understanding of regression to dependence to be able to recognise clients who are likely to enter a regressive process (Van Sweden, 1995). This process could be identified because of an indication of significant neglect in their early relational history, a history of repeated disruption in their later relationships with self or others, or from the therapist's countertransferential experiencing in initial interviews. Trainee therapists should be taught to recognise and acknowledge their limitations, or the limitations of their work setting, which may not allow for the sort of long term relational therapy needed to work with regression to dependence. This sort of psychotherapy is a relational, interpersonal process and it does not fit with some models of psychotherapy (Elkins, 2007). Observations of potential regression should be discussed in supervision in order to discuss the appropriateness or otherwise of working with any particular client. Integrative trainee therapists should be taught about human psychological development and may benefit from some form of infant observation as it relates to the regressive process. They should be provided with case material relating to clients who have experienced regression to dependence, in order to be able to appropriately facilitate regression to dependence when they have had sufficient experience. Upon qualification graduates should have awareness that it is often not appropriate or advisable to finish personal therapy at the end of training. One of my participants will elucidate further:

> I think the biggest problem is that most therapists haven't done their work themselves that they really need to do and they are afraid of their own regression and they project that right into the theory, they project that right into the methods and they criticise those therapists who would do those methods.

The relevance of shame to the practice of psychotherapy should be fully explored and discussed, particularly with regressive processes to enable the trainee to have sufficient theory, understanding, and experiencing to work with regression to dependence. The regressive experiences and therapeutic interventions described by participants indicate a wide, varied and sometimes messy and apparently disorganised process. This way of working requires the ability to tolerate ambiguities, to live without knowing, and to be comfortable with something that may look to outsiders as chaotic.

I would want my students to be aware of the possibility of regressive experiences when they came across them after training. Experience is an important factor when working with such clients, however, trainees and newly qualified therapists must be aware of the processes that some clients experience, and what to do about them, even if that means referral to a more experienced practitioner. Van Sweden (1995, p. 203) comments "regression to dependence as a concept should also be a part of the curriculum of training institutes". When I taught the basic understanding of regression to dependence to my final year Masters students other professionals commented on my "wrongness", seeing that such knowledge should only be available to the experienced practitioner.

I am reminded of the quotation from Pasteur's (1854) lecture regarding the sharing of knowledge, "In the fields of observation chance favors only the prepared mind".

The comments of my well-respected peers shamed me, and I was also fearful of exposing my own processes to others and being seen as unsuitable as a therapist, trainer, and researcher. Johns (2009) comments have foundations in history where practitioners have been ostracised for failing to adhere to the traditional path. I was conscious that Margaret Little, in revealing her therapy with Winnicott, had been viewed by her peers as unfit for practice. Yalom (1980, p. 402) recognises such shame for practitioners and the training of practitioners:

> During the course of effective psychotherapy the therapist frequently reaches out to the patient in a human and deeply personal manner. Though this reaching out is often a critical event in therapy, it resides outside official ideological doctrine; it is generally not reported in psychiatric literature (usually because of shame or fear of censure) nor is it taught to students. (both because it lies outside of normal theory and because it might encourage "excesses")

Historically in the profession of psychotherapy the popular ideological doctrine demands adherence. Those who step outside of this are ostracised in one way or another, for example, at the moment cognitive behavioural therapy is the popular mode of therapy and those outside of this exalted position may be seen as inferior (Elkins, 2007). It is my firm recommendation that therapists, supervisors, and trainers of trainee integrative psychotherapists should have an intimate knowledge of a full spectrum of in-depth therapy including regression to dependence.

## The challenge of the cultural context

In the course of my research, two of my participants told me, off the record, of their experiences of clients making complaints about the use of touch. In all cases this was not upheld, but the cultural and social context of blame and claim in which we live appears to be becoming more litigious, and therefore therapists may be more reluctant to step outside of recognised guidelines. Psychotherapy as a profession, and particularly integrative psychotherapy, straddles the medical model and the Humanistic view of human behaviour which holds a hopeful, constructive view of human beings and of their capacity to be self-determining, considering diagnoses and treatment plans whilst at the same time recognising that relationship is the key factor. If a potential client with chronic anxiety symptoms attends for therapy I may see early relational failure as the root which may need several years to address in therapy. If the same client presented at their GP seeing their issues as a medical problem, they may be given a short course of CBT and perhaps medication to address the symptoms, leaving the causative issue underground only to re-emerge at a later point. Cost is an important factor in State provision for psychological help and may offer a short term treatment to alleviate symptomology whilst failing to address the living burden of extreme damage within the client's internal world. Winterson (2011, p. 140) acknowledges that "when money becomes the core value, then education drives towards utility, or that the life of the mind will not be counted as a good unless it produces measurable results". This research then attempts to lay out some of the foundations of what might constitute evidence in this area, evidence that can be used by therapists themselves to articulate a rationale, but which also could begin the process of change in health care provision.

Elkins (2007, p. 66) identifies the confusion resulting from the influence of the medical model, considering that "the medical model in psychotherapy is a descriptive schema borrowed from the practice of medicine and superimposed on the practices of psychotherapy". He considers that this model "obscures the fact that psychotherapy is an interpersonal process" and that it does not account "for the fact that the vast majority of clients use psychotherapy for support, guidance, and personal growth instead of treatment for mental illness". Elkins identified the difficulty in differentiating "problems in living" from "mental illness". Health care provision seeks to resolve mental illness, restoring the client to functionality rather than having an interest in seeking contentment and fulfilment, and so the development of potential long-term relational problems may not be addressed.

Cognitive interventions and short term therapies cannot address relational deprivation in infancy, they just cover it over leaving the client feeling that they have tried to get help, but it has not helped and adds to their feelings of failure. Thinking and theories around regression seem to have got lost in new waves of therapy. Mitchell (1988) has explored the development of new theories and comments on the spawning of one theoretical system after another which do not hold on to the validity of earlier theories, but present themselves as the latest development.

Some clients presenting for therapy may have already received short-term, symptom-relieving therapy, but Winterson (2011, p. 222) identifies the chronic inevitability of the re-emergence of early relational wounding:

> You cannot disown what is yours. Flung out, there is always the return, the reckoning, the revenge, perhaps the reconciliation. There is always the return. And the wound will take you there. It is a blood-trail.

My study offers a means for therapists and theorists to be able to move beyond mere symptom management via the construct of relational wounding towards more effective and thorough ways of addressing these kinds of experiences, which have long lasting effects and enable clients to progress.

As knowledge of psychology has developed, so has the ability to work with patients previously seen as unsuitable for psychotherapy. This however is not the main issue as I see it. Those whose lives could be changed by regression to dependence do not have the opportunity. To provide a free long term psychotherapy service might be too costly for society, but not to resolve these long term issues is too costly for the individual.

A way of viewing the process described in this research, which ties in with Balint's (1968) work *The Basic Fault,* is that foundations of a person are laid down in early infancy and are intended to support the structure. Where foundations are flawed and weakened it takes time, effort and energy to maintain them and keep the structure standing; this is the role of the defences. Viewed as a metaphor where a house stands on poor or inadequate foundations the structure itself is effected and may require frequent shoring up, which can be costly in both time and energy. Attending to problems in the foundations can involve undoing and taking apart, and making a mess, but will result in a stable structure which requires less time and energy, leaving time and energy to be devoted to living life. The psychotherapeutic aim then is to identify a fault or deficiency, to offer repair, thus removing the need for shoring up and enabling the person to move on with life.

Once the therapist has identified the level of the client's regression to early infancy then the facilitation of such a relationship requires the therapist's adaptation to the needs of the client. Of course, the whole object of working with regression to dependence is to work through to a place of progression, that is, where these aspects of the client which have been split off, restricted, retarded or disowned, are integrated into the client's sense of self. This process offers the hope of a new beginning, from an attachment perspective, the hope of developing a new attachment style, maybe a first taste of security within relationship.

## Practitioner as researcher

There is an untapped resource in the work of experienced practitioners which is only recently receiving attention. My interest guided my need to research so that I could help my clients more effectively. At a training course led by Stephen Johnson, (October 2009) a theorist and practitioner, who describes character styles and treatment plans in an Integrative and effective way, he described to me the reasons that he first started to research, starting from the question, "How can I most effectively help my patients?" This question led to his in-depth research into the development of personality and the treatment needed by individual character styles. I share this ambition; that my research and writing will assist myself and others to more effectively help the clients that we work with.

### Reflexivity and heuristic research

"There is another level to the demands that heuristic research makes on the researcher. Deeply engaging in these tacit processes changes the researcher" (West, 1998, p. 63).

I recognise that, as the researcher, I have also been a participant in this study. This would seem to be the appropriate place to reflect upon the effect that conducting this research has had upon my practice. My understanding of the topic of this study has developed greatly, whilst my previous understanding contained some theoretical concepts and a large amount of intuition, I am now more able to articulate why I do what I do. This helped me to be more confident in my actions and in relation to boundary. In the process of reflecting upon my personal psychology I have learned more about myself, my own fear of intimacy, and difficulty with not knowing. Overall I am left with two conclusions about the process of regression to dependence, first, how essential it is for some people to revisit a time before their interpersonal damage occurred, and secondly, what a difficult process this can be.

Palmer (2008, p. 477) presents the notion that reflection on therapeutic work can reveal "the analyst's work to himself, and as such, is a valuable technique for self-analysis". It will be evident to the reader how my reflection has revealed my work to me. When I began this study I had no concept how much self-reflection and exploration of my personal experience would feature and that it would develop an autoethnographical nature.

During the process of this study I have constantly analysed my own therapy. This has had both negative and positive connotations. Analysis has resulted in some difficulty in my being able to be just a client, and I have often viewed my therapist's responses to me negatively, however, this study has also aided my personal growth in and out of therapy. I have lived with quite long periods of regression as a result of the immersion into the material of this study, both theory and data. I have also benefited in terms of my client work as I have gained more understanding and experience over this period. Dickson-Swift et al. (2007) and Cromby (2012) have identified the challenges for qualitative research when dealing with emotive issues. Dickson-Swift et al. (p. 342) acknowledge the emotional costs involved in sensitive research "Feelings of vulnerability for these researchers often came from the fact that in doing the research they were sometimes learning things about themselves". Cromby (2012, p. 9) recognises that "there are issues for qualitative clinical research that flow from the ineffability of embodied experience, the way its totality cannot be expressed or described in words".

I do not consider myself to be an academic even though I teach; my teaching style and my writing style are based on my experiences and reflexivity. As a person with dyspraxia I have found the organised chaos of researching very difficult, and I have become overwhelmed at times by trying to hold large amounts of information, and at the same time trying to organise them. This, together with the regressive nature of the work, has often left me unable to continue, and has undoubtedly effected the writing up of this project. When I am teaching I hope that my passion and the depth of my experiencing bring the work alive to my students, in the same way that the intuitive and attuned mother gives of her inner experiencing rather than that which is only consciously learned. I hope that this same depth and quality is available to the reader.

Benezer (2012) identifies his connection with the work of Winnicott. He uses Winnicott's concept of potential space as a principle for inter-cultural psychotherapy, seeing that the co-creation of potential space can become a mutual creative space, integrative psychotherapists view the relational as a co-created space. Formulating the origins of relational trauma and distress in adulthood as having their roots in infantile experiences enables both therapist and client to have a shared story, enabling them to make sense of their experiencing, developing a narrative within which the therapist can support clients more effectively and providing a space for the client to creatively explore their identity and relationships. It therefore makes sense to revisit these notions in the training and practice of psychotherapy.

In this work I have been exploring and describing the concept of regression to dependence, whereby the therapeutic setting is seen to facilitate a return to the earliest phases of early development, to infancy. This return is necessary for some clients because it results from damage caused to the developing self by failures in early relationships. As this putative trauma occurred pre-verbally, when it is experienced in therapy it may be difficult for both client and therapist to find words to describe the experience. The development of a narrative helps to develop meaning and also provides a language through which the experience can be understood, enabling shared language as ultimately "both the baby and the regressed patient in the end have no choice but to learn to speak the language—i.e. vocabulary and grammar—of the adult on whom they are dependent, the baby for his life, the regressed patient for his restoration!" (Balint, 1959, p. 72).

*Summary of findings relating to the process of regression to dependence*

I list below a simple summary of my research findings. My recommendations for the practice of integrative psychotherapy when working with regression to dependence are based on data from participants, but are supported by my own experiences and that of theorists writing about this subject:

- The therapist must be able to recognise a regressive process in a client, and understand the need to facilitate this process.
- The therapist must have an understanding of what this need to regress represents developmentally, and be able to identify the unmet needs.
- The therapist must be able to recognise the developmental need to be met by the therapist, and be able to take on some aspects of the role of primary caregiver.
- The therapist must have experienced care first hand so that they have a knowledge of the client's developmental need experientially.
- The therapist must be able to enter into the very experience of the transference relationship, being sufficiently in the enacted transference relationship to recognise and meet the unmet need, but at the same time hold an awareness of their own boundary.
- The therapist must be able to help the client to have a narrative for the experience of being in the moment in the therapy, and begin to describe that process.
- The therapist must also be able to give voice to the likely narrative of both mother and child, so that what is missing can be known and understood.
- The therapist should be able to engage with the regressive process at any point that the client is available, that is, emotionally, physically and psychologically and either symbolically or literally.
- The therapist must attend to the relationship and be a safe, containing, holding, attentive, and loving other, having an awareness of boundaries, safety, touch, and malignance.
- The therapist must have the capacity for, and be able to tolerate, profound distress and emotional pain in self and other.
- The therapist must be an object of transformation, helping the client to turn emotional pain into understanding, and able to offer the client a reparative experience.

## Epilogue

It is difficult to finish this work when there is so much understanding still to be gained. Whilst I have tried to illuminate this important aspect of therapy my hope is that others will continue this work, and that understanding will continue to develop beyond my present understanding.

The reader will observe that I have frequently used the words of others to say what I have been unable to say. I think that spending a large proportion of my life with inadequate words to describe my experiences has taught me that even if I do not have the words, words can be found that speak for me. Margaret Little has been an important model for my development and I shall use her words to express my personal position:

> It comes down to our fundamental honesty or hypocrisy, integrity or the lack of it. We have to admit the limitations of our knowledge, skill, and insight. We may have to act on the principle of the "balance of good over bad"; we may be using what we have faute de mieux. Or we may use what we have because it is worth using. What we have is what is in ourselves and in our patients: bodies, sensations, and emotions; movement and actions; words, ideas, thoughts, intelligence, and imagination. And that is quite a lot. (Little, 1981, p. 153)

# Research findings table

The following table identifies the key findings that emerged from my research study, completed 2014. The implications for the practice of psychotherapy are identified, and my recommendations, which have emerged from this study, are shown.

Key findings and the resulting implications for those involved in psychotherapy:

| *Key findings* | *Recommendations* |
| --- | --- |
| The significance of the process of regression to dependence | The potential for personal integration of aspects of self<br>The potential for growth as a result of regression to dependence<br>The presence of anxiety as an indicator of spontaneous regression<br>The importance of the therapeutic relationship<br>The therapist's use of self as facilitative partner |

*(Continued)*

189

(Continued)

| Implications for the client | Length of needed therapy<br>Cost<br>Personal challenge |
|---|---|
| Implications and recommendations for the therapist | Necessity for theoretical understanding of regression to dependence<br>A recognition and understanding of issues of boundary with this client group<br>The need for support for the therapist<br>Personal therapy<br>Supervision<br>The need for a high level of skill and experience in the therapist |
| Implications and recommendations for psychotherapy training | The theoretical base should include such theory that will provide a structure for the experience of regression to dependence<br>Provision of specific training to support the process<br>Facilitators should be experienced as both trainers and practitioners to enable the application of theory to practice to be taught effectively and facilitate development of trainees |
| Implications and recommendations for supervisors | The need to understand and support the process as appropriate<br>The importance of knowing the limitations of the supervisee<br>A sufficiently shared understanding of the process |

# REFERENCES

Adams, K. A. (2006). Falling for ever: The price of chronic shock. *International Journal of Group Psychotherapy, 56*: 2.

Adams, K. A. (2009). The abject self: Self-states of relentless despair. *International Journal of Group Psychotherapy, 61(3)*: 32–64.

Akhtar, S. (1999). The distinction between needs and wishes: Implications for psychoanalytic theory and technique. *Journal of the American Psychoanalysis Association, 47*: 113–151.

BACP (2010). Ethical framework for good practice in counselling and psychotherapy. Accessed 13th April 2011. Available online at: www.bacp. co.uk/ethical_framework/

Balint, M. (1959). *Thrills and Regression.* New York: International Universities Press.

Balint, M. (1968). *The Basic Fault.* USA: North Western University Press.

Basch, M. F. (1985). Some Clinical and Theoretical Implications of Infant Research. *Psychoanalytic Inquiry 5*: 509–516.

Benedek, T. (1953). Dynamics of the countertransference. *Bulletin of the Menninger Clinic, 17*: 201–208.

Benezer, G. (2012). From Winnicott's potential space to mutual creative space: A principal for intercultural psychotherapy. *Transcultural Psychiatry, 4(2)*: 323. Accessed 5th May 2013. Available online at: http:// tps.sagepub.com/content/49/2/323

Berenstein, R. (1995). *Lost Boys: Reflections on Psychoanalysis and Countertransference*. New York: Norton Press.

Bick, E. (1968). The experience of the skin in early object relations. In: Williams, M. H. (Ed.) *Collected Papers of Martha Harris and Esther Bick* (1987). UK: The Roland Harris Education Trust.

Bion, W. R. (1957). Differentiation of the psychotic from the non-psychotic personalities. In: *Second Thoughts: Selected Papers on Psychoanalysis*, (1967). New York: Jason Aronson.

Bion, W. R. (1962). *Learning from Experience*. London: Heinemann.

Bion, W. R. (1963). *Elements of Psycho-Analysis*. New York: Basic Books.

Blanchot, M. (1986). *The Writing of the Disaster*. Lincoln: University of Nebraska Press.

Bleuler, E. (1911). Dementia Praecox Oder Gruppe der Schizophrenien. In: Aschaffenburg, G. (Ed.) *Handbuch der Psychiatrie*. Leipzig: Deuticke (Germany).

Blum, H. P. (2004). Psychic trauma and traumatic object loss. In: Knafo, D. (Ed.) *Living with Terror, Working with Trauma: A Clinician's Handbook*. USA: Jason Aronson.

Bokanowski, T. (2004). Variations on the concept of traumatism: Traumatism, traumatic, trauma. *International Journal of Psycho-Analysis, 86*: 251–265.

Bollas, C. (1987). *The Shadow of the Object: Psychoanalysis of the Unthought Known*. New York: Columbia University Press.

Bollas, C. (2013). *Catch Them Before They Fall*. Sussex, UK: Routledge.

Borgogno, F. (2005). Ferenczi's clinical and theoretical conception of trauma: A brief introductory map. *American Journal of Psychoanalysis, 67(2)*: 141–149.

Borgogno, F. (2006). Ferenczi and Winnicott: Searching for a "missing link" (of the soul). *American Journal of Psychoanalysis, 67*: 221–224.

Borgogno, F., & Vigna-Taglianti, M. (2008). Role-reversal: A somewhat neglected mirror of heritages of the past. *American Journal of Psychoanalysis, 68*: 313–324.

Bornstein, M. (2013). Prologue: Winnicott's Legacy. *Psychoanalytic Enquiry: Topical Journal for Mental Health Professionals, 33(1)*: 1–2.

Bornstein, R. F. (1993). The Dependent Personality. New York: The Guilford Press.

Bornstein, R. F., & Bowen, R. F. (1995). Dependency in psychotherapy: Toward an integrated treatment approach. *Psychotherapy, 32*: 520–534.

Botella, C., & Botella, S. (2001). *The Work of Psychic Figureability: Mental States without Representation*. Hove and New York: Brunner—Routledge.

Bowlby, J. (1969). *Attachment*. London: The Hogarth Press.

Bowlby, J. (1973). *Attachment and Loss, Vol. 2, Separation, Anxiety and Anger*. London: The Hogarth Press.

Bowlby, J. (1980). *Attachment and Loss: Vol. 3, Loss: Sadness and Depression*. London: Hogarth Press.

Bradshaw, J. (1988). *Healing the Shame that Binds You*. USA: Health Communications Inc.

Braudel, F. (1995). *The Mediterranean and the Mediterranean World in the Age of Philip II, Volume 1*. London: University of California Press Ltd.

Breuer, J., & Freud, S. (1895d). *Studies on Hysteria. The Standard Edition of the Complete Psychological Works of Sigmund Freud Vol. 2*. London: Hogarth, pp. 1–335.

Bromberg, P. M. (1991). On knowing one's patient inside out: The aesthetics of unconscious communication. *Psychoanalytic Dialogues*, 1: 399–422.

Bromberg, P. M. (2012). Stumbling along and hanging in: If this be technique, make the most of it! *Psychoanalytic Enquiry. 32*, 1.

Brown, B. (2010). *The Gifts of Imperfection: Let Go of Who You Think You're Supposed to be and Embrace Who You Are*. Minnesota, USA: Hazelden.

Bryce Boyer, L. (1993). Introduction: Countertransference—brief history and clinical issues with regressed patients. In: Bryce Boyer, L., & Giovacchini, P. L. (Eds.) *Master Clinicians on Treating the Regressed Patient, Vol. 2*. USA: Jason Aronson.

Bryce Boyer, L., & Giovacchini, P. L. (Eds.) (1990). *Master Clinicians on Treating the Regressed Patient*. USA: Jason Aronson.

Bryce Boyer, L., & Giovacchini, P. L. (Eds.) (1993). *Master Clinicians on Treating the Regressed Patient, Vol. 2*. USA: Jason Aronson.

Buber, M. (1958). *I and Thou*. New York: Scribner.

Cashdan, S. (1989). *Object Relations Theory: Using the Relationship*. New York: Norton.

Chu, J. A. (1998). *Rebuilding Shattered Lives: The Responsible Treatment of Complex PTSD and Dissociative Disorders*. New York: Guilford.

Clark, B. D. (1993). Use of empathic transactions in the treatment of shame. 31st Annual ITAA Conference. *The Minneapolis Papers*.

Clarkson, P. (2003). *The Therapeutic Relationship*. London: Whurr Publishers Ltd.

Cohen, J. (1985). Trauma and repression. *Psychoanalytic Enquiry, 5*: 164–189.

Cozolino, L. (2006). *The Neuroscience of Human Relationships: Attachment and the Developing Brain*. London and New York: Norton.

Cromby, J. (2012). Feeling the way: Qualitative clinical research and the affective turn. *Qualitative Research in Psychology, Special Issue on Qualitative Research, 9(1)*: 88–98.

Dale, S. (2010). *Where Angels Fear to Tread: An Exploration of having Conversations about Suicide in a Counselling Context.* Newcastle upon Tyne, UK: Cambridge Scholars Publishing.

Dalenberg, C. J. (2000). *Countertransference and the Treatment of Trauma.* Washington, DC: American Psychological Association.

Darwin, C. (1979). *The Expressions of Emotions in Animals and Man.* London: Julian Friedman, 1872.

Dickson-Swift, V., James, E. L., Kippen, S., & Liamputtong, P. (2007). Doing sensitive research: What challenges do qualitative researchers face? *Qualitative Research, 7*: 327.

Dosamantes, I. (1992). The intersubjective relationship between therapist and patient: a key to understanding denied and denigrated aspects of the patient's self. *The Arts in Psychotherapy 19(5)*: 359–365.

Dunbar, H. F. (1947). *Mind and Body: Psychosomatic Medicine.* New York: Random House.

Duquette, P. (2011). What place does the real-relationship have in the process of therapeutic character change? Accessed 1st January 2014. Available online at: jdc.jefferson.edu/cgi/viewcontent.cgi?article=1359& context …

Durana, C. (1998). The use of touch in psychotherapy: Ethical and clinical guidelines. *Psychotherapy: Theory, Research, and Practice, 35(2)*: 269–280.

Eigen, M. (2001). *Damaged Bonds.* London and New York: Other Press.

Eigen, M. (2004). No amount of suffering. In: Knafo, D. (Ed.) *Living with Terror, Working with Trauma: A Clinician's Handbook.* USA: Jason Aronson.

Elkins, D. N. (2007). The medical model in psychotherapy: Its limitations and failures. *Journal of Humanistic Psychology.* Accessed 5th May 2013. Available online at: http://jhp.sagepub.com/content/49/1/66

Ellman, S. J. (2007). Analytic trust and transference: Love, healing ruptures and facilitating repairs. *Psychoanalytic Enquiry: A Topical Journal for Mental Health Professionals, 27(3)*: 246–263.

Erikson, E. (1950). *Childhood and Society.* Great Britain: Imago Publishing Company.

Erskine, R. G. (1993). Inquiry, attunement and involvement in the psychotherapy of dissociation. *Transactional Analysis Journal, 23*: 4.

Erskine, R. G. (1994). Shame and self-righteousness: Transactional analysis perspectives and clinical interventions. *Transactional Analysis Journal, 24*: 86–102.

Erskine, R. G. (1995). A Gestalt Therapy Approach to Shame and Self-Righteousness: Theory and Methods. *British Gestalt Journal, 4*: 107–117.

Erskine, R. G. (1998). Attunement and involvement: Therapeutic response to relational needs. *International Journal of Psychotherapy 3(5)*: 3.

Erskine, R. G. (2001a). The schizoid process. *Transactional Analysis Journal*, *31*: 4–6.

Erskine, R. G. (2001b). The psychotherapist's myths, dreams, and realities. Accessed 30th June 2013. Available online at: www.integrativetherapy.com/en/articles.php?id=33

Erskine, R. G. (2007). Life scripts: Unconscious relational patterns and psychotherapeutic involvement. Accessed 28th September 2011. Available online at: http://www.integrativetherapy.com

Erskine, R. G. (2011). Attachment, Relational Needs, and Psychotherapeutic Presence. Accessed 28th September 2011. Available online at: www.integrativetherapy.com

Erskine, R. G., & Criswell, G. E. (2012). Psychotherapy of contact-in-relationship: Conversations with Richard. Accessed 24th August 2013. Available online at: www.integrativepsychotherapy.com

Erskine, R. G., & Moursund, J. P. (2004). *Integrative Psychotherapy: The Art and Science of Relationship*. USA: Brooks/Cole.

Erskine, R. G., & Trautmann, R. L. (2002). *The Process of Integrative Psychotherapy*. New York: Institute for Integrative Psychotherapy.

Erskine, R. G., Moursund, J. P. & Trautmann, R. L. (1999). *Beyond Empathy: A Therapy of Contact-in-Relationship*. New York: Brunner-Routledge.

Etherington, K. (2000). *Narrative Approaches to Working with Male Survivors of Sexual Abuse; The Clients', Counsellors', and Researchers' Story*. London: Jessica Kingsley Publishers.

Etherington, K. (2003) (Ed.). *Trauma, the Body and Transformation: A Narrative Inquiry*. UK: Jessica Kingsley Publishers.

Evans, K. R. (1994). Healing Shame: A Gestalt Perspective. *The Transactional Analysis Journal*, *24*: 2.

Fairbairn, W. R. D. (1952). *An Object-Relations Theory of the Personality*. New York: Basic Books.

Federn, P. (1952). *Ego Psychology and the Psychoses*. New York: Basic Books.

Ferenczi, S. (1923). The dream of the "clever baby". In: Richman, J. (Ed.), Suttie, J. (Trans.). *Further Contributions to the Theory and Technique of Psycho-Analysis*. (1980). London: Karnac.

Ferenczi, S. (1930). The principle of relaxation and neocatharsis. In: Balint, M. (Ed.), Mosbacher, E. (Trans.). *Final Contributions to the Problems and Methods of Psycho-Analysis*. (1980). London: Karnac.

Ferenczi, S. (1931). Child analysis in the analysis of adults. In: *Final Contributions to the Problems and Methods of Psychoanalysis*. New York: Basic Books.

Ferenczi, S. (1932/1988). *The Clinical Diary*. Dupont, J. (Ed.), Balint, M. & Zarday Jackson, N. (Trans.) (1988). MA: Harvard University Press.

Ferenczi, S. (1933). Confusion of tongues between adults and the child. In: Balint, M. (Ed.), Mosbacher, E. (Trans.). *Final Contributions to the Problems and Methods of Psycho-Analysis*. (1980). London: Karnac.

Ferenczi, S. (1953). *The Theory and Technique of Psychoanalysis*. New York: Basic Books.

Fisher, J. (2015). Excerpt from Website Janina Fisher. Accessed 1/7/15. Available online at: www.janinafisher.com/about.php

Fosha, D. (2002). The activation of affective change processes in aedp—(accelerated experiential–dynamic psychotherapy). In: Magnavita, J. J. (Ed.). *Comprehensive Book of Psychotherapy, Vol. 1: Psycho-Dynamic and Object Relations Psychotherapies*. New York: Wiley.

Fosha, D. (2003). Dyadic regulation & experiential work with emotion & relatedness in trauma and disorganised attachment. In: Solomon, M. F., & Siegel, D. J. (Eds.) *Healing Trauma: Attachment, Trauma, the Brain, and the Mind*. New York: Norton.

Frank, A. (1995). *The Wounded Storyteller: Body, Illness and Ethics*. London: University of Chicago Press.

Freud, S. (1900a). *The Interpretation of Dreams. The Standard Edition of the Complete Psychological Works of Sigmund Freud, Vol. 5*. London: Hogarth.

Freud, S. (1905d). *Three Essays on the Theory of Sexuality. The Standard Edition of the Complete Psychological Works of Sigmund Freud Vol. 7*. London: Hogarth pp. 125–243.

Freud, S. (1915c). Instincts and their Vicissitudes. *The Standard Edition of the Complete Psychological Works of Sigmund Freud Vol. 14*. London: Hogarth, pp. 111–140.

Freud, S. (1920g). Beyond the Pleasure Principle. *The Standard Edition of the Complete Psychological Works of Sigmund Freud Vol. 18*. London: Hogarth.

Freud, S. (1933a). *New Introductory Lectures on Psycho-analysis. The Standard Edition of the Complete Psychological Works of Sigmund Freud Vol. 2*. London: Hogarth.

Freud, S. (1940a). *An Outline of Psycho-analysis. The Standard Edition of the Complete Psychological Works of Sigmund Freud Vol. 23*. London: Hogarth, pp. 141–207.

Fromm, M. G. (2004). On being the other person: Clare Winnicott, psychoanalyst and social worker. *Beyond The Couch, March*, 1.

Gabbard, G. O. (Ed.) (1989). *Sexual Exploitation in Professional Relationships*. Washington, DC: American Psychiatric Press.

Gergen, K. J., & Gergen, M. (1987). Narratives as relationships. In: Burnett, R., McGee, P., & Clarke, D. C. (Eds.). *Accounting for Relationships*. London: Methuen.

Gilbert, P. & Andrews, B. (Eds.) (1988). *Shame: Interpersonal Behavior, Psychopathology and Culture*. New York: Oxford University Press.

Gill, M. M. (1982). *Analysis of Transference. Vol. 1.* New York: International Universities Press.

Gill, M. M. (1991). A re-experiencing therapy. In: Kahn, M. *Between Therapist and Client.* USA: W. H. Freeman.

Giovacchini, P. L. (1972). Interpretation and definition of the analytic setting. In: *Tactics and Techniques in Psychoanalytic Therapy, 1.* New York: Science House, pp. 291–304.

Giovacchini, P. L. (1990). Interpretation, fusion, and psychic synthesis. In: Bryce Boyer, L. & Giovacchini, P. (Eds.). *Master Clinicians on Treating the Regressed Patient.* USA: Jason Aronson.

Goleman, D. (1996). *Emotional Intelligence: Why It Can Matter More Than IQ.* UK: Bloomsbury Publications.

Gorkin, M. (1985). Varieties of Sexualized Countertransference. *Psychoanalytic Review, 72:* 421–440.

Gorkin, M. (1987). *The Uses of Countertransference.* North Vale, New Jersey: Jason Aronson.

Gottlieb, S. (1992). Failures in the Transformational Object. *British Journal of Psychotherapy, 8:* 3.

Greenacre, P. (1967). The influence of psychic trauma on genetic patterns. In: Furst, S. (Ed.). *Psychic Trauma.* New York: Basic Books.

Greenson, R. R. (1967). *The Technique and Practice of Psychoanalysis, 1.* New York: International Universities Press.

Greenson, R. R. (1978). *Explorations in Psychoanalysis.* New York: International Universities Press.

Grotstein, J. (1984). Forgery of the Soul. In: Nelson, C., & Eigen, M. (Eds.). *Evil, Self and Culture.* New York: Human Scientists Press, pp. 203–226.

Grotstein, J. (1990). Nothingness, meaninglessness, chaos, and the "black hole", part I. *Contemporary Psychoanalysis, 26:* 257–290.

Grotstein, J. (1994). The foreword. In: Hedges, L. E. *Working the Organising Experience.* USA: Jason Aronson.

Guntrip, H. (1969). *Schizoid Phenomena, Object Relations and the Self.* New York: International Universities Press, and London: Hogarth.

Guntrip, H. (1971). *Psychoanalytic Theory, Therapy and the Self.* New York: International University Press.

Gutheil, T. G., & Gabbard, G. O. (1993). The concept of boundaries in clinical practice: Theoretical and risk-management dimensions. *American Journal of Psychiatry, 1(50):* 188–196.

Hartley, L. P. (1953). *The Go-Between.* UK: Hamish Hamilton.

Hedges, L. E. (1992). *Interpreting the Countertransference.* USA: Jason Aronson.

Hedges, L. E. (1994a). *Working the Organising Experience: Transforming Psychotic, Schizoid, and Autistic States.* USA: Jason Aronson.

Hedges, L. E. (1994b). *In Search of the Lost Mother of Infancy.* USA: Jason Aronson.

Heimann, P. (1950). On countertransference. *International Journal of Psychoanalysis,* 31.

Heimann, P. (1956). Dynamics of Transference Interpretations. *International Journal of Psychoanalysis, 37*: 303–310.

Hofer, M. A. (1978). Hidden regulatory processes in early social relationships. In: Bateson, P. P. G., & Klopfer, P. H. (Eds.). *Perspectives in Ethology, Vol. 3.* New York: Plenum Press.

Hofer, M. A. (1981). Towards a developmental basis for disease predisposition: the effects of early maternal separation on brain, behavior, and cardio-vascular system. In: Weiner, H., Hofer, M. A., & Stunkard, A. J. (Eds.). *Brain, Behavior, and Bodily Disease.* New York: Raven Press.

Hofer, M. A. (1982). Seeing is believing: A personal perspective on research strategy in developmental psychobiology. *Developmental Psychobiology 15*: 339–408.

Hofer, M. A. (1983a). On the relationship between attachment and separation processes in infancy. In: Plutchik, R. (Ed.). *Emotion: Theory, Research, and Experience, Vol. 2: Early Development.* New York: Academic Press.

Hofer, M. A. (1983b). The mother/infant interaction as a regulator of infant physiology and behavior. In: Rosenblum, L., & Moltz, H. (Eds.). *Symbiosis in Parent-Offspring Interactions.* New York: Plenum Press.

Hofer, M. A. (1984). Relationships as Regulators: A psychobiologic perspective on bereavement. *Psychosomatic Medicine, 46*: 183–197.

Holub, E., & Lee, S. (1990). Therapists' use of non-erotic physical contact: Ethical concerns. *Professional Psychology: Research and Practice, 21(20)*: 115–117.

Hopper, E. (2003). *Traumatic Experience in the Unconscious Life of Groups: The Fourth Basic Assumption: Incohesion: Aggregation/Massification or (BA) 1: A/M.* New York: Jessica Kingsley Publishers.

Hudnall Stamm, B., Higson-Smith, C., & Hudnall, A. C. (2004). The complexities of working with terror. In: Knafo, D. (Ed.). *Living with Terror, Working with Trauma: A Clinician's Handbook.* USA: Jason Aronson.

Hunter, M., & Struve, J. (1998). *The Ethical Use of Touch in Psychotherapy.* Thousand Oaks, California: Sage Publications.

Hurvich, M. (1989). Psychic Trauma, annihilation anxieties and psychodynamic treatment. For New Orleans APA Panel, *Trauma: Obvious and Hidden; Possibilities for Treatment.* Accessed 1 st January 2014. Available online at: www.45.pair.com/divisdyp/sec-com-pdfs/HurvichPSY-CHICTRAUMA.pdf.

Hurvich, M. (2000). Fear of being overwhelmed and psychoanalytic theories of anxiety. *Psychoanalytic Review, 87(5)*: 615. Proquest Medical Library.

Hurvich, M. (2004). Psychic trauma and feats of annihilation. In: Knafo, D. (Ed.). *Living with Terror, Working with Trauma: A Clinician's Handbook*. USA: Jason Aronson.

Jacobs, L. (1995). Shame in the therapeutic dialogue. *British Gestalt Journal, 4(2)*: 86–90.

Jacobs, M. (1988). *The Presenting Past* (2nd Edition). Buckingham: Open University Press.

Jacoby, M. (1984). *The Analytic Encounter*. Canada: Inner City Books.

Janet, P. (1904). L'Amnesie et la Dissociation des Souvenirs par L'Emotion [Amnesia and the dissociation of memories by emotions]. *Journal de Psychologie, 1*: 417–453.

Janet, P. (1919). *Les Medications Psychologiques*. Paris: Felix Alcan.

Johns, J. (2009). How do you get where you want to be when you don't know where you want to be? *Psychoanalytic Enquiry: A Topical Journal for Mental Health Professionals, 29(3)*: 223–235, doi: 10.1080/07351690802275154.

Johnson, S. M. (1985). *Characterological Transformation: The Hard Work Miracle*. New York: W. W. Norton & Company, Inc.

Johnson, S. M. (1994). *Character Styles*. New York: W. W. Norton & Company Inc.

Johnson, S. (2009). Character and complexity. National Council for Voluntary Organisations, London, 9th—11th October.

Johnston, S. H., & Farber, B. A. (1996). The maintenance of boundaries in psychotherapeutic practice. *Psychotherapy, 33(3)*: 391–402.

Josselson, R. (1992). *The Space Between Us: Exploring the Dimensions of Human Relationships*. San Francisco: Jossey Bass.

Jung, C. G. (1928). The therapeutic value of abreaction. *Collected Works 16*.

Kahn, M. (1991/2001). *Between Therapist and Client*. USA: W. H. Freeman.

Kalsched, D. (1996). *The Inner World of Trauma*. UK: Routledge.

Kaufman, G. (1992). *Shame: The Power of Caring*. Vermont: Schenkman Books.

Kaufman, G. (1993). *The Psychology of Shame*. London: Routledge.

Kaufman, J. (1994). Group thanatropics. In: Schermer, V. L., & Pines, M. (Eds.). *Ring of Fire—Primitive Affects and Object Relations in Group Psychotherapy*. London: Routledge.

Keller, H. (1904). *The Story of My Life*. New York: Grosset and Dunlap.

Khan, M. (1963). The concept of cumulative trauma. In: Khan, M. *The Privacy of the Self*. New York: International Universities Press.

Khan, M. (1984). Introduction to Winnicott, D. W. *Through Paediatrics to Psychoanalysis*. UK: The Winnicott Trust.

Kierkegaard, S. A. (1849). *Fear, Trembling and the Sickness unto Death*. Lowrie, W. (Trans.) (1941). Princeton: Princeton University Press.

Killingmo, B. (1989). Conflict and deficit: Implications for technique. *International Journal of Psychoanalysis, 70*: 65–79.

Klein, J. (1987). *Our Need for Others and its Roots in Infancy*. London: Routledge.

Klein, M. (1935). A contribution to the psychogenesis of manic-depressive states. In: *Love, Guilt and Reparation and Other Works 1921–1945*, 1975. New York: Delacorte Press, pp. 262–289.

Klein, M. (1957). *Envy and Gratitude*. London: Tavistock.

Klein, M. (1959). Our adult world and its roots in infancy. *Human Development, 12*.

Kohut, H. (1971). *The Analysis of the Self*. New York: International Universities Press.

Kohut, H. (1977). *The Restoration of the Self*. New York: International Universities Press.

Krowski, S. (1997). Working with adult incest survivors. In: Lawrence, M., & Maguire, M. (Eds.). *Psychotherapy with Women: Feminist Perspectives*. London: Macmillan.

Krystal, H. (1988). *Integration and Self-Healing: Affect, Trauma, Alexithymia*. *Hillsdale*. New Jersey: Analytic Press.

Laing, R. D. (1960). *The Divided Self: An Existential Study in Sanity and Madness*. Harmondsworth: Penguin.

Langs, R. (1976). *The Bipersonal Field*. New York: Jason Aronson.

Lansky, M. R. (1994). Commentary on Andrew Morrison's "The breadth and boundaries of a self-psychological immersion in shame". *Psychoanalytic Dialogues 4*: 45–50.

Lazarus, A. A. (1994). How certain boundaries and ethics diminish therapeutic effectiveness. *Ethics and Behaviour, 4(3)*: 255–261.

Leijssen, M. (2006). Validation of the body in psychotherapy. *Journal of Humanistic Psychology*. Accessed 5th May 2013 Available online at: http://jhp.sagepub.com/content/46/2/126

Levy, K. N. (2009). Psychodynamic and psychoanalytic psychotherapies. In: Richard, D., & Huprich, S. (Eds.). *Clinical Psychology Assessment, Treatment, and Research*. Burlington, MA: Elsevier Academic Press.

Levy, K. N., & Scala, J. W. (2012). Transference, transference interpretations, and transference-focused psychotherapies. *Psychotherapy, 49(3)*: 391–403.

Lewis, H. B. (1971). Shame and guilt in neurosis. *Psychoanalytic Review 58*: 419–438.

Lewis, H. B. (1987) Shame and the narcissistic personality. In: Nathanson, D. L. (Ed.). *The Many Faces of Shame*. London: The Guilford Press.

Lewis, R. (1981). The psychosomatic basis of premature ego development. *Comprehensive Psychotherapy, 3*.

Lewis, R. A. (2004). The psychosomatic basis of premature ego development. Accessed 5th October 2011. Available online at: www.bodymindcentral. com/pdf/pubs/LewisPub-PrematureEgoDevelopment.pdf

Lipton, S. (1977). The advantages of Freud's technique as shown in his analysis of the Rat Man. *International Journal of Psychoanalysis, 58*: 255–273.

Litt, C. (1986). Theories of transitional object attachment: An overview. *International Journal of Behavioural Development, 9(3)*: 383–399.

Little, M. (1958). On delusion transference (transference psychosis). *International Journal of Psychoanalysis, 39*: 134–138.

Little, M. I. (1981). *Transference Neurosis and Transference Psychosis*. USA: Jason Aronson.

Little, M. I. (1990). *Psychotic Anxieties and Containment*. USA: Jason Aronson.

Loue, S. (2008). *The Transformative Power of Metaphor in Therapy*. New York: Springer Publishing Company.

Lourie, J. B. (1996). Cumulative trauma: The non-problem problem. *Transactional Analysis Journal, Vol. 26*: 4.

Lynd, H. M. (1958). *On Shame and the Search for Identity*. London: Routledge and Kegan Paul.

Mahler, M. (1952). On child psychosis and schizophrenia: Autistic and symbiotic infantile psychoses. *Psychoanalytical Study of the Child 7*: 286–305.

Mahler, M (1958). Autism and symbiosis, two extreme disturbances of identity. *International Journal of Psychoanalysis, 39*: 77–83.

Mahler, M. (1968). *On Human Symbiosis and the Vicissitudes of Individuation. Infantile Psychoses, Vol. 1*. New York: International Universities Press.

Mahler, M. (1972). Rapprochement subphase of the separation-individuation process. *Psychoanalytic Quarterly, 41*: 487–506.

Mahler, M., Pine, F., & Bergman, A. (1975). *The Psychological Birth of the Human Infant*. New York: Basic Books.

Mair, K. (1992). The myth of therapist expertise. In: Dryden, W., & Feltham, C. (Eds.). *Psychotherapy and its Discontents*. Buckingham: University Press.

Mann, D. (1997). *Psychotherapy: A Neurotic Relationship*. London: Routledge.

Maroda, K. J. (1991). The power of the counter-transference: innovations in analytical technique. *Wiley Series in Psychotherapy and Counselling*. Chichester: Wiley.

McDougall, J. (1989). *Theaters of the Body. A Psychoanalytic Approach to Psychosomatic Illness*. New York: Norton.

Maroda, K. J. (2004). *The Power of Counter-Transference*. Hillside, New Jersey: The Analytic Press.

Milner, M. (1952). Aspects of symbolism and comprehension of the not-self. *International Journal of Psychoanalysis, 33*: 181–185.

Mitchell, S. A. (1988). *Relational Concepts in Psychoanalysis: An Integration*. USA: Harvard University Press.

Mitchell, S. A. (1991). *Relational Concepts in Psychoanalysis*. Cambridge, MA: Harvard University Press.

Modell, A. (1969). *Object Love and Reality*. London: Hogarth.

Nathanson, D. L. (1987). Shaming systems in couples, families and institutions. In:

Nathanson, D. L. (1992). *Shame and Pride: Affect, Sex, and the Birth of the Self*. New York: Norton.

Norcross, J. C. (2011). *Psychotherapy Relationships that Work*. USA: Oxford University Press.

Norcross, J. C., & Prochaska, J. O. (1986). Psychotherapist heal thyself: 1. The psychological distress and self-change of psychologists, counsellors and laypersons. *Psychotherapy, 23*: 102–114.

Ogden, P., Minton, K., & Pain, C. (2006). *Trauma and the Body—A Sensorimotor Approach to Psychotherapy*. New York and London: Norton.

Palmer, J. (2008). Forging an analytic identity through clinical writing. *Psychoanalytic Enquiry: A Topical Journal for Mental Health Professionals, 28(4)*: 477–492.

Pao, P. N. (1979). *Schizophrenic Disorders*. New York: International Universities Press.

Pasteur, L. (1854). Lecture, University of Lille (7th December).

Perls, F., Hefferline, R., & Goodman, P. (1951). *Gestalt Therapy—Excitement and Growth in the Human Personality*. New York: The Gestalt Journal Press.

Phelps, J. L., Belskg, J., & Cmic, K. (1998). Earned security, daily stress, and parenting: A comparison of five alternative models. *Development and Psychopathology, 10*: 21–38.

Polanyi, M. (1969). *Knowing and Being*. Grene, M. (Ed.). Chicago: University of Chicago Press.

Polanyi, M. (1983). *The Tacit Dimension*. Gloucester, MA: Peter Smith.

Polster, E., & Polster, M. (1974). *Gestalt Therapy Integrated*. New York: Vintage.

Pope, K. S., & Keith-Spiegel, P. (2008). Dual relationships, multiple relationships, and boundary decisions: A practical approach to boundaries in psychotherapy: Making decisions, bypassing blunders, and mending fences. *Journal of Clinical Psychology 64(5)*: 638–652.

Price, L. (2014). *Back to the Beginning: An exploration of the treatment and effects of therapeutic regression to dependence in psychotherapeutic practice*, PhD thesis, De Montfort University. Available online at: http://hdl.handle.net/2086/10510

Putnam, F. W. (1997). *Dissociation in Children and Adolescents: A Developmental Perspective*. New York: Guilford.

Racker, H. (1968/1982). *Transference and Countertransference*. England: Hogarth Press.

Rennie, D. L. (1992). Qualitative analysis of the client's experience of psychotherapy. In: Toukmanian, S. G., & Rennie, D. L. (Eds.). *Psychotherapy Process Research: Paradigmatic and Narrative Approaches*. Newbury Park: Sage Publications.

Roisman, G. I., Padron, E., Sroufe, L. A., & Egeland, B. (2002). Earned-secure attachment status in retrospect and prospect. *Child Development, 73(4)*: 1204–1219.

Rothstein, A. (1983). *The Structural Hypothesis: An Evolutionary Perspective*. New York: International Universities Press.

Sandler, J. (1983). Reflections on some relations between psychoanalytic concepts and psychoanalytic practice. *International Journal of Psychoanalysis, 64*: 35–45.

Santayana, G. (1905). The Life of Reason. Accessed 1st January 2014. Available online at: https://archive.org/details/lifeofreason01sant

Santayana, G. (1921). The Suppressed Madness of Sane Men. In: Pearsall Smith, L. (Ed.) *The Collection of Little Essays*, with the collaboration of the author.

Sartre, J.-P. (1957). *Being and Nothingness*. Barnes, H. (Trans.). London: Methuen.

Schneider, C. D. (1977). *Shame, Exposure and Privacy*. London: Norton.

Schore, A. N. (2003). Early relational trauma, disorganised attachment, and the development of pre-disposition to violence. In: Solomon, M. F., & Siegel, D. J. (Eds.). *Healing Trauma: Attachment, Mind, Body, and Brain*. New York: Norton.

Schur, M. (1953). The ego in anxiety. In: Loewenstein, R. (Ed.) *Drives, Affects and Behaviour*. New York: International Universities Press.

Searles, H. (1965). *Collected Papers on Schizophrenia and Related Subjects*. New York: International Universities Press.

Shaw, R. (1998). Shame: An integrated approach to the pre-verbal becoming verbal. *Changes, 16(4)*: 294–308.

Shaw, R. (2008). The Practitioner-Researcher. *The Psychotherapist, 38*: 8–10: UKCP.

Sherwood Psychotherapy Training Institute (2003). *MA Integrative Psychotherapy Handbook*. SPTI/Derby University.

Siegel, D. J. (1999). *The Developing Mind: How Our Relationships and the Brain Interact to Shape Who We Are*. New York: Guilford Press.

Siegel, D. J. (2003). An interpersonal neurobiology of psychotherapy: The developing mind and the resolution of trauma. In: Solomon, M. F. & Siegel, D. J. (Eds.). *Healing Trauma: Attachment, Mind, Body, and Brain*. New York: Norton.

Siegel, D. J. (2015). Interpersonal neurobiology. Seminar 24/4/15. London.

Simon, S. N., & Geib, P. (1996). When therapists cause shame: Rupture and repair at the contact boundary. In: Lee, R. G. and Wheeler, G. (Eds.). *The Voice of Shame*. Hillsdale, New Jersey, USA: Gestalt Press.

Smith, D., & Fitzpatrick, M. (1995). Patient–therapist boundary issues: An integrative review of theory and research. *Professional Psychology: Research and Practice, 26(5)*: 499–506.

Solomon, M. F., & Siegel, D. J. (Eds.) (2003). *Healing Trauma: Attachment, Mind, Body, and Brain*. New York: Norton.

Spitz, R. (1957). *The First Year of Life*. New York: International Universities Press.

Steele, K., Van der Hart, O., & Nijenhuis, E. R. S. (2001). Dependency in the treatment of complex post traumatic stress disorder and dissociative disorders. *Journal of Trauma and Dissociation, 2(4)*: 79–116.

Steinbeck, J. (1952). *East of Eden*. USA: The Viking Press.

Stern, D. N. (1985). *The Interpersonal World of the Infant*. New York: Basic Books.

Stewart, H. (1992). *Psychic Experience and Problems of Technique*. London: Routledge.

Stewart, H. (2003). Winnicott, Balint, and the independent tradition. Accessed 31st May 2005. Available online at: Http:/Datastarweb.Com/ Nhs/20050531_102350_F2dd9_9/Wbform/1005/720.

Stewart, I., & Joines, V. (1987). *TA Today: A New Introduction to Transactional Analysis*. Nottingham, England: Lifespace Publishing.

Stewart, L. (2011). Weaving the fabric of attachment. In: *International Journal of Psychotherapy*. USA: The International Integrative Psychotherapy Association.

Stolorow, R. D., & Atwood, G. E. (1992). *Context of Being: The Intersubjective Foundations of Psychological Life*. Hillsdale, New Jersey: Analytic Press.

Suttie, I. D. (1935). *The Origins of Love and Hate*. Great Britain: Penguin Books.

Symington, J. (1985). The survival function of primitive omnipotence. *International Journal of Psychoanalysis, 66*: 481–488.

Symington, J., & Symington, N. (1996). *The Clinical Thinking of Wilfred Bion*. London: Routledge.

Symington, N. (1986). *The Analytic Experience: Lectures from the Tavistock*. Free Association Books.

Tarantelli, C. B. (2003). Life within death: Towards a metapsychology of catastrophic psychic trauma. *International Journal of Psychoanalysis, 84*: 915–928.

*The Shorter Oxford English Dictionary* (1983). London: Book Club Associates by arrangement with Oxford University Press.

Thompson, C. (1943). The Technique of Sandor Ferenczi: A Comment. *International Journal of Psychoanalysis 24*: 64–66.

Tomkins, S. S. (1962). *Affect/Imagery/Consciousness. Vol. 1: The Positive Affects.* New York: Springer.

Tomkins, S. S. (1963). *Affect/Imagery/Consciousness. Vol. 2: The Negative Affects.* New York: Springer.

Tompkins, P., Sullivan, W., & Lawley, J. (2005). Tangled spaghetti in my head: Making use of metaphor. *Therapy Today, BACP,* October.

Toronto, E. (2001). The human touch: An exploration of the role and meaning of physical touch in psychoanalysis. *Psychoanalytical Psychology, 18(1)*: 37–54.

Totton, N. (2012). Boundaries and boundlessness. In: *Therapy Today.* Accessed 14th April 2013. Available online at: www.Therapytoday.net/article/show2101/

Tustin, F. (1966). A significant element in the development of autism. *Journal of Child Psychology and Psychiatry, 7*: 53–67.

Tustin, F. (1972). *Autism and Childhood Psychosis.* London: Hogarth.

Tustin, F. (1981). *Autistic States in Children.* London: Routledge and Kegan Paul.

Tustin, F. (1984). Autistic shapes. *International Review of Psycho-Analysis II*: 279–288.

Tustin, F. (1986). Autistic barriers in neurotic patients. *Topique, May*: 9–23.

Tustin, F. (1990). Autistic encapsulation in neurotic patients. In: Bryce Boyer, L., & Giovacchini, P. L. (Eds.). *Master Clinicians on Treating the Regressed Patient.* USA: Jason Aronson.

Tustin, F. (1994). The perpetuation of an error. *Journal of Child Psychotherapy 20(3)*: 3–23.

UKCP (United Kingdom Council for Psychotherapy) (2009). Ethical Principles and Code of Conduct.

Van der Hart, O., Steele, K., Boon, S., & Brown, P. (1993). The treatment of traumatic memories: Synthesis, realization, and integration. Accessed 15th July 2013. Available online at: www.Trauma-Pages.Com/A/Vdhart-93.Php.

Van der Kolk, B. A., & Fisler, R. (1994). Childhood Abuse & neglect and loss of self-regulation. *Bulletin of Menninger Clinic, 58*: 145–168.

Van der Kolk, B. A., & Fisler, R. (1995). Dissociation and the fragmentary nature of traumatic memories: Overview & exploratory study. *Journal of Traumatic Stress, 8(4)*: 505–525.

Van Sweden, R. (1995). *Regression to Dependence.* USA: Jason Aronson.

Volkan, V. D. (2006). *Killing in the Name of Identity.* Charlottesville, USA: Pitchstone Publishing.

Wachtel, P. L. (2008). *Relational Theory and the Practice of Psychotherapy*. USA: The Guilford Press.

Wallin, D. (2007). *Attachment in Psychotherapy*. USA: Guilford Press.

Weil, A. M. (1970). The basic core. *Psychoanalytical Study of the Child, 2*: 142–460.

Weiss, A. G. (2002). The lost role of dependency in psychotherapy. *Gestalt Review, 6(1)*: 6–17.

West, W. (1998). Passionate research: Heuristics and the use of self in counselling research. *Changes, 16*: 60–66.

Wilkinson, M. (2010). *Changing Minds in Therapy: Emotion, Attachment, Trauma, & Neurobiology*. London and New York: Norton.

Winnicott, C. (1980). Fear of breakdown: A clinical example. *International Journal of Psychoanalysis, 61*: 351–357. Republished in: Kanter, J. (Ed.) (2004). *Face to Face with Children: The Life and Work of Clare Winnicott*. London: Karnac.

Winnicott, C., Shepherd, R., & Davis, M. (Eds.) (1989). *Psychoanalytic Explorations*. Cambridge, MA: Harvard University Press.

Winnicott, D. W. (1949). *The Ordinary Devoted Mother and Her Baby. Nine Broadcast Talks*. London: Julkaisematon Käsikirjoitus.

Winnicott, D. W. (1952/1984). Anxiety associated with insecurity. In: *Collected Papers: Through Paediatrics to Psycho-Analysis*, (1958/1984). New York: Basic Books, pp. 97–100.

Winnicott, D. W. (1953). Transitional objects and transitional phenomena. In: *Playing and Reality*, (1971). London: Tavistock, pp. 1–26.

Winnicott, D. W. (1958a/1984). Metapsychological and clinical aspects of regression within the psycho-analytic set-up. In: *Through Paediatrics to Psycho-Analysis*, (1958b/1984). New York: Basic Books, pp. 278–294.

Winnicott, D. W. (1958b/1984). *Through Paediatrics to Psychoanalysis*. (Winnicott Trust) London: Karnac.

Winnicott, D. W. (1958c/1984). Clinical varieties of transference. In: *Through Paediatrics to Psycho-Analysis*, (1958b/1984). New York: Basic Books.

Winnicott, D. W. (1960). The family and emotional maturity. In: *The Family and Individual Development*, (1989). London: Routledge, pp. 88–96.

Winnicott, D. W. (1963a). Dependence in infant care, in child care, and in the psychoanalytic setting. *International Journal of Psychoanalysis*, xiiv.

Winnicott, D. W. (1963b). Fear of breakdown, In: Winnicott, C., Shepherd, R., & Davis, M. (Eds.). *Psychoanalytic Explorations*, (1989). Cambridge, MA: Harvard University Press, pp. 87–95.

Winnicott, D. W. (1965a/1984). Ego distortion in terms of true and false self. In: Winnicott, D. W. *The Maturational Processes and the Facilitating Environment*. New York: Basic Books.

Winnicott, D. W. (1965b/1984). *The Maturational Processes and the Facilitating Environment*. London: The Hogarth Press.

Winnicott, D. W. (1967). Mirror role of mother and family in child development. In: Lomas, P. (Ed.). *The Predicament of the Family: A Psycho-Analytical Symposium*. London: Hogarth Press, pp. 29–33.

Winnicott, D. W. (1971). *Playing and Reality*. London: Routledge.

Winnicott, D. W. (1974). Fear of breakdown. *International Review of Psychoanalysis, 1*: 103–107.

Winnicott, D. W. (1988). *Babies and their Mothers*. London: Free Association Press.

Winnicott, D. W. (1989). *Psychoanalytic Explorations*. London: Karnac Books; Cambridge, Mass: Harvard University Press.

Winterson, J. (1985). *Oranges Are Not the Only Fruit*. London: Vintage.

Winterson, J. (2011). *Why Be Happy When You Could Be Normal?* London: Vintage.

Wosket, V. (1999). *The Therapeutic Use of Self: Counselling Practice, Research and Supervision*. London: Routledge.

Wright, K. (1991). *Vision and Separation: Between Mother and Baby*. USA: Jason Aronson.

Wurmser, L. (1981). *The Mask of Shame*. London: The Johns Hopkins Press.

Wurmser, L. (1987). Shame: The veiled companion of narcissism. In: Nathanson, D. L. (Ed.). *The Many Faces of Shame*. London: The Guilford Press.

Yalom, I. D. (1980). *Existential Psychotherapy*. New York: Basic Books.

Yorke, C. (1986). Reflections on the problem of psychic trauma. *Psychoanalytical Study of the Child. 41*: 221–238. New Haven, CT: Yale University Press.

Young, R. M. (2005). The analytic frame, abstinence and acting out. Accessed 14th April 2010. Available online at: Human-Nature.Com/Rmyoung/Papers/Pap110h.html

Zeig, J. (1980). Erickson's use of anecdotes. In: Zeig, J. (Ed.). *A Teaching Seminar with Milton H. Erickson*. New York: Brunner/Mazel.

Zilber, T. B., Tuval-Mashiach, R., & Lieblich, A. (2008). The embedded narrative: Navigating through multiple contexts. *Qualitative Inquiry, 14(6)*: 1047–1069.

# INDEX

abandonment, xv, 2, 10, 52, 61, 89, 95, 122, 163
abstinence, 13, 88
abuse, 2, 29, 34, 44, 60, 66, 76, 78, 86, 93, 100–101, 117, 127, 145, 159, 161
Adams, K. A., 70, 72, 74–76
adaptation, 10, 154
adjustment, 102, 149, 154–155, 169
Akhtar, S., 36
alienation, 10, 73
annihilation, 26–32, 50, 59, 64–70, 73–74, 128
anxiety, xiii–xiv, xx, 1–2, 10, 23–24, 27, 30–32, 40, 49, 58, 60–71, 74–75, 78, 80, 86–87, 94–96, 100, 103, 128, 134–136, 140–141, 169–172, 181, 189
   and panic attacks, xiii, 1, 24, 32, 58, 169–170

annihilation, 27, 60, 65–70
   unthinkable, 31, 60, 64, 66, 69, 80, 87
attachment, 12, 23, 28, 30, 35–38, 44–45, 58, 71, 83
   insecure, 35
   relationship, 94–95, 99, 102
   secure, 66, 89, 132–133
attunement
   affective, 106–108, 130, 144
   empathic, xvi, 51
   failures of, 2, 29, 94
   mis-, 28–29, 44, 63, 73, 76–77, 88, 90, 94, 121–122, 140

BACP (British Association for Counselling and Psychotherapy), 146
Balint, M., xix, 2, 4, 6, 13, 16–17, 27, 30, 36–37, 39, 64, 84, 90, 135,

209